CHIEF EXECUTIVE
COACH

Why Executives Need Coaches and the Kind of Coaches They Need

Corrie Jonn Block,
PhD, DBA

Chief Executive Coach
Why Executives Need Coaches and the Kind of Coaches They Need
by **Corrie Jonn Block, PhD, DBA**

Paperback ISBN: 978-1-962825-47-4

First published in 2025

Cover design by Michael Beas
Publishing, design, and production facilitated by

Atlas Elite Publishing Partners, LLC.

www.atlaselitepublishing.com

ATLAS ELITE
PARTNERS
PUBLISHING

Powered by **C-Suite Network**

https://c-suitenetwork.com

C-SUITE NETWORK™

PRAISE FOR CHIEF EXECUTIVE COACH

Chief Executive Coach by Corrie Jonn Block is a groundbreaking guide that every executive and aspiring leader should have on their bookshelf. Corrie **masterfully combines decades of experience with cutting-edge research** to deliver insights that are both profound and practical. This book is not just about coaching; it's about transforming the very essence of leadership in the modern corporate world. What sets this book apart is Corrie's ability to **blend strategic thinking with deep empathy**. He understands that behind every successful executive is a human being grappling with immense pressures and responsibilities. **Chief Executive Coach** is a testament to the power of coaching in unlocking potential and driving sustainable success. If you're serious about elevating your leadership game and making a lasting impact, this book is an indispensable resource. Corrie Jonn Block has **truly written an executive coaching masterpiece** that will resonate with leaders for years to come.

Dr. Marshall Goldsmith, the Thinkers50 #1 Executive Coach and New York Times bestselling author of The Earned Life, Triggers, and What Got You Here Won't Get You There.

Exactly the kind of bold, no-nonsense guidance the executive coaching industry needs right now. Dr. Corrie Block challenges traditional coaching, pushing coaches to elevate their practice and inspire trust at the highest level. His call to go beyond questioning and deliver real, actionable value is both unconventional and critical for transforming CXO coaching. This book **redefines true executive coaching** and is a must-read for those seeking to impact and elevate the effectiveness and contributions of senior leaders everywhere.

Stephen M. R. Covey, the New York Times and #1 Wall Street Journal bestselling author of The Speed of Trust and Trust & Inspire

Corrie Jonn Block's *Chief Executive Coach* is a **C-Suite performance manifesto**. It's raw, it's real, and it's exactly what every CXO needs to shatter the glass ceiling of their potential. This isn't your typical coaching fluff. It's a no-holds-barred guide that tells it like it is, pushing you to redefine what it means to lead. If you're ready to ditch the comfort zone and **embrace the chaos of true leadership**, this book is your playbook. It's not for the faint-hearted or the complacent. It's for those who dare to disrupt, innovate, and dominate. Get ready to be challenged, inspired, and transformed. This is the **coaching revolution** you didn't know you needed.

Jeffrey Hayzlett, Founder & Chairman of The C-Suite Network

Corrie Jonn Block has written a challenging book that working coaches need. From the description of what puts the "executive" in "Executive Coach" to a step-by-step roadmap for how to build out your toolkit, working coaches can assess what they bring to the conversation, focus on who they are, and lay out a unique offering to serve the exact client they want to serve. You'll find your emotions rising in multiple places (at least I did!), but **don't put the book down**. My advice to you is to read it in small doses. Give yourself time to react. Then, put what you discover into action in your coaching practice. You'll be glad you looked in the mirror and raised your game. This book will help you get hired and rehired. Bottom line, this book is **good for the coaching industry!**

Jonathan Reitz, CEO at FLUXIFY and Working Coach Labs, Member of the Coaches50

Chief Executive Coach is a standout in the field and one that I wholeheartedly recommend. What sets this book apart is its perfect blend of **rigorous research and practical, actionable advice**. Dr. Corrie doesn't just speak in theory - every chapter offers tangible insights and tools that can be immediately applied to real-world leadership and coaching scenarios. It's a guide that's as much about strategic thinking as it is about personal growth, making it invaluable for anyone who works with top-tier executives. Having worked with executives at the highest levels, I can attest to how valuable the framework in *Chief Executive Coach* can be in driving meaningful change, both for the individual leader and the organization as a whole. This is a book that doesn't just sit on a shelf; it's one you'll return to again and again for its wisdom and practical guidance. If you're looking for a book that will help you elevate your coaching practice and **make a true impact** on the leaders you work with, *Chief Executive Coach* is a must-read. Dr. Corrie has crafted something truly special - **an indispensable resource for any executive coach** or leader striving to be their best.

Mick Todd, Founder and Chairman 2b Limitless
2024 Professional Services Executive Coach of the Year

Demystifies executive coaching to appreciate the vast opportunity that CXOs and ECs partner to exploit to serve their organizations, customers, and the lives they aspire to lead. Well-researched and shared by **a realist storyteller**, this book invites CXOs and ECs to lean into the power of partnership, presence, and perception, essential to sustaining excellence.

Janet M. Harvey MCC, ACS
Coaches50 Executive Coach, CEO inviteCHANGE

Coaching the C-Suite requires a specific mindset, emotional fortitude, and strategic acumen to enhance the **fine-tuned coaching skills** you have developed. *Chief Executive Coach* is a complete guide to equip you with these requirements to coach at the highest levels of leadership. With a keen understanding of executive psychology, Dr. Corrie Jonn Block delivers a **bold, insightful, and refreshingly candid** roadmap to elevate your impact in the C-suite. If you want to transform executives, this is your playbook.

Dr. Marcia Reynolds, CEO of Covisioning,
Author of the international bestseller, *Coach the Person,* Not t*he Problem*

Finally!!!...As a former CEO and now mentor to current C-suites, I really enjoyed reading Corrie's book. Anyone who "coaches" a CEO needs to read this and then reflect on how they are turning up for their clients. The unique and challenging CEO role (and I would argue the broader C-suite as well) means that traditional/"pure" coaching plays a critical BUT NOT complete role in helping the CEO be the best leader they can be. Questions help ... but they are not enough, and Corrie gets it. **Practical & engaging** read. Kudos.

Howard Gough, Executive Mentor & Coach, CMi Merryck

Loved every word! Looking to develop the essential skill as a CEO coach? This is an essential read.

Andrew Stotter-Brooks, Chief Learner, ADNOC Group

Chief Executive Coach strikes a **perfect balance between theoretical knowledge and practical advice**, making it an essential read for both aspiring executive coaches and CXOs looking to elevate their coaching experiences. Corrie's extensive experience and expertise in the field shine through in every chapter, offering readers a comprehensive understanding of the unique challenges faced by executive coaches and their clients. I particularly enjoyed the case studies and real-life examples, which added depth and relatability to the content – a must read for anyone looking to gain a deeper understanding of executive coaching and for CXOs wanting to optimize their performance.

Leah Cotterill, CEO, Cigna Healthcare

Dr. Corrie Block has written **the book that every CEO coach wishes they had written** (including me) and every aspiring C-suite coach needs. It's a bible of success-critical content and great contextual stories. Great job.

Matthew Lewis, Managing Director and CEO Coach, Hinsta Performance.

Chief Executive Coach is **a thought-provoking, powerful tool** that any executive coach, CEO or CHRO should be able to understand if they intend to create strong, top performing executive teams. It not only **calls**

out critical gaps in the executive coaching industry but also highlights the myriads of tools, research and knowledge that every effective EC should be using to coach their "Olympic athlete."

Rodha Alharthi, Group Head of L&D, E&

Having supported over 30 CXOs transitioning into public listed organizations, one of the biggest challenges is sourcing the right coach for them and being clear on the coaching need purpose. Dr. Corrie Block's approach to **psychological recalibration to bring about the high performing corporate athlete** assures personal transformation and adaption towards personal success. Dr. Corrie's approach opens the CXO mind and positions them for success across all stakeholder groups. His 10 Principles for Coaching are insightful. It's **a must read** for any CEO, CEO coach, and HR executive who seeks to make a difference to CXO optimum performance.

Graham Almond, CEO, Culture Synergy

Chief Executive Coach by Dr. Corrie Block is a very **versatile and comprehensive** handbook for coaching leaders entrusted with overall responsibility for delivering strategic success for an organization. It is written in a conversational, very readable but thought provoking style that makes it easy to absorb while enhancing both understanding and ability for a coach. I particularly appreciate Dr. Block's advocacy of engaging in active "advisory coaching" to support and guide CXOs for actual and specific issue resolution. Chief Executive Coach is an **absolutely invaluable reference guide**. I am sure that vastly experienced coaches will also find it a handy fount of refreshing insight and perspective.

Mansoor Tirmzi, Mentor CMi Merryck and former CFO, HSBC

A **transformative resource** for anyone aspiring to elevate their coaching practice to the C-suite. With deep insights into the unique challenges faced by high-level executives, Dr. Corrie masterfully combines practical tools, strategic methodologies, and a wealth of real-world experience to redefine what it means to coach at the top. This book is not just a guide; it's **a blueprint for shaping the future of executive performance.**

Christian Farioli, CEO, ESD Marketing

Chief Executive Coach offers valuable insight and perspective into the spiraling yet unregulated executive coaching space. **Balanced and forthright**, it considers coach and client perspectives and, by intention, invites questions and provides answers in similar measures. Whether a CXO, seasoned executive coach or aspiring newcomer, *Chief Executive Coach* has something for you.

Chris Lake, EC & Program Development Lead, The Advantage Coach

A great reminder of **all that it takes to be a great coach** to a leading business executive. This can be both inspiring and daunting!

Fraser Gregory, Executive Mentor & Coach, CMiMerryck

Chief Executive Coach is a transformative guide that tackles one of the most critical yet overlooked challenges in the coaching industry: the lack of alignment between executive coaches and CXOs. Dr. Corrie Block **brilliantly dissects the root causes of mismatched coaching relationships**, offering profound insights and practical solutions to bridge the gap. It will challenge your assumptions, refine your approach, and equip you with tools to create real-world success. Don't miss it!

Hadeer Khorshid, CEO, SocialDar

Dr. Corrie Jonn Block's *Chief Executive Coach* is a transformative guide for those coaching senior leaders. With **unflinching honesty, practical tools, and thought-provoking insights**, this book is a must-read for anyone aspiring to elevate CXO performance and redefine the coaching landscape.

Kate Barker, Chief Future of Work Officer, NEOM

Chief Executive Coach is a powerful call to action for the executive coaching industry – a timely resource that challenges leaders and coaches alike to rethink their approach. Through a **compelling narrative rich with real-world experiences and actionable insights**, Dr. Corrie offers a masterclass in navigating leadership with purpose. **Balancing scientific rigor with accessible guidance**, this book serves as an invaluable blueprint for CXOs, HR teams, and emerging leaders who aspire to build lasting legacies through effective, purpose-driven coaching. A transformative read, *Chief Executive Coach* is **not just a leadership book; it's a coaching revolution**.

Nejib Ben Kheder, SVP, Emirates

Dr. Corrie Block's *Chief Executive Coach* is **a bold and invaluable addition to the field of executive coaching**, challenging conventional coaching orthodoxy and offering practical tools for coaches working at the highest executive levels. With courage and insight, Dr. Block breaks away from the traditional "one-size-fits-all" approach, advocating for a versatile, advisory-based model that aligns more closely with the realities CXOs face. *Chief Executive Coach* is **a groundbreaking resource that positions coaches as true strategic partners for executives**. Dr. Block's willingness to disrupt the status quo in coaching, combined with the practical, adaptable nature of his toolkit, makes this a must-read for anyone invested in the future of executive leadership.

Paul Peplow, General Manager, CMiMerryck

This concise book is **theory led and practice focused** and it will certainly be beneficial to executive coaches, learning and development professionals, top executives and others that are willing to continuously and boldly widen their perspective and create/add significant value to self, others, their team and organization while maximizing their return on investment. Therefore, if you want to continuously make the deemed impossible capabilities possible, read the *Chief Executive Coach* and get/become a blatantly honest, adept, and versatile coach.

Prof. Raymond Lihe, DeMontfort University

Corrie gives **a masterclass** into the world of Executive Coaching.

Richard Steward, CEO, Value Mastered

I am thrilled to endorse *Chief Executive Coach* by Dr. Corrie Jonn Block: a mentor, friend, and long-time supporter who has significantly impacted my professional journey. Corrie's unwavering commitment to sharing his deep knowledge and passion for inspiring others has guided me through some very critical growth moments. While collaborating with him, I've witnessed firsthand his dedication to **empowering leaders to embrace authenticity, drive high performance, and create real impact.** This book is a true gift to anyone seeking to elevate their leadership and drive real transformation. Thank you, Corrie, for your wisdom, generosity, and friendship.

Shereen Qutob, Dir. Talent Management & Culture,
Majid Al Futtaim Group

Chief Executive Coach is **a comprehensive guide for both aspiring and experienced executive coaches**. It blends theory with practical strategies, offering a deep dive into the nuances of coaching high-level professionals. The book covers key techniques like goal setting, emotional intelligence, and leadership development, providing actionable insights for coaching executives to unlock their potential. With real-world case studies, it's a valuable resource for understanding the challenges faced by top leaders. The writing is clear and accessible, making it **an essential read** for anyone looking to deepen their understanding of executive coaching and leadership dynamics.

Talat Sheerazi Goldie, CHRO, Taaleem

If you are a coach or a consultant, **this book must be on your reading list!** While coaches are trained to not provide advice, Corrie neatly sums up how that will fall flat on its face if you are coaching the C-suite. Corrie's book captures the challenges CX Officers face and equips you the reader with the knowledge and tools to support your client in a way that adds value and develops an effective long-term relationship. Consultants who are often advising clients will learn another way to enable CX Officers to own and execute on the advice they have sought.

Tina Chugani, Managing Director, Proxis

If you've questioned as a coach the rigidity of a singular coaching approach, or how basic some coaching approaches are compared to the needs of an executive, this book shows you're not alone! Corrie's book gives a step-by-step guide to building the tools that an executive needs you to have, **developed by walking the walk for many years**. Simply laid out, interspersed with great stories of being in the room where it happens, this book will help coaches and leaders alike understand **what is needed at the highest levels of coaching** to have impact. As coaches, all we need to do is follow the learning steps to develop the skills and knowledge needed. And if you're a C-suite member, this book shows what you should expect from your coach at this level. By following these steps, we will all get better!

Tony Evans, EMEA Marketing Science Director, Meta

DEDICATION

For my parents:

Ernie and Joni Block

ACKNOWLEDGEMENTS

I dedicate this book to my parents, who have dedicated much of their lives to me. Their unconditional support has been a solid foundation upon which I've charted my maverick and often fantastically unorthodox journey. Though they have not always understood me, they have always loved me.

I'm so grateful for my amazing economic partners: Amy Sharman, Ely Fangonil, Bianca Saraum, Wey Magluyan, Hadeer Khorshid, Hany Gawad, Shereen Qutob, Adrian Manansala, Kayla Jacobs, and Simone Chrystal. Their support makes it possible for me to focus on the materials, and on executing well for our clients.

Thanks as well to Dr. Nathalie Awad, my sanity checker. She's the first person to have read this book before it went out for a wider review. Her wisdom improved its quality immensely and saved me from a lot of embarrassment.

I'd also like to extend my thanks to Ridma Wali, Founder at Nyra Leadership Consulting, and her incredible team for their help with some of the background research. Their consistent hard work and commitment to excellence really enabled me to bring this book together.

Thanks to Paul Peplow and the team of Mentors at CMiMerryck for their feedback and engagement on the material during the review process. They helped me to hone this into something more relevant for practitioners like us. I appreciate being able to think out loud with such a strong group of talented ECs (Executive Coaches).

My greatest source of mentorship in recent years has been my coachees. Whether GCEOs of multinational conglomerates or small business owners, each of them is a source of wisdom for me. As we work together to maximize their performance, the echo effect is that our conversations maximize my performance as well. I'm grateful for all of them.

I can't express how much I've leaned on my covenant partner and best friend, Nicole. I'm so grateful for her patience and encouragement. You wouldn't believe what she puts up with from me during the writing process. And I'm grateful to my dear friend Laura for continuing to fill my life with song and dance.

TABLE OF CONTENTS

INTRODUCTION

"He is a master tactician; he can break a swim stroke down so that any swimmer, young or old, novice or Olympic-level, can understand the method behind the madness. But calling Bob a swimming tactician undervalues his true calling. He is a motivator and a teacher. He is someone who can take people with a passion and show them how far they can go with it. He's developed a formula for helping people go from one level to the next, and through his method, they learn more about who they actually are. In short, he makes people better. I'm proof. … I don't believe any other coach could have brought me to where I am today. Bob is one-of-a-kind."

– Michael Phelps

Spanning five Olympic games, Michael Phelps broke 39 World Records and won 28 Olympic medals, 23 of which were gold. He is arguably the best Olympian of all time.

Michael's coach, through all of his success, was Bob Bowman. Sure, Bowman was a competitive swimmer for a couple of years in the mid-1980s, but do you really think his swimming experience was relevant to the sport when he brought Michael to their first Olympic games in 2004? Nope, but his 20 years of coaching experience sure was.

"The best coaches," writes Bowman, "are the ones who show their people not just how to get better but how to motivate themselves to get better."[1] According to him, coaches "show how." According to Michael Phelps, coaches have formulas and methods that blend the disciplines of motivator, teacher, and master tactician. It's probably best for the sport of swimming overall that Bob didn't just "hold space" for Michael to figure out for himself how to fix his butterfly stroke.

The Problem with Coaching

My issue with executive coaching today is simple: no one seems to know what qualifies someone to call themselves an "Executive Coach."

When do athletic coaches get to call themselves Olympic coaches? Is it when they've first coached an experienced Olympic athlete? Or when one of the athletes they've coached makes the Olympics? Or does the person have to attend the Olympics as an official coach to call themselves an Olympic Coach? If I coached an Olympic athlete for a couple of months one time, would I get to call myself an Olympic coach, too? What if I was coaching them in mindset and not in athletics?

Honestly, I'm not quite sure. I suppose it's a matter of honor and ego. For coaches who have been heavily involved in the development and successes of Olympic athletes, I think it's a matter of honor to call themselves Olympic coaches. And for those claiming that title while knowing they haven't really added a lot of differentiating value to Olympians, it's a matter of ego.

Similarly, what qualifies someone to call themselves an executive coach? When does honor require us to acknowledge the impact we have made? When does ego grasp an accolade prematurely through overconfidence?

Like Olympians, today's business executives need more than someone to simply ask, "What would you like to work on today?" They need strategic advisors who know their game and can raise their level of performance. Executive coaching isn't the same as coaching; it's a subset of coaching and a niche. And let's be honest, most coaches aren't ready to handle the weight of the corner office. But for those who are, this

---

[1] Bowman, B., & Butler, C. (2016). *The golden rules: 10 steps to world-class excellence in your life and work*. Little, Brown Book Group. (Online information for entries can be found in the Reference and Further Reading list at the end of this book)

book is your blueprint for coaching (or being coached) at the highest level.

Bob's level. The Olympic level.

Before we get to that, though, I need to vent. There are three huge obstacles in the way of good executive coaching: arrogant executives, underqualified coaches, and a lack of definition. Let's start here.

Obstacle 1: Arrogant (or Ignorant) Executives

Q: What do you call an Olympic athlete without a coach?

A: Retired.

Why is it then that so many executives still simply do not recognize the value of executive coaching?

Howard Gough, former EMEA CEO of global health company Cigna Group admits that during his 30+ year executive tenure he never sought out executive coaching for himself personally, even though he procured coaching for many of his direct reports. From those I have spoken with Howard was very much an inspirational and successful leader, but ego, stubbornness, and competitiveness got in the way of his own development.

As a CEO he thought of coaching for himself personally as a reflection of weakness, or perhaps as a punishment exacted by a Board of Directors upon CEOs for remedial performance. After all, what could a coach possibly help him with? And how could he find the time for coaching relative to his other priorities? It wasn't until he resigned his position at his company and completed his professional certification in executive coaching from Henley Business that he realized his (and his shareholders') monumental missed opportunity. He reflected with me over coffee that he'd had, "An exciting and rewarding career, lots accomplished – but how much more did I leave on the table by not having a coach by my side?!"

Coaching isn't something you get because you're broken and need to be fixed. That's therapy, and that is not my job. Coaching is something you get because you're talented and you think you might be a world-class competitor in your domain. Still, many people fail to make this distinction and confuse coaching with counseling, a grave mistake that no reader of this book will ever again make.

Executives who don't think they need coaching for performance are either ignorant of the craft or arrogant in their character. And worse, they're leaving profitability and shareholder value on the table as a result. They're not the only ones they're letting down.

> Q: What do you call an executive without a coach?

> A: Remedial.

Howard now coaches for CMi Merryck. Ask him – he'll tell you.

[He's amazing to spend time with. You should look him up.}

Obstacle 2: Underqualified Coaches

I know a lot of executives in my home city of Dubai and around the world. While many of them recognize the need for a good executive coach (EC) to improve their performance, finding a good fit can be a tough process.

There's certainly no shortage of coaches out there, and there are plenty of platforms to find them on, but what CEO has the time to sift through them all? Finding the right coaching partner in a sea of online profiles can be an exhausting and disheartening journey. They might schedule several chemistry calls, meet with a few coaches, and even commit for six months just to see what will happen. Too often, they don't find what they need in the relationship, and sadly, some of them have given up.

I know HR (Human Resources) does their level best here, but even in the best circumstances, they'll tend to present three candidate coaches to their executives and ask them to pick one. Sometimes, they'll provide a mail-order catalog from BCG or McKinsey to sift through. Chemistry calls are a bit like blind dates, though; three might not be enough to find a good fit for a relationship of this magnitude, even if the candidates are pre-qualified.

It's a real problem.

So, I called Adam.

Adam Ashcroft has become a close friend over the last few years. He's an EC in Dubai, and like me, he's been a bit disheartened by the sheer volume of people calling themselves "Executive Coach" online. Most of his executive friends, too, would consider the majority of "Executive Coaches" as swipe-left coaches rather than swipe-right (if you know, you know). He's building a roster of high-quality coaches with The Advantage Coach to try to mitigate this challenge.

Others, like CMi Merryck in Australia and 100 Coaches in the US, have done the same. Like exclusive matchmaking services, some organizations are working hard to connect earnest executives with qualified coaches. When the right connection is made, it changes careers, businesses, and lives. We can't just give up. I like that. I want to help.

Obstacle 3: Lack of Definition

My search on LinkedIn today for people claiming the title of "Executive Coach" returned more than 386,000 results. What I can't find is an agreed-upon set of criteria that qualifies someone to use the EC title. So, what's preventing anyone and everyone from putting that job title on their profile?

Nothing.

[That can't be good, right?}

Pause...

BTW, I'll use [this bracketing format} when I want to share my inner thoughts and opinions with you, so you get a bit of a view into my less polished internal commentary. The square bracket is [formal], like a placeholder in a legal contract. The brace is {informal} and sets off incidental or optional information. I use them in combination [... } as an expression of my *Business is Personal* style of branding to let you know I'm thinking out loud.

Unpause...

How can executives find good executive coaches if anyone and everyone can use that title? It's no wonder they often simply give up. We need to come to some agreement, first, on what coaching is and then on what executive coaching is as a sub-category. It's remarkable to me that the executive coaching industry has been so successful with such a lack of clarity on its basic definitions. And it will become clear in what follows that even a formal certificate that literally says "Executive Coach" on it, is likely to be insufficient for the demands of the executive coaching role.

I'll get into granular detail on the art and science of executive coaching in this book. For now, I'll present my working definition of this discipline:

> *Executive coaching is a co-creative process in which a coach and an executive elicit insights and actions from each other to optimize the mindset and skillset required for the executive to perform at their personal best in their executive role.*

Does that sound like *remedial* work to you?

Me neither.

Insert Random Coaching Statistics Here

My purpose in this book is to bring together two kinds of people I love and value equally: executives and coaches. The partnerships that result from good executive coaching are often career-altering and even life-changing. So, here's a quick overview of the science of executive coaching results.

The International Coaching Federation (ICF) found that 86% of organizations report positive ROI from coaching, and 96% of executives who tried it would do it again.[2] Another study of more than 100 executives from 56 organizations found that "The majority of the 43 participants ... reported between $100,000 and $1 million as the return on investment in executive coaching."[3]

Executive coaching results in better personal management, self-control, and enhanced leadership skills."[4] Almost everyone knows MetrixGlobal's study that found 77% of executives said coaching had a significant impact on their performance, with the average ROI on executive coaching at 788%.[5] McGovern's EC study averaged 6x ROI.[6]

Some researchers found that only about 14% of executive coaching purchasers considered ROI in their decision, favoring other metrics, like retention and engagement, in their evaluations of coaching's effectiveness.[7] Others argue for a Balanced Scorecard approach to measuring EC outcomes.[8]

[2] The ROI of business coaching: Executive coaching ROI statistics. (2023 Updated). www.rhythmsystems.com.

[3] Boysen, S., Cherry, M., Amerie, W. & Takagawa, M. (2018). Organisational coaching outcomes: A comparison of a practitioner survey and key findings from the literature. *International Journal of Evidence Based Coaching and Mentoring, 16.* 159–166.

[4] Athanasopoulou, A., & Dopson, S. (2016). *Executive coaching outcomes and how organizations can capitalize on them.* In 2016 AOM Symposium on Coaching & Competencies. Said Business School – University of Oxford.

[5] Anderson, M., & Metrixglobal. (n.d.). Executive briefing: Case study on the return on investment of executive coaching.

[6] McGovern, J., Lindemann, M., Vergara, M., Murphy, S., Barker, L., & Warrenfeltz, R. (2001). Maximizing the impact of executive coaching: Behavioral change, organizational outcomes, and return on investment. *Manchester Review, 6*(1).

[7] Lawrence P., & Whyte A. (2014). Return on investment in executive coaching: A practical model for measuring ROI in organisations. *Coach Int J Theory Res Pract, 2014,* 7, 4–17.

[8] Fernández-Llano, C., Bernardo Vilamitjana, M., & Kasperskaya Riabenko, Y. (2023). Assessing the impact of executive coaching on business results applying a Balanced Scorecard Framework. *International Journal of Evidence Based Coaching and Mentoring, 21*(1), 4–16.

Then there's that Manchester Inc study that found that executive coaching resulted in a ton of other business improvements, including:[9]

- Productivity (reported by 53% of executives)
- Quality (reported by 48% of executives)
- Organizational strength (reported by 48% of executives)
- Customer service (reported by 39% of executives)
- Reducing customer complaints (reported by 34% of executives)
- Retaining executives who received coaching (reported by 32% of executives)
- Cost reductions (reported by 23% of executives)
- Bottom-line profitability (reported by 22% of executives)

And the executives themselves reported individual improvements in:

- Working relationships with direct reports (reported by 77% of executives)
- Working relationships with immediate supervisors (reported by 71% of executives)
- Teamwork (reported by 67% of executives)
- Working relationships with peers (reported by 63% of executives)
- Job satisfaction (reported by 61% of executives)
- Conflict reduction (reported by 52% of executives)
- Organizational commitment (reported by 44%)
- Working relationships with clients (reported by 37%)

Empirical studies from the perspectives of executives themselves consistently indicate that they "included improved executive focus, better alignment of key leadership behaviors, candid and ongoing feedback, accountability for appropriate leader behaviors, improved emotional intelligence and ego control and personal support and

---

[9] McGovern, J., Lindemann, M., Vergara, M., Murphy, S., Barker, L., & Warrenfeltz, R. (2001). Maximizing the impact of executive coaching: Behavioral change, organizational outcomes, and return on investment. *Manchester Review, 6*(1).

encouragement, among others."[10] All of these are intensely profitable for both the executive and their organization.

One meta-analysis of the effects of executive coaching found that across six different studies, executives indicated a massive average effect size of 1.27 (that's 1.27 standard deviations above the mean performance level before the intervention).[11]

In my personal practice, I use four different ROI models to determine the financial impact of my executive coaching on the organizations I serve. Each client chooses the model they prefer, and they fill in the numbers. Over a year, the ROI on my coaching is regularly over 30x, often as high as 70x, and in one major group of companies with 80,000+ employees, the ROI was a staggering 900x this year. There's a coaching ROI course on my block[forge} academy (www.learn.corrieblock.com) if you want to know how to calculate these figures.

Ok, the stats section is over. I hope you're on board with the general profitability of executive coaching. Now, let's make sure you're reading the right book on the subject.

Is This Book for You?

This book isn't for everyone, and that's intentional. It's written specifically for three groups of people:

1. **Coaches**: Specifically, those who aspire to work with CXOs and those who already coach executives but want to sharpen their edge. If you're outside of the executive coaching niche, you may find some of the concepts challenging. But if you're ready to take your coaching game to the highest level in business, you're in the right place. If you're a coach of any kind, this book will help prepare you to be an executive coach, and it'll clarify how you

---

[10] Longenecker, C. & McCartney, M. (2020). The benefits of executive coaching: Voices from the C-suite. *Strategic HR Review, 19*(1), 22–27.

[11] Grover, S., & Furnham, A. (2016). Coaching as a developmental intervention in organisations: A systematic review of its effectiveness and the mechanisms underlying it. *PLOS ONE, 11*(7).

can qualify yourself to confidently wear the "Executive Coach" title on LinkedIn.

2. **CXOs**: If you have the words Chief, Director, or President in your job title, you're a CXO, and this book will help you understand the benefits of coaching, as it addresses the major differences between senior management and executive functions. It'll also clarify the services that your EC should be providing for you based on the challenges you are facing. It will help you to choose a good one so you don't miss out on the impact of this powerful relationship.

3. **CHROs, Learning and Development (L&D) Professionals, and Talent Management Professionals**: I'm counting on you to be the matchmakers here. If you are interested in how coaching can benefit your executive-level learning and development strategy, this book is for you. It will serve as a guide for how to sell an executive coaching program to your executives, and it will also show you how to choose great coaches to facilitate strong coaching outcomes for your business. I have a lot more to add for HR professionals about how you can effectively facilitate executive coaching, including corporate executive coaching strategy templates, ROI calculators, and evaluation tools – but due to space constraints, I'll have to save them for another book. Just email me if you want to learn more. I'm not hard to find.

The primary goal of this book is to help you understand why executives require a certain kind of coach and the kind of coach they require.

If you're a **CXO**, imagine having someone you can talk to freely and *transparently* about all of your career aspirations, the office politics that are driving you crazy, your imposter syndrome, insecurities, and even how tired you are in general because your new baby still isn't sleeping through the night (yes, I've addressed this challenge as an EC). Imagine having a confidant beside you who understands business, organizational dynamics, human behavior, leadership, and management; someone who has an above-average understanding of AI and psychology and is laser-focused on your personal happiness and professional success.

Would that improve the quality of your life?

If you're a **coach** who really wants to add that value to the executives in your market, imagine knowing for sure that you can do so consistently over time in all the domains I mentioned above. Then imagine adding a zero to your coaching fees as a result of being able to coach at that highest level – and imagine being able to provide a 50x+ ROI to your clients' companies because of your influence on their leaders.

Would that improve the quality of your life?

Awesome.

But Corrie, What's a CXO?

Right. I should probably expand on the definition here. We've got a working definition of executive coaching; now let's get specific about what we mean by "executive."

I know the abbreviation CXO is sometimes used for Chief Experience Officer these days, but I'm using the X as a placeholder for everything between the Chief and Officer titles. An executive, as I define it in this book (a CXO), is anyone holding a C-suite position. Anyone in any organization who has the word Chief, Director, or President in their job title. This includes CEOs, CFOs, CHROs, CMOs, CIOs, COOs, CITOs, CSOs, C3POs, etc. I know some organizations shy away from "Chief" titles, and others prefer President, Vice President (VP), and Senior Vice President (SVP), or Managing Director (MD), Director, and Deputy Director. In management studies, we sometimes refer to these roles as N and N-1, or L0 and L1.

I'll refer to each of these roles as CXOs and to the Executive Committee, which includes all of these roles in an organization such as the EXCO.

CXO	N	L0	CEO	President	Managing Director
CXO	N-1	L1	CFO, CHRO, CMO, COO, etc.	(Senior) Vice President	Director
C-1	N-2	L2	Deputy CFO, Deputy COO, etc.	(Deputy) Vice President	Deputy Director

I haven't included Board Members because, as individuals, they rarely face the same challenges that CXOs face, which I'll discuss in this book. However, Board Members should have coaching as well, considering the weight of decisions they make and the quality of information challenges they face. I'll leave it to you to decide if your Board of Directors is included in the CXO definition, though it certainly will be in our discussion in Chapter 7.

I'm not militant or precious about the CXO definition. After reading this book, you should decide for your organization which roles are included in the term as I employ it here. For ease and consistency, I'll use the C-suite language, but please adapt it to your Directorial or Presidential structure (or otherwise) if it's not in line with the job titles at the top of your company's organization chart.

There are now hundreds of C-level role titles. Each of them is held by the person responsible for the highest level of competency and authority in their particular discipline in the organization. This pinnacle position is the differentiator that sets them apart from their direct reports and bonds them to each other as colleagues at the executive level.

I'm primarily referring to CXOs in medium to large organizations, both private and public sector, though most of the concepts apply to entrepreneurial leaders and CXOs in small enterprises as well. The size of the organization doesn't matter much. Whether a startup of 100 employees or a multinational of 100,000, all organizations are included because they're all made up of humans, and they're all structured as some kind of collaborative hierarchy, generally with a CEO (or equivalent) at the top.

Who's Speaking Truth to Jack?

"Good coaches provide a truly important service. They tell you the truth when no one else will."

– Jack Welch, Chair and CEO of General Electric (1981-2001)

It's important for both coaches and executives to understand and appreciate the impact of someone like Jack saying something like this.

I agree with Jack, of course. When you're coaching a CXO, you're not just influencing one person; you're influencing the direction of entire organizations, industries, and economies. This isn't just coaching; this is shaping the future of business in the same way that Bob Bowman shaped the future of swimming. So, how do we tell the difference between someone who calls themselves an "Executive Coach" on LinkedIn and someone Jack might have called *his* executive coach?

Let's agree for now that the shareholders of General Electric during Jack Welch's 20-year tenure as CEO would probably want to know the qualifications of any person Jack trusted to provide "the truly important service" of telling him the truth "when no one else will."

And if you're one of those people (as I am) calling yourself an EC on LinkedIn, does that mean Jack was talking about *you* (or *me*)? Could you have provided the important service of telling Jack the truth when no one else would, without posing a risk to his team, his Board of Directors, or GE's stock price?

[Shit. This *is* hard. I think this is probably going to irritate people, but it still needs to be said.}

Why I'm Passionate About This

I'm not exactly sure what qualifies someone to write a book like this, but it needs to be done. I've invested more than 30 years of my life in leadership development, corporate strategy, and executive coaching. I've studied human psychology and behavior, along with history, business, artificial intelligence, neuroscience, and finance. I've buried two of my own failed startups and exited five other successful ones. And I'm widely recognized to be the top EC in the UAE.

[I didn't say it, BTW. Marshall Goldsmith did. And Forbes, SHRM, ATD, CIPD, and a few others. Don't get me wrong, I'm honored, but I'm a bit uneasy about the #1 EC title. I'll get to that in Chapter 8.}

In any case, someone needs to help my executive friends find good executive coaches, so I'm taking on that challenge.

Mostly, though, if you decide to listen to what I have to say, let it be because I care. No, seriously. I literally wrote a book called *Love@Work: The Final Frontier of Empathy in Leadership* in 2023, and it became an Amazon Global #1 Bestseller in Management. I care *a lot* about the leaders in the organizations I serve and about their people. I care enough to do thousands of hours of research on the impact of caring on profitability and publish it as a management science book.

[It's also a pretty fun TEDx talk. You should watch that. It's not hard to find online.}

The most practical expression of my caring for leaders is through my coaching. All of my clients will tell you that I don't rent my time; I rent space in my head. I have an hourly rate, but it's pretty meaningless when I spend my whole CrossFit WOD on a Tuesday morning thinking about how to better help a CEO navigate a major merger and a personal divorce at the same time. That's not a billable hour.

This book, too, is perhaps my most incisive expression of my concern for my clients. The time I've dedicated to coaching research and developing Olympic-level coaches is my way of raising the general level of care we provide for executives.

High-performance athletes train 90% of the time and compete 10% of the time. But for high-performance executives, it's exactly the opposite. They're on the field 90% of the time and spend maybe 10% in training (if at all, including coaching). The training-to-performing ratio is dramatically unbalanced, which makes the choice of coaching at least nine times more critical. The fact that some companies still don't invest in tailored coaching for their executives and that some executives still don't understand the value of coaching for their performance is monumentally stupid.

We now know that an industry downturn will knock 1.5 years off of a CEO's lifespan.[12] It's no wonder Deloitte's recent survey across the US, UK, Canada and Australia found that 70% of CXOs "are seriously considering quitting for a job that better supports their well-being," and 81% of CXOs "say improving their well-being is more important than advancing their career."[13] CXOs are supposed to be taking care of everyone, but who's taking care of them? Who's paying attention to the unique challenges they face and helping them maximize that 10% training time to keep them in 90% high-performance mode?

I am.

[And maybe you are, too. After all, you're reading this book. Good job for a good job!}

How This Book Is Structured

There are many systemic and collective challenges that executives face, but to keep the book to a reasonable length, I've concentrated on seven particular individual challenges and on one-on-one coaching as the core coaching modality.

[I may need to write a companion book on group coaching once this is done.}

In each of the first seven chapters, I'll try to explain one of the major differences between executive coaching and coaching other kinds of managers and leaders in organizations. They're mostly based on challenges that CXOs face that their direct reports (C-1s) won't

---

[12] Borgschulte, M., Guenzel, M., Liu, C., & Malmendier, U. (2021). *CEO stress, aging, and death.* National Bureau of Economic Research.

[13] Fisher, J., & Silverglate, P. H. (2022). The C-suite's role in well-being. *Deloitte Insights.*

encounter nearly as often. In Chapter 8, I'll concentrate on the kind of coach that CXOs need.

The narrative of these chapters runs something like this: Executives need:

1. **Advisory Coaching** tailored for
2. **Peak Performance**, where the
3. **Language Barrier** contributes to a
4. **Defensive Shift**, resulting in
5. **Executive Isolation**, which requires
6. **External Objectivity**, because
7. **High-Stakes Decisions** reinforce the case for ...
   Advisory Coaching. But what kind of advisory coaching exactly?
8. **Wizard Expertise**.

At the end of each chapter is a section called *The CXO Coach Toolkit*, which is designed to:

1. Help executives and talent management professionals figure out what kind of coach they should be looking for to manage the particular challenge outlined in that chapter, and in light of that challenge,
2. Provide guidelines for what coaches should learn and be capable of doing in order to put the "Executive" in their "Coach" title. Please note that these suggestions are exemplary, not exhaustive. It would be nearly impossible to learn all the tools. I just want to give you a solid starting place for your own development.

That's it. Super simple. If you're a coach, that's how we'll put the "Executive" into your "Coach" title on LinkedIn. And if you're an executive, that's how we'll elevate your "remedial" status to "Olympic."

Also note that I haven't bothered to add any fluff to even out the chapter lengths. Some are longer than others because I felt that they needed to be, that's all. Although all of the stories are true, I've sometimes left out last names or changed names completely to protect the identities of those involved.

Oh! And I'm likely going to challenge a lot of what you've heard about coaching … especially the idea that ICF (International Coaching Federation) coaching is the gold standard. If you've built your practice on that foundation, some of this might sting. But I invite you to stay open, question your assumptions, and consider the possibility that CXOs need something more.

Awkward Transition to Chapter 1

Ultimately, what most of my coaching clients are looking for is to be happier, more successful, and make more money. So that's what I'll aim to do for you. When good CXOs find good executive coaches, they both grow, personally and professionally. Whether you're the CXO or the EC in the equation, finding this partnership should result in exactly that.

So yeah: more money and a better career for executives and their coaches.

That's what I'm aiming for here.

Let's begin.

1.

ADVISORY COACHING

"What is the least I need to do today for this person to feel seen and heard and have new insights into their own stuff?"
— **Claire Pedrick and Lucia Baldelli,**
The Human Behind the Coach

Think about that quote for a second. What is the *least* I need to do? Is that *really* what I should be asking myself before I step into my CXO client's office for a coaching session?

Total. Nonsense.

I'll preface this chapter by saying that I have a lot of strict non-advisory coaches as friends and colleagues. I love them, and I strongly believe that non-advisory coaching is both a valid discipline during the initial stages of executive coaching, and a generally effective coaching style outside of the C-suite.

If you're ICF certified you may be having an emotional allergy to this already. Breathe. Please come with me, I want to show you something interesting.

Remember that in each chapter I'll be discussing a particular kind of challenge that CXOs face and that C-1s don't experience quite so intensely. That's not to say that these challenges aren't present in lower levels of management in organizations, just that their potency goes up exponentially as soon as a manager is called a "Chief."

The first thing that a CXO will need that a C-1 won't is an advisory coach.

I often hear from executives that they're challenged to find off-the-shelf training that's suitable for them. They don't want to take a week-long leadership program, even if it is from Harvard or Cambridge, because their role is too nuanced, their industry too specialized, their experience too personal, and their time too valuable.

So, how can executives who are already playing at the highest level continue to develop themselves? The same way Olympic athletes do. They need a development strategy specifically designed for them as individuals.

Those CXOs looking for continued development often take a step toward coaching and invite an executive coach to meet with them. With an open mind and a sincere heart, the CXO might then welcome a coach into their corner office. Let's imagine a coach stepping in for their first session together with a CEO:

"Tell me, what would you like to work on today?"

"I've been having trouble with a member of my Board of Directors bypassing me and conspiring with one of my EXCO members to sabotage an acquisition I'm pursuing."

"What's the outcome you're looking for?"

"I want him to back off and let me do my job."

"Ok, and what have you tried?"

"I sent him an email, called him, tried confronting the CFO, and I'm about ready to lose my shit."

"Ok, and what haven't you tried?"

"What do you mean? If I knew what I hadn't tried, I'd try it. Uh, I suppose I haven't tried actual violence, or firing the CFO, though I did consider it. The problem is, the CFO is really good at her job, and I don't want to lose her talent."

"Great, and what else?"

"And what else what?"

"And what else haven't you tried? And what else haven't you thought of yet?"

"Aren't you supposed to tell me that?"

"No, my job as a coach is to ask you provocative questions to help you realize that the answers you need are already inside you. You've known what to do the whole time, you just weren't aware of it. I'm not here to give you advice, I'm here to help you reach a moment of insight when you discover the solution on your own."

"Look, not to be a jerk here, but if I knew what to do, I wouldn't need a coach. I didn't get to be the CEO of a two-billion-dollar company by being unsure of myself or not reviewing all of my options. What I need is something that's *not* inside me. I need tactics, strategy ideas, leadership plays I'm not aware of."

"That's not what executive coaching is. I'm ethically bound by my coaching organization to not give you any advice or provide any solutions."

"Then I don't need you. Sorry. This is a waste of my time. I don't think coaching is for me."

And just like that, the CEO has been inoculated against executive coaching by a well-meaning, non-advisory coach who thinks non-advisory coaching is the only kind of coaching there is. Subsequently immune to executive coaching, the CEO then spends the rest of their career thinking, "Well, I tried coaching once; it wasn't my thing." And they're right.

Non-advisory coaching has a place in the roster of coaching modalities. But it's not the only one. Too often executives are not presented with the variety of coaching modalities available to them. When coaches present non-advisory coaching as the only "pure" form of coaching, many executives opt out of the service altogether.

The Gold Standard in Coaching

Organizations like the ICF[14] and the Co-Active Training Institute[15] promote active listening, powerful questioning, creating awareness, and designing actions. These are all good tools, but layered on top of them are strict ethical guidelines discouraging coaches from offering advice or potential solutions. They often present non-advisory coaching as the very definition of coaching altogether.

The closest the ICF ever gets to encouraging the coach to add value outside of deep questioning is in permitting observations.[16] These are four of the Professional Certified Coach (PCC) markers, which provide the ethical framework for ICF PCC coaches:

- 4.4: Coach partners with the client by inviting the client to respond in any way to the coach's contributions and accepts the client's response.
- 6.1: Coach's questions and observations are customized by using what the coach has learned about who the client is or the client's situation.

---

[14] International Coaching Federation (ICF). (2024). *International Coaching Federation: Empowering the world through coaching.* ICF.
[15] Co-Active Coaching and Leadership Training. (n.d.). *Co-active.*
[16] International Coaching Federation. (2020). PCC Markers. *ICF.*

- 6.6: Coach allows the client to complete speaking without interrupting unless there is a stated coaching purpose to do so.
- 7.5: Coach shares – with no attachment – observations, intuitions, comments, thoughts or feelings, and invites the client's exploration through verbal or tonal invitation.

Observations are not advice. Under these principles, the coach can make an observation only if the client decides that the observation is helpful – and knows what to do with it. So the first chair violin player's coach might say, "May I make an observation?" and the violin player may accept, after which the coach might say, "You're not moving quickly enough along the fingerboard in this section." The player might then reply, "No shit. What do I do about it?" The coach then is ethically bound to say, "That's your call. What do you *think* you should do about it?"

Of course, the coach is not allowed to proceed from there. They've made their observation. Tactical advice is beyond the scope of the PCC markers. Even if the violin coach knows that a small turn of the wrist is required to succeed, they are ethically restricted by the ICF from offering advice, only observations.

Hmm … perhaps the ICF PCC certification might not apply to top-tier violin coaching.

While writing this book, I reached out to Magdalena Mook, CEO of the ICF, to ensure I represented the ICF fairly. Magdalena was generous enough to take the time to respond, emphasizing that the ICF's core philosophy is to "meet the client where they are," providing flexibility for clients to choose a coach with the necessary domain knowledge. She also acknowledged that advisory coaching might be valuable depending on the client's needs, stating, "If the client is seeking advisory, they can look for a coach with deep experience in the role or industry."[17]

However, this perspective raises critical questions: firstly, is advisory coaching restricted to coaches with previous in-role and/or industrial experience? The answer is no, but I'll discuss knowledge half-life in Chapter 8. Anything skillset oriented, such as leadership and

---

[17] Personal communication, January 3, 2025.

management, time and task mastery, strategic thinking, focus and flow neuro-skills … These are all advisory coaching toolkits with multiple specialized certification programs, and none require previous in-role or industrial experience to align between the coach and coachee.

Secondly, does this flexibility dilute the ICF's claim as a gold standard? As I responded in our exchange, "The ICF might be the most popular certification among executive coaches, but that popularity is correlative, not causative, to what qualifies someone as an effective executive coach." While the ICF provides a valuable foundation, I contend that the self-proclaimed gold standard in coaching is insufficient for coaching at the Olympic-level standard of the executive suite.

ICF certification is not irrelevant, just insufficient for the executive coaching niche.

Magdalena also cautioned against the biases and blind spots inherent in advisory coaching, referencing research (which I've requested and hope to include in future revisions). My initial observation, however, is that cognitive bias risk exists across all coaching styles and is mitigated through continuous learning, ethical practices, and self-awareness, qualities just as critical to advisory coaching as to non-advisory methods. I'll address cognitive bias risk again in Chapter 7.

I really wanted to include more of Magdalena's email dialogue with me, but she ghosted me after our first exchange.[18] I really like her as a person, she was warm in her email and made a sincere effort to connect with me and address my concerns. I know she's doing her best to represent ICF, and I'm not at all offended.

[Magdalena, if you're reading this: Thank you.}

---

[18] [Perhaps I went too far in the email where I said "I would certainly consider McDonald's definition of "burger" in my definition of "burger," but I'm not likely to give McDonald's much weight in my definition of a "Craft Burger." Certainly McDonald's sells many more burgers than any establishment defining its burgers as "Craft Burgers," but their right to define stops at burger, short of craft. All craft burgers are burgers by category, but not all burgers are craft burgers, and it's not the burger maker with the highest production volume that defines the niche. Volume and niche are inversely correlated." Maybe *that's* why she didn't write back to me.}

The Two Most Popular Coaching Books

John Whitmore's *Coaching for Performance* was the bible of coaching in the 20th Century. Whitmore presents coaching as something that can be done by anyone, with anyone else, in any domain.[19] And in the best-selling coaching book of the 21st century, *The Coaching Habit*, author Michael Bungay Stanier clearly defines coaching as a discipline in direct opposition to advisory work.

> Coaching is an art, and it's far easier said than done. It takes courage to ask a question rather than offer up advice, provide an answer, or unleash a solution. Giving another person the opportunity to find their own way, make their own mistakes, and create their own wisdom is both brave and vulnerable.[20]

I met Michael at the Thinkers50 event in London in the fall of 2023. He was dressed for a black-tie dinner in an elaborately decorated, brightly colored Hefneresque gown. I, in my equally rebellious (but far less dramatic) VANS skate shoes, fell in love with him immediately. He's very tall, eccentric, funny AF ... I enjoyed his company a lot. I'm sure he'll be more honored than irritated by my calling him out on this blind spot.

Michael, I think you're a little too narrow in your definition of coaching.

I think what you've defined isn't coaching, but *one type* of coaching. I do appreciate you qualifying your methodology with this quote: "There's a place for giving advice, of course. [*The Coaching Habit*] isn't suggesting that you never give anyone an answer ever again. But it's an overused and often ineffective response."[21] But even this sets advice and answers outside of your definition of coaching. And I don't see a distinction made between advising and coaching in any other human domain where the term "coaching" is used, either formally or informally.

---

[19] Whitmore, J. (2002). *Coaching for performance: GROWing people, performance and purpose.* Nicholas Brealey.

[20] Bungay Stanier, M. (2016). *The coaching habit: Say less, ask more & change the way you lead forever.* Box of Crayons Press.

[21] Bungay Stanier, M. (2016). *The coaching habit: Say less, ask more & change the way you lead forever.* Box of Crayons Press, p. 60.

I agree with Michael that "it takes courage to ask a question rather than offer up advice" and that managers, leaders, CXOs, and coaches often move into solution mode too quickly or wrap up the conversation to gain control. However, I don't see these practices (even prematurely executed) as outside of the coaching practice.

What would it mean for coaches in all other human domains if Michael's (or the ICF's) was the universally accepted definition of coaching? What would the impact be on professional tennis players if their coaches weren't allowed to provide tactics? What happens to the first-chair violin player when her coach refuses to offer a solution to the section of the concerto that's challenging her the most? What happens to the performance of the surgeon whose coach doesn't understand medicine?

I would absolutely love it if Michael had begun his above definition with "Non-advisory coaching is an art..." and simply continued from there. To me, that would have solved this challenge. But the fact is that unlike the domains of championship tennis or concert violin, coaching in the business domain has been recently and popularly defined *de facto* as "non-advisory coaching."

I sent Michael a copy of this book for review before forwarding it to my editor. In our brief email exchange, he politely declined my invitation to contribute the Foreword to this book, although he did ultimately "agree that good coaching is a mix of questions, and advice, and teaching ... and what's needed depends on the context."[22]

[Thank you, Michael. That was gracious of you.}

I completely understand why it makes sense to present non-advisory coaching as *the* definition of coaching, though: you'll sell more books. And if your company's coaching

Michael Bungay Stanier and me at Thinkers50 in London in 2023

---

[22] Personal communication, December 28, 2024.

credential is based on Whitmore's idea that anyone can coach anyone else in anything, then the world's population has become your market, and the remainder of the world's population has become your client's market. The idea that coaching is non-advisory by definition and that, therefore, anyone can coach anyone in anything ... well, it makes great business sense (for the coach and their credentialing organization).

The gold standard is gold for the coaches. But it's not gold for the clients.

Non-Advisory Coaching Modalities

Non-advisory coaching alleviates the need for coaches to be competent in the client/coachee's domain (e.g. leadership and management). And I want to be clear that there are a number of truly great non-advisory coaching modalities in addition to those from ICF. Briefly, here are a few:

1. **Positive Psychology Coaching** – Scott Barry Kaufman's *Self-Actualization Coaching* is my favorite expression of this style.[23] It's evidence-based coaching informed by research in positive psychology to enhance resilience, achievement, and well-being. It focuses on facilitating clients' self-discovery of strengths and promoting well-being without directing specific actions.[24]

2. **Motivational Interviewing** – This collaborative, person-centered form elicits and strengthens motivation for change, without providing direct advice.[25]

3. **Person-Centered Coaching** – A non-directive approach based on the belief that individuals are their own best experts and are intrinsically motivated to become more autonomous and optimally functioning.[26]

---

[23] Kaufman, S. B. (2021). Center for human potential.

[24] Palmer, S., & Green, S. (Eds.). (2018). *Positive psychology coaching in practice* (1st ed.). Routledge; van Zyl, L. E., Roll, L. C., Stander, M. W., & Richter, S. (2020). Positive psychological coaching definitions and models: A systematic literature review. *Frontiers in Psychology, 11*, 793.

[25] Abuse Treatment. (1999). Motivational interviewing as a counseling style. In *Enhancing motivation for change in substance abuse treatment (Treatment Improvement Protocol* (TIP) Series, No. 35, Chapter 3). Substance Abuse and Mental Health Services Administration; Souders, B. (2019). *17 Motivational Interviewing Questions and Skills*. positivepsychology.com.

[26] Palmer, S., & Cavanagh, M. (2006) Editorial – Coaching psychology: Its time has finally come. *International Coaching Psychology Review, 1*(1); de Haan, E., & Burger, Y. (2014). Person-centred coaching: Facilitating the coachee. In *Coaching with colleagues*. Palgrave Macmillan.

4. **Somatic Coaching** – I'm not an expert in this discipline myself, but it involves working through the body to identify and release physical blocks, integrating new paradigm shifts to make them habitual for transformation.[27]

5. **Cognitive Developmental (a.k.a. Transpersonal) Coaching** – This style stimulates and facilitates personal development through awareness of developmental trajectories and patterns influencing one's capacity for change and self-directed growth.[28]

6. **Narrative Coaching** – I really like this approach. It's a co-creative process enabling clients to reflect on and understand their experiences and interactions, leading to new ways of acting in specific contexts. When I use it, I encourage my clients to reflect on and re-author their personal narratives, with me acting as a facilitator rather than an advisor.[29]

I've been picking on Michael because his book is this century's best-selling book on coaching, and on ICF because they're the most popular coaching credentialing organization on the planet. Pop-coaching culture has successfully marketed the idea that these and other non-advisory disciplines are the only valid form of coaching in business. Although non-advisory coaching works for a lot of coaches and many of their clients (including some of mine), it often reaches its limits in the executive office.

Don't get me wrong here: Michael's 7 Coaching Questions are truly brilliant. They are wizard-like. They're exactly what managers and executives need to be using with their teams, and all organizational leaders should know them. But they're not what executives themselves

---

[27] Strozzi-Heckler, R. (2014). *The art of somatic coaching: Embodying skillful action, wisdom, and compassion.* North Atlantic Books; Hamill, P. (2013). *Embodied leadership: The somatic approach to developing your leadership* (1st ed.). Kogan Page.

[28] Bachkirova, T. (2009). Cognitive-developmental approach to coaching: An interview with Robert Kegan. *Coaching: An International Journal of Theory, Research and Practice, 2*(1), 10–22. Laske, O. E. (1999). An integrated model of developmental coaching. *Consulting Psychology Journal: Practice and Research, 51*(3), 139–159; Cox, E. & Bachkirova, T. (2016). A cognitive-developmental approach for coach development. In *The complete handbook of coaching* (3rd ed.). Sage.

[29] Drake, D. B. (2017). *Narrative coaching: The definitive guide to bringing new stories to life* (2nd ed.). CNC Press; Cox, E., Bachkirova, T., & Clutterbuck, D. (Eds.). (2023). *The complete handbook of coaching* (3rd ed.). Sage.

need the most, and nowhere in the book did he say that his methodology was simply *a kind of* coaching.

Advisory Coaching Modalities

Although I, too, often begin my executive coaching engagements using non-advisory techniques and deep questioning, I don't stick to them as an ethical mandate or dominant long-term practice. Once I have a deep enough understanding of my client's character and context, I shift to advisory coaching, because that's what my clients really need.

When attempting to raise the performance of already high-performers – such as Grand Slam tennis players, first-chair violin players, or high-performing executives – the coach is ethically required to know the game. And they're required to offer real psychological and tactical value to the coachee, beyond mere questioning and self-discovery. The coach doesn't have to be able to play the game as well as their executive, but they must be competent enough to coach at their executive's level of play.

The niche domain of surgical medicine has its own coaching methodologies and styles, too. The Wisconsin Surgical Coaching Framework is a well-known example. It includes various non-advisory coaching practices such as directive feedback, but it includes a whole range of advisory modalities as well, including technical and cognitive skills, modeling, and advising. If surgeons aren't well coached, people may die, and good surgical coaching is clearly defined as advisory in nature.

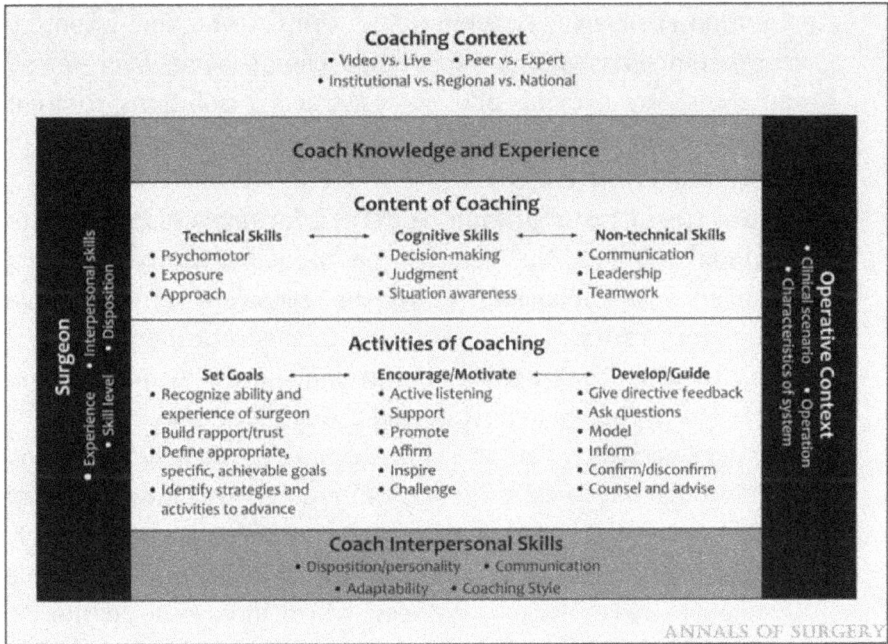

Wisconsin Surgical Coaching Framework[30]

There's a whole range of advisory coaching modalities out there. I won't get sidetracked by listing all of the potential domains in addition to surgery, such as sports, music, leadership, mathematics, public speaking, chess … etc. I'll just stick to a few domain-agnostic advisory coaching modalities to highlight this point.

1. **Cognitive Behavioral Coaching (CBC)** – I use this a lot with my clients. It's an integrative approach using cognitive, behavioral, imaginal, and problem-solving techniques to help clients achieve realistic goals. While CBC can be collaborative, it often involves the coach guiding clients through specific cognitive and behavioral techniques to achieve goals.[31]

---

[30] Greenberg, C. C., Ghousseini, H. N., Pavuluri Quamme, S. R., Beasley, H. L., & Wiegmann, D. A. (2015). Surgical coaching for individual performance improvement. *Annals of Surgery, 261*(1), 32–34.

[31] Neenan, M., & Palmer, S. (2001). Cognitive-behavioral coaching. *Stress News, 13*(15), 15–18; Ducharme, M. J. (2004). The cognitive-behavioral approach to executive coaching. *Consulting Psychology Journal: Practice and Research, 56*(4), 214–224; Ratiu, L., David, O. A., & Baban, A. (2017). Developing managerial skills through coaching: Efficacy of a cognitive-behavioral coaching program. *Journal of Rational-Emotive & Cognitive-Behavior Therapy, 35*, 88–110.

2. **Solution-Focused Coaching** – This outcome-oriented, competence-based approach helps clients achieve preferred outcomes by evoking and co-constructing solutions to their problems. Coaches actively help clients identify solutions and set specific, actionable steps.[32]

3. **Neuro-Linguistic Programming (NLP) Coaching** – Also a favorite toolbox of mine, NLP focuses on modelling and replicating excellence in behavior, using the structure of subjective experience rather than committing to theoretical constructs. I use NLP often to direct clients through specific techniques and exercises to change behaviors and thought patterns.[33]

4. **Gestalt Coaching** – Gestalt focuses on becoming fully aware and turning that awareness into action, creating a positive cycle of resolution and emergence of new focuses. Although commonly thought of as non-advisory, it often involves more directive elements when raising awareness, which then leads to specific actions.[34]

5. **Psychodynamic Coaching** – This modality is based on understanding the mental forces operating within and between individuals and groups, influencing their thinking and behavior. The coach interprets and provides insights into the unconscious motivations and patterns influencing their client.[35]

And there are many more. My personal coaching warehouse includes some really obscure sets of tools from disciplines like Evolutionary Psychological Coaching, Neuroplastic Coaching, and my own Love-Based Coaching. I'm not going to go into those in detail in this book. My point is that they are all advisory methodologies, they all produce positive

---

[32] Greene, J., & Grant, A. M. (2006). *Solution-focused coaching: Managing people in a complex world.* Momentum; Szabó, P. (2012). Making a positive change: A randomized study comparing solution-focused vs. problem-focused coaching questions. *Journal of Systemic Therapies, 31*(2), 21–35.

[33] Passmore, J., & Rowson, T. S. (2019). Neuro-linguistic-programming: A critical review of NLP research and the application of NLP in coaching. *International Coaching Psychology Review, 14*(1), 57–69; Grimley, B. N. (2016). What is NLP? The development of a grounded theory of Neuro-Linguistic Programming, (NLP), within an action research journey. Implications for the use of NLP in coaching psychology. *International Coaching Psychology Review, 11*(2), 166–178.

[34] Siminovitch, D. (2017). *A gestalt coaching primer: The path toward awareness IQ.* Dorothy Siminovitch.

[35] Nagel, C. (2019). *Psychodynamic coaching: Distinctive features* (1st ed.). Routledge; Sandler, C. (2011). *Executive coaching: A psychodynamic approach.* Open University Press..

results in the lives of my clients, and they are all equally valid expressions of the discipline of coaching.

Here's how I see some of the best voices, books, and programs I've studied in the coaching discipline – and where I think the definition of executive coaching should sit.

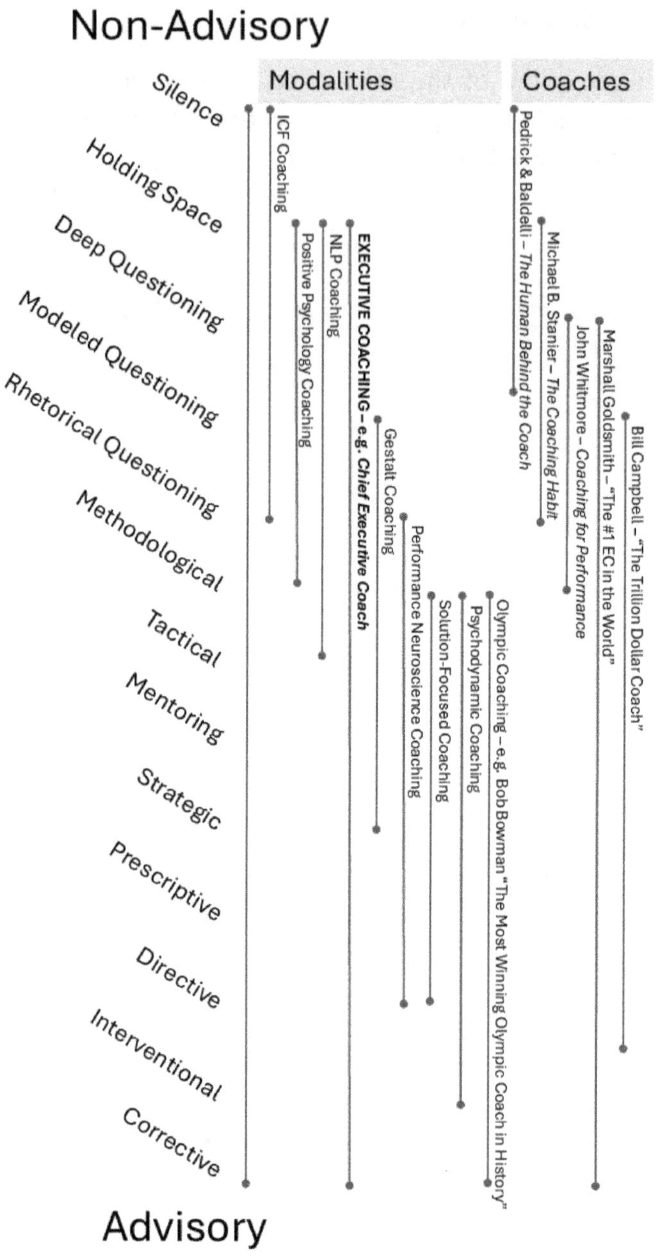
Non-Advisory
Modalities
Coaches
Silence
Holding Space
Deep Questioning
Modeled Questioning
Rhetorical Questioning
Methodological
Tactical
Mentoring
Strategic
Prescriptive
Directive
Interventional
Corrective
ICF Coaching
Positive Psychology Coaching
NLP Coaching
EXECUTIVE COACHING – e.g. Chief Executive Coach
Gestalt Coaching
Performance Neuroscience Coaching
Solution-Focused Coaching
Psychodynamic Coaching
Olympic Coaching – e.g. Bob Bowman "The Most Winning Olympic Coach in History"
Pedrick & Baldelli – The Human Behind the Coach
Michael B. Stanier – The Coaching Habit
John Whitmore – Coaching for Performance
Marshall Goldsmith – "The #1 EC in the World"
Bill Campbell – "The Trillion Dollar Coach"
Advisory

The Coaching Spectrum

On the far-right side of the spectrum you'll see corrective coaching. Don't freak out, corrective coaching is not the whole definition of coaching, it's just a *kind of* coaching (like ICF).

Corrective and interventional coaching are typically initiated by the Board of Directors for the CEO, or by the CEO for an EXCO member. Specific performance expectations or behavior change requests become the mandate of the executive coach. With interventional coaching the coachee typically recognizes their need for change and (sometimes reluctantly) accepts the process. In corrective coaching the coachee is typically resistant to the coaching process and may even interpret it as punitive. The time and effort invested in these kinds of coaching is offset against the attrition cost of a key executive, and the ongoing missed-opportunity cost of their particularly unhelpful style of management or leadership.

I've executed both interventional and corrective executive coaching contracts. They're exceedingly rare, and very challenging as the coachee is often both highly intelligent and hostile to the process. It's up to the coach to earn the executive's trust, which usually starts in a deficit position. Coaching at this extreme advisory level requires a whole new set of tools, most of which you won't find in *The Coaching Habit*, *Coaching for Performance*, or *The Human Behind the Coach*.

Corrective coaching was what Howard from Cigna was wary of, coaching that he perceived as interfering when he didn't need it, so he resisted. For some CXOs the fear that coaching is (or is perhaps perceived by their peers as) a punishment for bad behavior or poor performance becomes the lens through which all executive coaching is perceived. Corrective coaching is a niche within a niche, but for Howard the entire executive coaching industry was equated with the corrective coaching discipline. But this is just as fallacious of a generalization as the equation of non-advisory coaching with the entire industry.

I empathize with CXOs like Howard who bought the fake news on this, but it really must stop here and now. Could you imagine the entire Major League Baseball industry's top players all thinking that coaching was an indication of weakness and a punishment for poor performance? Yet that's the common misconception we're dealing with in business. It's ridiculous. Howard agrees, which is why he's an executive coach now. He doesn't want other CXOs missing out on the performance benefits of coaching like he did.

My point here is that there's a whole other side of the coaching spectrum that isn't addressed by non-advisory pop-coaching certifications like ICF, with equally misguided grandiose perceptions of importance. None of the points on the spectrum are sufficient as a complete definition of coaching, and yet we have ICF on one side saying their definition is the entire spectrum, and executives on the other side thinking their definition is the entire spectrum.

Let's all just take a breath, and step back.

Coaching is a big discipline, and executive coaching is a niche.

The executive coaching niche requires multiple sets of tools from holding space (strategic non-judgmental silence) all the way to corrective intervention. It's a big niche. It took me decades to collect the tools I have now. That's decades of education, certification, training, and experience that someone who can coach anyone in anything wouldn't have to bother with. And that's why so many executives don't find the value they're looking for in a non-advisory coach.

Olympic Athletes Need Olympic Coaches

In the modern age, there's no such thing as an Olympic athlete without an Olympic coach ... with two recent and notable exceptions. During the 2024 Olympics in Paris, Goh Jin Weh from Malaysia was not allowed to bring her coach, Nova Armada, due to accreditation restrictions. She subsequently failed to advance to the top-16 in women's badminton.[36] Munehiro Kugimiya, the coach of the Philippines' gymnast Carlos Yulo, was also notably absent, as the pair had parted ways due to personal

---

[36] Kirubashini, R. (2024, July 31). Jin Wei wins cheers after going down fighting in Olympics debut. *The Star.*

differences.[37] Kugimiya watched from the sidelines as Yulo won gold in both the floor exercise and the vault.

I guess if you show up to the Olympics as an athlete without a coach it could go either way for you. You might miss the finals, and you might win double gold. In any case, all of the other 10,498 athletes competing in the Paris Olympics had coaches with them.

Olympic athletes need Olympic coaches, and you'll never see an Olympic coach asking their athlete, "What do you think you should do?" or "What exercises have you not tried yet?" Why? Because at the highest level of play, the top performers often have all the talent they need, but not all the strategy or information required to develop themselves further. They need to focus on training and their execution, so having a coach as a competent confidant and strategy filter makes sense.

The highest level of human performance, breaking a world record (or disrupting an industry), requires a coach-athlete conversation that moves beyond all the ideas that have been had. They're doing something that, by definition, has never been done before. An athlete might make the regional or national team on their own steam, but if they want to make the Olympics or break a world record, they'll need an Olympic-level coach.

And Olympic level coaches don't ask, "And What Else?" [Yes, I'm picking on A.W.E., sorry Michael. I couldn't help myself. I love you, mate.}

> Q: What difference can a good coach make when off-the-shelf training and non-advisory coaching are simply not providing value at the executive's level of play?

> A: Good advice.

The shift from non-advisory to advisory coaching is the first major difference between coaching CXOs and C-1s. It's a major shift, as major as that from regional to Olympic athletics, and to provide value it requires a coach with an adequate understanding of the game their

---

[37] Kantaro, S. (2024). Carlos Yulo's former Japanese coach proudly watches from Paris Games sidelines. *Rappler*.

player is in, the latest scientific and technological advances in that game, and tools for both strategy and mindset. Throughout this book, we'll return to the athlete-executive metaphor, to offer a lens through which CXO coaching should be separated from coaching C-1s.

The CXO Coach Toolkit

I'll include this section at the end of each chapter to help coaches know what they need to know, to help CXOs know what to look for in their coach, and to help talent management professionals come up with clear qualifications for executive coaches they invite to meet with their executives. Again, this isn't an exhaustive list; it's just a few examples to get you started. Don't feel you need to learn all of them. I expect that would take a lifetime. I'll start with a few of my favorite toolkits, then I'll add a checklist of others you can consider at the end of this section.

The Coaching Habit

For all my critiques of Michael's narrow definition of coaching above, his 7 Coaching Questions are amazing in practice, and I can see why *The Coaching Habit* has sold millions of copies. The book is very simple to read, learn, and apply. I won't spoil it for you here, just buy it.

A Warehouse, Not a Roadmap

CXOs are finding limited benefit in off-the-shelf training and cookie-cutter methodologies. The nature of their work is too specific, too nuanced. The CXO coach is unlikely to succeed with any single established methodology, no matter how well prepared they are or how many steps it has.

So, once you start coaching CXOs, step away from the 10 steps to success or whatever your slickly packaged methodology has been. This is one of those times when what got you here won't get you there.[38] Don't walk in with a plan. Walk in with a closed mouth, an open mind, and a warehouse of tools at your disposal.

---

[38] Goldsmith, M., & Reiter, M. (2007). *What got you here won't get you there: How successful people become even more successful.* Hyperion.

I'm lucky to count Marshall Goldsmith as one of my friends. He has twice been honored as the Thinkers50 #1 Executive Coach and is, in my opinion, the best EC to have lived. For the record, Marshall is an advisory coach. So are my friends Stephen M. R. Covey, and Mark C. Thompson, and so was *"The Trillion Dollar Coach"* Bill Campbell. [R.I.P., Bill.} According to my friends Scott Osman and Jacquelyn Lane at 100 Coaches, so are the vast majority of CXO coaches in their network.

So, if you want to coach an Olympic-level executive, you'll need to behave like an Olympic-level executive coach. I'll go into much more depth on EC qualifications in Chapter 8.

Stop Asking Questions and Start Adding Value
As I mentioned above, I always *start* with a lot of questions, empathy, and active listening. Asking questions for clarification to get your coachee to think from outside of their biases and heuristics is a good thing. Just remember that CXOs earn their way to the top by being strategic, tactical, thoughtful, and decisive. They are a *kind of* person, requiring a *kind of* coach. They're already adept at brainstorming and contingency planning. So, once you have a good understanding of the picture, it's time to add value.

Consider that your history of education, experience, and context are valuable sources of potential enlightenment for your client. You need to stop asking questions and start doing what Olympic coaches do for Olympic athletes: recommend new plays, prescribe new exercises, and suggest new mindset shifts. That's right. At the CXO level, you are ethically obligated to be prepared with enough education, experience, and contextual knowledge to provide good tactical advice and to offer it.

Bottom Line

Non-advisory coaching isn't the definition of coaching, it's a category of coaching. The shift from non-advisory to advisory coaching is essential when working with CXOs. In the next chapter, we'll look at the peak performance pressures that advisory coaching addresses. While non-advisory methods have their place, at the highest level of executive performance coaches must move beyond questioning and into providing real value: strategic, tactical, and psychological.

Here's a good way of looking at it. At the CXO level, it's not you who should be asking, "And what else?" of your clients. They should be asking it of you. Your CXOs should be looking to you for negotiation tools, political strategies, ideas for a work-life blend, psychological tips, and leadership advice.

When an Olympic athlete asks their coach, "And what else can we try?" The Olympic coach always has an idea. That's their job.

That's YOUR job.

The Checklist
This is a list of the major competencies executive coaches should be aware of to address the challenge in this chapter. If you're a coach, you can review the list and consider where you might like to develop your coaching competencies. If you're a CXO, this list will give you an idea of what you should be looking for in your EC's profile.

I've included some links to sample programs for these and other coaching modalities in the resource pack on my block[forge} academy online. You'll find a recommended reading list, including books and academic papers relating to the CXO coach competencies discussed.

You'll also be able to submit your recommendations for programs, organizations, books, and papers for other readers of the *Chief Executive Coach* on the site.

It's completely free of charge. Just follow the QR code.

SCAN ME

www.learn.corrieblock.com/courses/CECresources

Formal Expertise:

- Certification in Non-Advisory Modalities
  - International Coaching Federation (ICF) Certification
  - Motivational Interviewing
  - Person-Centered Coaching
  - Somatic Coaching
  - Positive Psychology Coaching
- Certification in Advisory Coaching Modalities
  - Cognitive Behavioral Coaching Programs
  - Emotional Intelligence Training Programs
  - Narrative Coaching
  - Solution-Focused Coaching
  - Gestalt Coaching
  - Psychodynamic Coaching
  - Stakeholder Centered Coaching
- Advanced degrees in business administration, psychology, or related fields
- Understanding of business strategy, operations, and organizational behavior
- Training in cognitive-behavioral techniques and positive psychology

Informal Expertise:

- Ability to ask deep, clarifying questions
- Skill in providing tactical advice and strategic insights
- Experience in executive roles or working with executives
- Strong interpersonal and communication skills
- Ability to build trust and rapport quickly
- Empathy and active listening skills

2.

PEAK PERFORMANCE

"The purpose of coaching is to close the gap between potential and performance."
– Keith Webb, author of *The COACH Model for Christian Leaders*

The second challenge CXOs face that C-1s won't deal with as much is the pressure of peak performance and the role that mindset plays in facing that pressure. Just a reminder that while there is a lot of room to expand the ideas in this book to team coaching, in the interest of space, I've focused on individual executive coaching.

In this chapter we'll look at positive and negative, and internal and external, influences on peak performance in the C-suite. The negative inner voice is called the critical voice, and its counterpart is self-efficacy. The negative external effect of the self-fulfilling prophecy is called the Golem Effect, and its counterpart is the Pygmalion Effect. We'll get to each of these, but first pause for a second to hear the crack of the shuttlecock

	INTERNAL (the inner game)	EXTERNAL (the self-fulfilling prophecy)
NEGATIVE	Critical Voice	Golem Effect
POSITIVE	Self-Efficacy	Pygmalion Effect

Internal and External Narratives

as it taps just inside the rear line and skips to the back of the court.

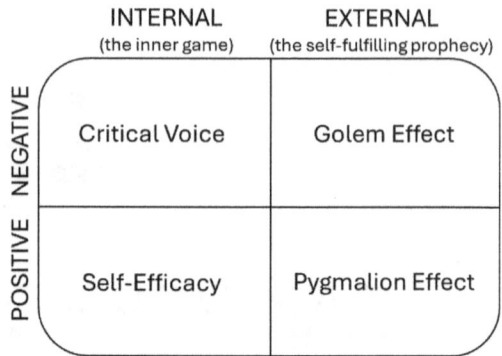

This was it, the moment of truth.

PV Sindhu faced Nozomi Okuhara in the women's singles final of the 2018 Badminton World Federation (BWF) Championships. It was the intense culmination of both women's journeys; they'd beaten out all the other 355 opponents to face each other once again.

They had met a year prior in the 2017 World Championships final, an epic clash lasting 110 minutes—the longest women's singles match in history. Okuhara had won that year, and now this was Sindhu's opportunity for revenge.

Sindhu came out strong, taking the first game 21-19. Tension built as the two Titans fought relentlessly, exchanging powerful smashes and lightning-fast net shots. Okuhara managed to level the match by winning the second game 22-20.

The third game was a nail-biter. The audience perched on the edge of their seats, leaning in. Sindhu and Okuhara pushed each other to the limits, refusing to give a hair's width on the line. The moment of truth had finally come. Sindhu had match point at 20-19. With her foot on the neck of her opponent, the crowd held its breath.

But Okuhara responded with incredible resilience, retrieving a deep shot from Sindhu and leveling the score. At 20-20, it was sudden death. One golden point to decide the champion. Okuhara unleashed a powerful cross-court smash that Sindhu couldn't reach. The shuttlecock kissed the line, and Okuhara collapsed in joy.

Sindhu, devastated, sank to her knees. It was another heartbreak, a second consecutive World Championships final loss. Sindhu's courage and sportsmanship were commendable, but the elusive gold medal had slipped through her fingers once again. Was it the pressure of the game, or something inside?

The Inner Game

Having reached the finals and been defeated by Okuhara in 2017 and 2018, Sindhu had been widely panned by the media as "final-phobic" and a "choker."[39] She had buckled at the finish line twice.

How do you get up after that? What more can you possibly do?

In April 2019, just five months ahead of the BWF Championships, Sindhu replaced her longtime coach, Pullela Gopichand, with Korean coach Kim Ji-Hyun.[40] Kim quickly figured out the cause of her defeat and pulled her attention toward the one big stone that sat in her path: her lack of aggression.

Sindhu was a defensive player. Kim trained Sindhu in channeling all her energy into leveraging her taller-than-average stature to add more power to her attacks, and focusing on maintaining dominance over her opponent during the game.

It wasn't a skill she'd had to learn; it was a tactical shift that started with a new mindset and leveraged a pre-existing asset. It paid off: Sindhu was finally crowned BWF World Champion in 2019. But it wasn't just a win, it was a reckoning. She crushed Okuhara in straight games of 21-7 and 21-7, in only 38 minutes.

---

[39] How PV Sindhu definitively shed off the tag of second best. (2019) *Times Now News*; (2018). PV Sindhu response on her final phobia (BWC 2018). *YouTube.*
[40] PV Sindhu's new Korean coach Kim Ji-hyun focused on producing champions. (n.d.). *India Today. Sportstar.*

No third game required, no new skill learned. Just a new coach. And a new mindset.

It's important to note that improving your performance at such high levels entails less skill development and more psychological recalibration. For executives, it's often not the kind of development that can be learned from Coursera, or even Cambridge; it needs to be teased out by a competent and experienced executive coach.

I'm reminded of former tennis coach Tim Gallwey's description in *The Inner Game* (1974).[41] He suggested that each player (and every one of us, for that matter) has a critical self that continuously berates us from this inside, dismissive of everything that our successful self accomplishes. In addition to reminding us of the consequences of past failures, the critical self also causes the anxiety and stress that typically accompanies facing a big challenge. The critical self is the one causing the most difficulties, yet it assigns blame for those challenges to the successful self through internal diatribes such as "you're gonna blow it. You're going to let everyone down."

It was less than a month ago as I write this that one of my CEO clients said exactly this to me. She was working on a $100 million equity fundraising deal and feared that she might fail in the attempt. If she failed, she'd need to radically shift her strategy, and likely need to restructure her company. All eyes were on her, and her internal narrative was self-critical.

In any high-performance domain, it's internal interference that poses the greatest threat to success, yet these kinds of feelings are often magnified by external pressures and expectations. In both sports and business operations, the limelight shines on every executive action, and every decision is magnified by the weight of external expectations. C-1s don't have to face that kind of limelight, or scrutiny. So, let's add external pressure to the mix.

---

[41] Kimblin, A. (2009). The inner game of coaching. *International Journal of Evidence Based Coaching and Mentoring SpecIssue, 3*, 38–50.; Gallwey, W. T. (1974). *The inner game of tennis.* Random House.

The Divine Ponytail

How much time have you spent in the public limelight, or under the investigator's spotlight? Elite athletes and executives both have to manage this transition to public scrutiny. Even if you're not in a globally recognized or publicly traded company, once you're in the C-suite all eyes are on you. From the entry-level employee to the most remote shareholder, everyone knows who the executives are. Why? Because their livelihoods are tied to the executive's performance. This shifts the pressure narrative from the inner game (internal) to the self-fulfilling prophecy (external).

Roberto Baggio was the all-star in Italy's 1994 FIFA World Cup campaign, and instrumental in the team's advance to the finals. The media called him "Il Divin Codino" (the Divine Ponytail), to reflect his god-like status among his fans. The pressure was intense during the closing penalty kicks in the final game against Brazil. Baggio stepped up to the ball.

[Insert *Lose Yourself* by Eminem here.}

You only get one shot. Do not miss! Once in a lifetime!

[Mom's spaghetti!}

Ok, so he missed. So what? Maybe it was an inner game issue that held him back, or maybe he was just having an off day. That's not my point here. My point is that what happened afterward was nothing like Sindhu's recovery.

Baggio was instantly demonized by the very fans who had moments earlier deified him. In the months that followed, his every step was scrutinized by the press. His private hobbies and personal beliefs became subject to football punditry. An Italian Catholic magazine insisted Baggio be excommunicated for taking up Buddhism. And Italy's Anti-Vivisection League demanded to know what a Buddhist was doing playing football in the first place.

The pressure of that one kick was just the beginning.

When asked about it years later, Baggio sighed, "It is a wound that never closes. I had dreamt of playing in a World Cup final since I was a little boy, but I never thought it could end like that."[42]

No one is a god, no matter how good their hair looks! Despite his efforts to move forward, the miss heard around the world continued to overshadow his professional and personal life. His mental health deteriorated, which took a visible toll on his performance, manifesting in injuries and self-doubt that plagued him on the field for the remainder of his career.

People feel betrayed when they find out their tiny gods are just humans wrapped in high expectations. A single spotlight failure in the public eye can fester into a vicious cycle of constant underperformance and self-doubt. In the realm of peak performance, business is no different from football.

The False Prophet

Marissa Mayer was well known as the design guru behind Google's minimalistic and user-friendly interface. In her 13 years with Google, she was an affectionately self-declared "geek" who left a legacy of successes that included Gmail, Google Maps, and Chrome. She had overseen more than 50 acquisitions and was instrumental in creating more than 40 billion dollars in shareholder value.[43]

Yahoo!, in contrast, was struggling throughout those years, and Mayer was hailed as its savior when she took over as CEO in 2012. Declining ad revenue, competition from Google and Facebook, and internal organizational issues plagued the tech superstar. Mayer resorted to micromanagement in the absence of a cohesive vision for Yahoo!'s future. Her acquisition of Tumblr and investment in Alibaba were incongruous with the company's core business. The media latched on to these challenges, and the pressure to perform intensified with every

---

[42] FourFourTwo. (n.d.). *World Cup icons: Roberto Baggio – The miss that haunted a career (1994).*
[43] ThoughtCo. (2017). Everything you need to know about new Yahoo! CEO Marissa Mayer. *ThoughtCo.*; Who is Marissa Mayer? Everything you need to know. (n.d.). Www.thefamouspeople.com.

headline.[44] In 2016 Variety Magazine bestowed upon the "geek" a terrible new nickname, "The False Prophet," depicting her image on the cover as a Christ-like character carrying a Y-shaped cross.[45]

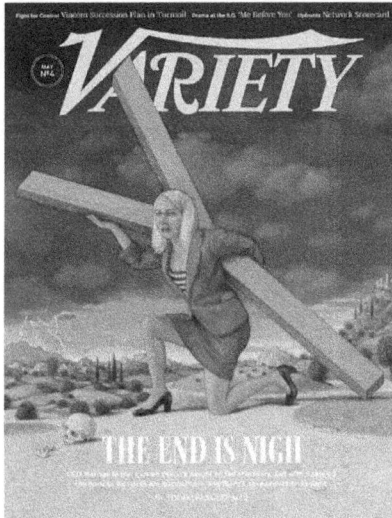

How Marissa Mayer failed to turn the company around.
(2016, May 24). Yahoo Entertainment.

Mayer stepped down when Yahoo! was acquired by Verizon in 2017.

The terrible truth is that the step into the C-suite isn't a step at all, it's a leap, akin to a footballer stepping onto a World Cup pitch for the very first time. It's a massive jump across a yawning chasm of expectations and accountabilities resulting in crushing pressures that the C-1 management layer doesn't experience until they've taken it. Mayer's last job title at Google was Vice President of Search Products and User Experience. Her shift to CEO proved to be too much, and the False Prophet of Yahoo! suffered the same fall from grace as the Divine Ponytail.

---

[44]Tobak, S. (2016, July 26). *RIP Yahoo: Why Marissa Mayer failed. FOXBusiness*; Snider, J. S., & Mike. (n.d.). Marissa Mayer's diminishing legacy at Yahoo. *USA Today.*
[45] Controversial magazine cover features Yahoo CEO. (n.d.). *ABC7 San Francisco*; Yahoo's false prophet: How Marissa Mayer failed to turn the company around. (2016, May 24). *Yahoo Entertainment.*

I don't know if Mayer had an executive coach; I do know that Baggio had at least four more coaches in his career after the 1994 World Cup. My point is simply that high-performance roles in any domain are tough for any human, with or without a coach.

The Self-Fulfilling Prophecy

The concept of self-fulfilling prophecy can be found in ancient Greek, Chinese, and Indian philosophies. But it wasn't until the 1950s that sociologist Robert K. Merton gave it a catchy name and a formal definition.[46] He described the self-fulfilling prophecy as an unfounded prediction that, either directly or indirectly, influences others and subsequently causes the prediction to manifest as true. It's like planting a seed of belief in your mind and then watching it sprout and grow into reality. It can take both positive and negative forms.

In Jewish folklore, a Rabbi is said to have carved a clay creature and brought it to life to protect the community. Over time, though, the Golem became uncontrollable and unruly. It eventually had to be destroyed. The Golem's creation led to unintended negative outcomes, so in research it's come to serve as a symbol of negative self-fulfilling prophecies.[47]

For Sindhu it was a defensive posture predicting critical failures on the badminton court.

For Baggio, it was a single missed opportunity predicting a career of underperformance. One missed kick in isolation shouldn't cause a future career of misses; when it does, that's the Golem Effect.

Mayer's focus on acquisition and doubling down on search had made her successful at Google, but they were outside of Yahoo!'s core business. It was the media's unrelenting mockery of these decisions that

---

[46]Merton, R. K. (1968). *Social theory and social structure*. Free Press.

[47] Babad, E. Y., Inbar, J., & Rosenthal, R. (1982). Pygmalion, Galatea, and the Golem: Investigations of biased and unbiased teachers. *Journal of Educational Psychology, 74*(4), 459.; Leung, A., & Sy, T. (2018). I am as incompetent as the prototypical group member: An investigation of naturally occurring Golem Effects in work groups. *Front. Psychol., 9*, 1581.

grew into a self-fulfilling prophecy resulting in an unstoppable decline of share value.

On an institutional scale, the Golem effect happens when an institution (such as a major bank or investment firm) becomes extremely large and influential, with an implicit assumption that it is crucial to the stability of the financial system. This impression leads investors, customers, and other market participants to start viewing these institutions as "too big to fail." They believe that if such an institution were to collapse, it would trigger a domino effect, leading to widespread panic, economic downturns, and job losses.

Because of this perception, such institutions may take on more risk than smaller players. They might engage in obscure investments, assuming that if things go wrong the government or central banks will step in to prevent their collapse. Regulators, aware of the systemic risk posed by these institutions, often provide bailouts or emergency support during times of crisis, which reinforces the belief that these institutions are indeed "too big to fail."

And the cycle continues.

Until one day, it doesn't.

I remember the 2008 Financial Crisis very well. After all, it was the first time I had experienced bankruptcy. My personal investment portfolio was completely tied up with a broker I thought was "too big to fail." I was wrong. I was as wrong about my broker as the Yahoo! Board of Directors was about Mayer.

Whether we begin with an omnipotent institute as too big to fail, a footballer's "Samsonesque" hair prompting his deification, or the untouchable demi-goddess of Google, the Golem Effect is usually the pin that bursts our tiny-god bubble.

[It sucks for us fans, but it's devastating for the tiny god.}

The good news is that the self-fulfilling prophecy phenomenon isn't all doom and gloom. If intentionally leveraged, it can influence peak performers In a positive direction as well. The CXO coach's role is to intentionally curate a positivity bias decoupled from external influences. There's a psych tool we can use for this, one that emerges poetically from the tale of another set of false gods.

The Pygmalion Effect

The Pygmalion Effect in psychology is when "one person's expectation for another person's behavior comes to serve as a self-fulfilling prophecy."[48] It comes from an ancient Greek story of a man from Cyprus named Pygmalion who created a sculpture of a woman so incredibly beautiful that he fell in love with it. He begged the gods to bring him a real woman of the same beauty, and the gods answered by bringing the statue to life. Pygmalion's positive expectation produced a positive result.

A couple of thousand years later, in 1964, researchers tested the Pygmalion Effect by conducting an IQ test among a group of elementary school kids. Next, they randomly selected some of the kids and told their teachers that these students were highly gifted. The teachers naturally treated them as gifted, resulting in higher expectations and more focused attention. At the end of the year, the researchers re-administered the same IQ test, and, sure enough, the randomly selected "gifted kids" outperformed their peers. Over and above intrinsic talent and intelligence, the teacher's expectation turned out to be the greatest indicator of higher performance among their students.[49]

Six decades after the gifted kids experiment, The Pygmalion Effect in business psychology is well known; it is most often referred to as an external influence on internal self-efficacy. It's the belief in one's own ability to perform, and in addition to pre-requisite skills and motivation (both intrinsic and extrinsic), self-efficacy is a major determinant of executive success. The impact of executive coaching as a Pygmalion

---

[48] Oxford Bibliographies. (n.d.) Self-fulfilling prophecy and the Pygmalion effect in management (Abstract). *Oxford bibliographies.*
[49] Rosenthal, R. (2003). Pygmalion in the classroom. *American Psychologist, 58*(3), 839.

influence on executive self-efficacy is very well established in the research.[50]

[Almost done with the science-y bit.}

Not surprisingly, a meta-analysis of thirteen studies on the Pygmalion Effect in organizations found that the influence of positive expectations is consistently effective, with the average effect close to that found by the original researchers' review of 345 previous studies based across a range of domains.[51] Essentially, positive expectations drive positive performance, whether the high performer is a badminton player or the CEO of Yahoo!.

That's why executives with coaches who believe in them tend to believe more strongly in themselves, and perform better as a result. The EC's expectations of the CXO can influence performance in a way that mitigates the negative influences of both the critical inner voice and the external Golem Effect. The impact of this on high-performance individuals in any organization cannot be overstated, so let's look at how to use this in executive coaching.

The Pygmalion-Olympic Executive Coach

"I can do that?" she asked me.

"Of course you can, all the rules are made up, by people not smarter than you. And you've earned the right to make up a few rules yourself."

Dina was the key person responsible for sustainability at EXPO 2020 in Dubai. It was a big job. She was immediately made Partner in one of the Big-4 consultancies, and she was now looking to pivot into starting her own eco-friendly VC. The short conversation recounted above happened

---

[50] Bandura, A. (1997). *Self-efficacy: The exercise of control.* Freeman; Stewart, L. J., Palmer, S., Wilkin, H., & Kerrin, M. (2008). The influence of coaching on self-efficacy. *International Journal of Coaching in Organizations,* 6(1), 13–22.
[51] Kierein, N. M., & Gold, M. A. (2000). Pygmalion in work organizations: A meta-analysis. *Journal of Organizational Behavior,* 21(8), 913–928; Rosenthal, R., & Rubin, D. B. (1978). Interpersonal expectancy effects: The first 345 studies. *Behavioral and Brain Sciences,* 1(3), 377–415.

at least a dozen times over the course of about six months as she was setting things up and getting ready to resign her partnership.

I told her she was strong enough to walk out of a negotiation, smart enough to lead people smarter than her, connected enough to out-maneuver some shady players, worthy enough to demand ridiculous amounts of money for her time and efforts, fast enough to outpace her competitors, and loved enough that she could just relax and let a few personal events unfold that were out of her control.

Did I know for a fact that she was strong enough, smart enough, connected enough, etc.? No. Of course not: there are no metrics for that. How could I have possibly known that? I'm just her coach.

What I did know is that she trusts me, and if I tell her that she's all kinds of globally capable, and I treat her like an eternal wellspring of wisdom and capacity, she's more likely to believe my truth about her than her own, and more likely to perform accordingly. Just like the gifted kids.

They weren't necessarily gifted until they were treated like they were gifted.

Then they became gifted.

Teachers teach.

Coaches coach.

Having someone on the sidelines who knows you well and is telling you that you're capable of more than you think you are, is a massive strategic advantage. Coaches need to understand how deeply their voice can influence not just self-esteem but self-efficacy and, ultimately, performance. A good coach's consistent positive affirmations and focused interventions can help executives gradually change their perspective from one of imposter syndrome to one of empowerment.

I've seen this personally dozens of times – when my CXO clients start to free themselves from their critical inner voice or the echoes of Golemic prophecies and carve a path toward significant personal growth by adopting a more optimistic perspective on their performance than their own.

Whose perspective do they adopt instead?

Mine.

I'm that Pygmalion influence. It's not deep questioning, and it's not non-directive. It's pure positive psychology.

What was Kim's breakthrough influence on Sindhu? It wasn't a set of plays or a new badminton skill. It was a shift from a defensive to an offensive mindset. It was a Pygmalion effect. He saw her as an aggressive player with a height advantage, and when she saw herself that way too, she behaved like one. That's why she won. That's good coaching.

Converting the Critical Inner Voice into Self-Efficacy

Let's look at C-1 positions. Who is it in the organization that sets positive expectations for a C-1? It's the CXO. For example, the Deputy CFO's performance will be positively influenced by the positive expectations of the CFO. That's clear science.

But who's setting those expectations for the CFO? Or the CEO?

The expectations of company owners are rarely aimed at positive leadership performance; they're usually aimed at financial results. Let's also be clear that management increasing KPIs does not qualify as Pygmalion influence. A nation's Olympic committee wants the gold medal, they're not typically interested in the positive psychology that influences the athlete's actual performance in achieving it.

That's the Olympic Coach's job.

Likewise, the Board of Directors might well be interested in the NPM (Net Profit Margin) and Share Value, but the positive psychology that influences the CEO's performance, and that of their EXCO team, is unlikely to be on the Board Meeting agenda.

[Again, it's the Executive Coach's job ... though sadly this role is often vacant.}

Now, the important question is, what can be done when the self-fulfilling prophecy is negative (Golem Effect) – the CXO silently questioning their performance and external pressures building an inevitable path toward failure, as happened to Mayer? Perhaps the only way to break the cycle of the self-fulfilling prophecy is by redefining the very assumptions upon which the prophecy was initially based, that is, by hijacking it with a Pygmalion voice and reversing the trend. This proactive approach entails issuing early, consistent, and positive statements or gestures to counteract negative beliefs and prevent them from taking root.

Someone the CXO trusts – even more than they trust the internal and external negative narratives – must be present.

Whose job is that on your organizational chart?

Name a Premier League football team whose Owner is regularly sitting with the Team Captain and investing in the Pygmalion Effect to influence them (and, vicariously, the whole team) to perform better. This doesn't happen. Why?

That's the coach's job. That's why.

The CEO of a company might have high expectations of themselves even as they are also struggling with their inner voice and staving off a self-fulfilling prophecy. The fact is, if they are being influenced by a competent EC with high expectations, they'll perform better.

[Don't follow me, follow the science, because that's what I'm doing.}

The CXO Coach Toolkit

Bear in mind the point I made earlier: while athletes train 90% of the time and perform 10%, for CXOs it's exactly the opposite. Athletes like Sindhu have annual world championship games they're working toward, but CEOs like Mayer don't have the

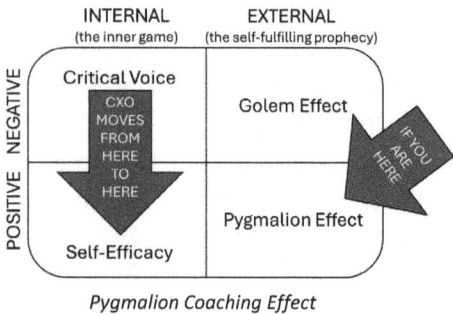

Pygmalion Coaching Effect

luxury of being able to absorb a bunch of training days between competitions when they can underperform without consequences. The C-suite is an "always-on" performance context.

Managing both the inner game and external performance pressures is typically a mindset challenge. Mayer's failure to drop her historical best practices in favor of her new operating environment echoes Sindhu's repeated championship game losses. But Sindhu had something Mayer didn't: a new coach, and a new mindset. Don't underestimate the Pygmalion Coaching Effect.

Clifton Strengths

Taking a page from Kim's coaching of Sindhu in this chapter, a good EC should focus on the strengths rather than the weaknesses of their coachees. Remember that focusing on fixing weaknesses comes from the assumption that with enough time and effort, we can all become perfect, like a god. The Divine Ponytail and the False Prophet are perfect examples of why godliness is too high an aspiration for any executive. It's a lot more effective to work with what you've got (like Sindu's height) to find the advantage. To do that, though, you need to know what you've got.

For that, I recommend Clifton Strengths Assessment.[52] I've been using it for years with my clients. It's well-researched, not difficult to learn, and very easy to apply. It'll give you lots of ammunition for your Pygmalion-Olympic approach to positively influence your clients' view of themselves, and it'll help you to see where your CXO clients are stepping outside of their wheelhouse in their leadership behaviors. It also comes from *them*. It's a product of their view of themselves, so it's easily leveraged as an alternative inner voice when they're facing negative narratives or imposter syndrome.

A focus on strengths is just one expression of Behavioral Tendency Coaching, which uses personality types and tools from psychology to identify behavioral tendencies. Having a clear view of one's tendencies helps to chart a path toward modification. But it also helps in seeing the

---

[52] Rath, T. (2007). *StrengthsFinder 2.0.* Gallup Press; Gallup. (2024). CliftonStrengths.

kinds of people who might balance out an individual CXO, so I also use this tool to help my clients chart a path to an omni-talented team. I encourage them to surround themselves with people whose strengths cover their weaknesses, and to trust them and collaborate with them. CXOs are often looking for better individual performance, but business is a team sport, and this is a good shortcut for building a strong leadership team.

Positive Psychology Coaching

I know that Positive Psychology Coaching is commonly pitched as non-advisory and non-directive, but the tools are easily repurposed for a Pygmalion coaching approach. If you're a geek like me, I recommend *Positive Psychology Coaching in Practice* as a reference,[53] or if you prefer training, consider the Foundations of Self-Actualization Coaching program.[54] In addition to a focus on strengths, positive psychology provides tools aimed at mindfulness, well-being, mental clarity, and optimism.

Pure optimism has its limits, though. In the neuroscience studies of positive psychology, we've learned that affirmations that don't line up with either our values or our view of ourselves are easily dismissed and can sometimes cause cognitive dissonance.[55] Basically, if we say something optimistic about ourselves that we don't believe is true, there's a part of our brain that calls "bullshit," and it causes more pain than positivity.

---

[53]Palmer, S., & Green, S. (Eds.). (2018). *Positive psychology coaching in practice* (1st ed.). Routledge; Also see van Zyl, L. E., Roll, L. C., Stander, M. W., & Richter, S. (2020). Positive psychological coaching definitions and models: A systematic literature review. *Frontiers in Psychology, 11,* 793; Seligman, M. E. P. (2011). *Flourish: A visionary new understanding of happiness and well-being.* Free Press.

[54]Kaufman, S. B. (2021). Center for human potential.

[55] Cascio, C. N., O'Donnell, M., Tinney, F. J., Lieberman, M. D., Taylor, S. E., Strecher, V., & Falk, E. B. (2016). Self-affirmation activates brain systems associated with self-related processing and reward and is reinforced by future orientation. *Social Cognitive and Affective Neuroscience, 11*(4), 621–629; Galinsky, A. D., Stone, J., & Cooper, J. (2000). The reinstatement of dissonance and psychological discomfort following failed affirmations. *European Journal of Social Psychology, 30*(1), 123–147.

The key to cracking this code is the Pygmalion approach. The positive voice needs to be external, and the coachee needs to trust the coach's voice as much as (or more than) they trust their critical inner voice.

Peak Performance Coaching
I hate this term. Peak performance is unsustainable, by definition, because it's "peak." No one can sprint at their highest speed for more than a few seconds. I agree that learning to sprint positively improves overall running pace and endurance, but many coaches and programs offering peak performance coaching tend to focus on sprint-only kinds of training.

Instead, I advocate optimum performance. It's not your top speed I'm interested in, but raising the level of your average day. For that, I have a few toolkits that I combine to help my clients. Executive coaches should have the following three toolkits:

1. **Evolutionary psychology**: Read everything you can get your hands on by David Buss and Robert Sapolsky. Having this knowledge base helps you to easily illuminate attitudes and behaviors that are inherited from a million years of successful survival and adaptation. The tools we (and our clients) often employ were designed to help us survive in a world that no longer exists: a world of relative scarcity and violence. We now live in a world of unfathomable abundance, a world our ancestors could not have imagined and have not prepared us for. You need to know the difference.

2. **Neuroscience**: Attitudes, behaviors, mindset, paradigm shifts, mental models ... all of it is built on a Lego-like foundation of electricity, chemistry, and proteins. You don't have to be a neuroscientist, but as an EC, you'll be a lot more effective if you understand the foundational concepts of neurochemistry, neuroplasticity, and neuroeconomics and can put them to use in your practice. I use these tools a lot In my practice, though I typically don't go into the science behind how or why they work with my clients.

3. **Time and Task Management**: I hope I don't have to tell you that the Eisenhower Matrix is completely outdated now. CXOs aren't sorting between important and unimportant anymore. Everything is important, and everything is urgent. The fact is, there are many more excellent and meaningful things to do every day than can ever be done. You'll need a toolkit for helping your clients with scheduling, prioritization, discipline, leverage, flow, and mitigating distractions and interruptions. I have a protocol for this that has transformed my clients' efficiency and effectiveness – but look out for it in my next book: *Undistractable*. For now, I also recommend *Eight Steps to High Performance* by Marc Effron.[56]

If you're looking for a good program to get a handle on how to apply these three disciplines in your coaching, I recommend connecting with the Flow Research Collective, and learning all you can from them.[57] The science is solid and the application is very effective. Also check out npnHub (npnhub.mn.co). It's a community of Neuroplasticians, and there's a lot of great material on there for learning how the brain wires itself, and how to apply the science to your coaching practice.

Bottom Line

CXO roles come with unique and intense pressures. Performance at that level isn't just about skill or strategy; it's about managing the internal and external pressures that accompany high-stakes roles. Whether in sports or business, the greatest challenges are very often psychological.

As we've seen, success at the highest level demands more than technical proficiency; it requires a mindset shift that can often only be facilitated by competent coaching. By focusing on strengths and positive expectations, and leveraging tools like the Pygmalion Effect,

---

[56] Effron, M. (2018). *8 steps to high performance: Focus on what you can change (ignore the rest)*. Harvard Business Review Press.
[57] Performance Neuroscience Coaching Certification - Apply Now. (2023). Flowresearchcollective.com.

neuroscience, and psychology, executive coaches can help leaders to rise above internal doubts and external pressures to achieve their best.

They'll need to be able to perform at their best, and lead at their best. The pressures of peak performance only amplify and exacerbate the already endemic C-Suite challenge of the language barrier. That's what we'll look at in the next chapter.

The Checklist

Here are the broad strokes of what an executive coach should be aware of when addressing peak performance pressures. There's a much more comprehensive list of sources in the online companion program. You can also submit your comments and suggested resources there. It's free of charge. Just follow the QR code at the end of Chapter 1 or at the end of the Conclusion of this book.

Formal Expertise:

- Training in positive psychology and cognitive-behavioral techniques
- Knowledge of performance coaching frameworks (e.g., Clifton Strengths, Positive Psychology Coaching)
- Certification in neuroscience or psychology-based coaching programs
- Understanding of motivational theories and techniques
- Strong expertise in time and task management
- Basic understanding of neuroscience
- Basic understanding of evolutionary psychology

Informal Expertise:

- Ability to foster self-efficacy and resilience
- Skill in mindset coaching and reframing techniques
- Experience in high-stakes decision-making environments
- Ability to identify and leverage individual strengths
- Knowledge of stress management and mindfulness practices
- Ability to create a supportive and motivating coaching environment

3.

LANGUAGE BARRIER

"Great coaches lie awake at night thinking about how to make you better. Most people don't spend a lot of time thinking about how they are going to make someone else better. But that's what coaches do."

– Ronnie Lott, about his coach, Bill Campbell in
The Trillion Dollar Coach

The third major challenge that CXOs tend to face and that C-1s are less likely to encounter is the inter-departmental foreign language problem. CXOs have to perform at peak levels consistently, but often this is hampered by considerable communication difficulty with their own team.

CXOs spend their entire careers becoming experts, and it's their niche competence in their area of discipline that earns them their seat at the EXCO table. They are the most competent they've ever been, yet at the same time, they can feel the most stupid and inadequate they've ever felt.

First-time CXOs are often the unwitting victims of an elaborate, hidden bait-and-switch plot. It's sinister, and yet no one seems to notice. They've been promoted and hired as a direct result of their excellence in their specialized field and its associated language, but as soon as they sit at the EXCO table, they're encouraged not to use it. This can be really confusing and disheartening.

A Problem of Language

Paul was the CEO of a multinational company with more than 50,000 employees. He called me in specifically to coach his new Chief Information Officer (CIO).

"Hey Paul, how can I help?" I started.

What You Think the Language Barrier Looks Like

"I asked Dennis to produce a new digital strategy for the company, and to present it at the 90-day point after he took office. I was excited. He was excited. But what he presented was 70 slides long and took an hour and a half. It was exhausting. And I could see that he was proud of himself, and he'd clearly put in a lot of work. I didn't want to deflate him, but I'm in my 60s, and I understand Blockchain well enough, but RPAs, APIs … Kubernetes? And I'll be honest with you, as a fisherman, a data lake sounds like an oxymoron to me. But look, I didn't want to discourage him. He's competent, I get that, otherwise I wouldn't have hired him. So, I told him I was struggling to understand his strategy and I asked him to take a week and come again with a more elegant and perhaps more comprehensible plan."

"Ok," I replied, "And did he?"

"Well, kind of? I guess? Maybe he confused comprehensible with comprehensive, but the new deck was 120 slides long and much more detailed, so I stopped him about an hour in. I told him I wasn't going to be able to sign off on any of it until I could understand at least half of it. He was shocked, and he left the boardroom visibly frustrated."

"So the coaching you want is for you? So you can understand the digital strategy language?"

"No. Understanding that vocabulary isn't a requirement of my job. It's a requirement of his. What I need is for him to stop peacocking around in a language I don't understand, and to show me something in a language I can."

"Right. Got it."

I met with Dennis the following week. I asked him to walk me through the 120-slide Digital-Monster-Deck. It took three hours, but it was in a language I understood, and I recognized very quickly how much effort, thought, and clear competency was embedded in his digital strategy.

The issue wasn't strategy or competency; it was language, and it had so far cost the company two weeks in delay cost at a value of roughly $49,000 (I'll explain that figure later).

Dennis had spent his entire career in the IT function. For more than 20 years, he had progressed from cybersecurity through digital services, and into managing major digital strategy projects. He had interacted predominantly with techies his whole adult life. This was the first time in his career that he reported directly to a boss who wasn't also a digital services guru.

In fact, all functional departments have their own vocabulary, values, beliefs, cultural artifacts, and these invariably influence the default (native) language of the functional CXO. However, none seem to be as dominant on the EXCO as the language of finance.

The Dominant Language of Finance

Eventual CFOs rarely start their careers outside of the finance function. As of 2023, only a fifth of CFOs didn't carry a CPA or MBA degree specifically, a figure in steady decline.[58] Accountants who eventually become CFOs rarely leave the finance function along the way.

An Accountant might become a Senior Accountant then an Accounting Manager before progressing through Financial Controller and Finance Director roles, eventually becoming a CFO only 20 or more years after starting their career. The successful first-time CFO has often had a career path solely charted in the finance department, and therefore, their organizational worldview and native language are also dominantly those of finance. They see the organization as a data lake, a visualization dashboard, and a series of spreadsheets, all of which lead to the Holy Grail of KPIs: Net Profit.

Finance is their native language. And it's currently the dominant language of most C-suites.

It's also compelling to note the abundance of finance professionals in CEO roles. According to a 2019 survey by Forbes, more than a fifth of Fortune 100 CEOs began their careers in finance.[59] In many corner offices, it's finance talk that rules. But it's important to recognize finance

---

[58] Strickland. B. (2024, January). From CFO to CEO: An increasingly popular path. *Journal of Accountancy.*

[59] Whitler, K. A. (2019, October 14). New study on CEOs: Is marketing, finance, operations, or engineering the best path to CEO? *Forbes.*

as a specialized language. It consists of numbers, charts, probabilities, and algorithms – a language that quite often the CEO and CFO speak fluently. But finance language is esoteric. To EXCO peers not raised in the finance function, it can be experienced as a kind of *secret* language between the CEO and CFO, one that keeps them at arm's length.

Translating IT into Finance

That was the case with Dennis. Finance was not Dennis's native tongue. He could barely speak it at all, in fact. Sure, the first-time CIO could write a budget for a DX project or IT department, but NPV? WACC? CAGR? Delay Cost? – these weren't tools Dennis had learned to use yet.

What the Language Barrier Actually Looks Like

Paul and Dennis were both highly competent and incredibly experienced. Both were industry titans, with great mutual respect and playing for the same team, but they spoke different departmental languages.

In their company, finance was the dominant language of decision-making. But IT was the language that had earned Dennis his seat at the table.

"I just want to make the plan as clear as possible," Dennis sighed.

"I get that," I responded, "and you did. For anyone with a history in digital strategy, your time on task, uptime, and cycle time improvement projections are amazing. And I can see how the changes you want to make will lead to those results."

"So what's the problem then? Why isn't Paul getting on board? I mean, isn't this what he hired me for?"

"Absolutely, but he needs it to be in his language. Can we convert a bunch of these outcomes into finance for him?"

"There's a budget in there already."

"That's not what I mean. Let's provide him with an NPV and Delay Cost calculation."

"I've never done that before."

We got to work converting the initiatives and milestones in the strategy into projected financial impact statements. We created a list of assumptions and probability-weighted each of them to bring up the level of accuracy. The CFO provided the WACC so we could find the NPV, and from that, the Delay Cost. And just like that, the digital strategy had been condensed into a small series of spreadsheets, most of which were in a language foreign to Dennis.

"I don't get it. Like, I actually don't understand what Discounted Cash Flow means, or how it's relevant to what I'm doing."

"There! It's right there." I pointed to the spreadsheet. "It's $3500 per day."

"What is?"

"The delay cost. Given all of our reasonable assumptions, probability-weighted and even insulated with a 25% general uncertainty adjustment, the cost of delay on this one section of your project is $3500 per day."

"That's how much we pay if we don't do it?"

"That's how much you paid today because you didn't start yesterday. It's an elaborate missed opportunity cost. This is what you take to Paul."

Another 10 days had gone by. This meant that the number of days between Dennis' initial presentation to Paul and now was roughly 24 days. At a delay cost of $3500 per day, that's $84,000 in unrecoverable missed opportunity value.

The CFO, Ahmed, took a week with Dennis and me to sharpen the assumptions and the projections. That week cost the company a further $24,500. Dennis and Ahmed then presented the plan together. Paul approved the plan the next day.

It's important to note here that Dennis' DX strategy did not change during the time between his initial presentation to Paul and Paul's approval of it almost a month later. The only thing that changed was the language, from IT to finance, and at a delay cost of $108,500.

This happens a lot more often than you'd think. In fact, if you're a CXO reading this book there's a pretty good chance this has happened in your EXCO this quarter already. So what's the root cause of all of this inefficient communication at the executive level?

Specialization.

Proving Your Worth

Finance and IT aren't the only specialized languages in organizations. The entry-level Recruiter might eventually become a CHRO, or an entry-level Market Researcher might mature into a CMO, each of them spending a decade or more of their lives, day after day, seeing the organization through the filters of their departmental priorities and speaking to their colleagues in their own native languages.

The new CXO eager to prove their worth to their EXCO peers often does so with a display of competency. Naturally, they do it in their own native language, the one they're most competent in. The CHRO talks about discretionary effort and retention plans. The CMO highlights brand recognition and influencer marketing. For many first-time CXOs, the shift to the C-suite is the first time that they are at the top of their field; they are the highest authority on HR or Marketing in the company. They want to show off what they can do, presenting the value they can add to their new team only to be confronted with departmental peers in the EXCO who do not speak, or sometimes even value, their native language.

Imagine the disappointment, frustration, and sense of bewilderment experienced by the new CHRO or CMO entering the EXCO without CFO-level finance skills, or even the vocabulary to converse?

It makes perfect sense that a new CIO, like Dennis, might present a 70-slide deck for digital strategy that the CEO, CFO, CHRO, and CMO simply do not appreciate. At a loss as to why such a detailed and competent roadmap received such a lackluster response from their new peers, their likely reaction will be to assume that it wasn't detailed enough. And the 120-slide deck that follows will only serve to alienate them even more from their new team.

A seasoned EC doesn't have to be an expert in all departmental languages, or possess the acumen to translate across them all. However, a good EC will be able to recognize this CXO-level challenge in communications and guide their coachee through the challenge of thinking through the creation of impact statements for new initiatives in the languages of each of the other EXCO members. This is especially true for first time CXOs entering the C-Suite, and should be a core competency for any CXO readiness program.

In my own interactions with finance professionals during coaching sessions, I've seen firsthand how their expertise in numbers can lead to a narrow perspective. Their focus on finance can sometimes blind them to the realities and challenges faced by other departments. Regardless of what you call your HR department, humans are not resources, nor do they behave like capital. Native finance speakers often fail to appreciate the behavior gaps between humans and all other kinds of capital.

Finance Rules?

Some of the biggest misunderstandings on the EXCO happen because of an assumptive default to finance language. How many times have you heard CFOs question the need for advertising and recruitment? It sounds like this: "Do we really need to spend so much on advertising?" or "Why are we hiring people when we already have enough?"

Honestly, how condescending is *that*?! Do you ever hear the CHRO ask the CFO, "Why did you add up those numbers?" or "Did you account for all of the expenses this month?"

Dear CFO, do you really consider yourself more competent than your CMO to make a judgment about advertising? And do you really think your CHRO is less professionally equipped than you are to make judgments about workforce planning requirements? Sometimes it seems like the CFO thinks being a finance expert makes them an automatic expert in everything else, too!

[Yeah, you know who you are! I've coached you before. Yes, *you*!}

Unfortunately, this kind of dismissiveness can breed resentment. When professionals of a specific expertise fail to see the value in initiatives outside their own domain, it often results in tension that hampers productivity. It's even worse when they casually question the competency of those presenting those initiatives.

When finance is the default language of the EXCO, and all other languages need to be translated into it to get projects moving, CFOs often think they run the EXCO. Isn't their domain expertise the common tongue?

But what if that changes? Tech leaders are increasingly rising to the CEO role, and tech is now threatening finance as the dominant tongue of EXCO decision-making. Remember, Uber was founded in 2009 but didn't turn a profit until 2023. And Twitter, founded in 2006, was bought by Elon Musk in 2022 for $44 billion without having ever reported positive EBITDA.

Finance isn't governing decision-making the way it used to. Technology is.

CFOs beware!

MIT Sloan Management Review defined tech-savvy as, "an understanding, developed through experience and education, of the impact that emerging technologies will have on a business's success over the next decade." Even with a definition as broad as this, they found that only 7% of the 2,000 large companies in their study had tech-savvy executive teams, and yet those that did outperformed their competitors in revenue growth and valuation by 48%. Only 23% of the CEOs in the study were considered tech-savvy.[60]

Undoubtedly, Paul falls in with the majority of CEOs who aren't tech-savvy – and this means it's likely that he and his company would be making more money if he were.

I had missed that as a coach. I should have seen it, and I failed. I'd solved the wrong problem.

I had helped Paul understand Dennis, but I should have insisted on a digital competency program for Paul at the same time. After all, it's Dennis' language, not Paul's, that fueled Microsoft's $10bn investment in OpenAI Global, a capped-profit company majority owned by a non-profit organization!

That was a tech-centric decision, not a financial one.

So … is finance really the dominant language of the EXCO now? It may be in your company. If so, is that ultimately helpful or unhelpful for your organization? It was good coaching for me to guide Dennis to translate his strategy from tech into finance so that he could communicate with Paul and Ahmed, but ultimately it was a missed opportunity for the company.

---

[60] Weill, P., Woerner, S. L., & Shah, A. M. (2021, March 3). Does your C-suite have enough digital smarts? *MIT Sloan Management Review.*

The Danger of Monolingual Leadership

The dominance of any particular departmental language can become a limiting influence on effective decision-making. The dominance of tech-centric perspectives sometimes leads to a narrowing of focus, or shiny toy syndrome, as leaders prioritize technological solutions over holistic considerations of inter-departmental and organizational objectives. Just like it is with finance, a singular focus on tech-driven outcomes can occasionally result in blind spots, overlooking critical aspects of business operations, customer needs, and stakeholder interests.[61]

In their own fields, tech-savvy leaders are no doubt geniuses, but each departmental language runs the risk of becoming a dominant filter that mutes the others. Leading an organization entails multifaceted challenges that require a broader perspective.

It's important to note that the trap of departmental language dominance is not a new phenomenon. Let's look back a century before the roles of CDO or CIO were ever conceived. And long before the terms tech-savvy or even "human resources" were ever a part of the corporate glossary.

Accounting CEO vs. Recruiting CEO

Herbert Hoover had a strong career as a mining engineer and businessman before becoming US President in 1929. His expertise in engineering and management earned him international recognition, particularly for his work in organizing relief efforts during World War I and his leadership in the American mining industry. However, when Hoover became president, he struggled to deal with the complexities of domestic and international politics during one of the biggest economic catastrophes in American history.[62] Balancing a crashing economy proved too difficult for the accountant-as-CEO.

---

[61] Block, C. (2022, March 16). 12 reasons your digital transformation will fail. *Forbes*.
[62] Herbert Hoover: The engineer-president. (2023, October 31). *Washington Examiner*.

Hoover was a numbers guy. He'd dropped out of high school but took night classes in accounting.[63] He failed every entrance exam into Stanford University, except math.[64] But he was accepted anyway, presumably because it was Stanford's first year in operation and they were in dire need of students. He majored in engineering and was elected student treasurer.

He went into mining after graduation, but as a manager, not as an engineer. He opposed HR initiatives like minimum wage and worker's compensation as he felt they impeded the rights of the owners.[65] He brought Italian immigrants to replace local workers to cut labor costs.[66] He became partner, then owner, then investor. After a long series of successful investments his financial management prowess was well established, resulting in his appointment as US Secretary of Commerce under President Warren Harding. Hoover was a finance guy with an obvious allergy to HR, and at the age of 46, he was CFO of the United States of America.

Nine years later, he became President (i.e. CEO), just in time for the Great Depression.

His background in engineering and finance shaped his approach to governance. He believed in individual initiative, self-reliance, and limited government intervention in the economy. Consequently, when the stock market crashed Hoover predictably responded with policies attempting to restore confidence in the market and encourage voluntary cooperation among businesses.

His reluctance to pursue more aggressive government intervention and his CFO-level addiction to balancing the federal budget in the face of economic collapse earned him criticism from both the public and his political opponents. He was stuck in his own native language, unable to hear the voices of experts around him speaking other languages. Many argued that his engineering mindset and commitment to *laissez-faire*

---

[63] Leuchtenburg, William E. (2009). *Herbert Hoover*. Times Books.
[64] Burner, David. (1996) [1979]. *Herbert Hoover: The public life*. Easton Press.
[65] Leuchtenburg, William E. (2009). *Herbert Hoover*. Times Books.
[66] Hoover's Gold. (2005). *Australian Broadcasting Corporation*.

economics prevented him from adequately addressing the root causes of the Depression and providing sufficient relief to the millions of Americans suffering from unemployment and abject poverty.[67]

The language he needed wasn't that of Finance, but that of Human Resources – the language of people and culture.

Despite sincere efforts and dedication to public service, Hoover's inability to adapt his leadership language and policies to address the Great Depression ultimately led to his defeat in the 1932 election, paving the way for Franklin D. Roosevelt and the New Deal era.

Roosevelt spoke HR fluently. He studied philosophy, history, and languages at Harvard. Instead of being class treasurer, he taught religious studies in his spare time.

As President, he immediately began investing in public works projects that drove employment. He formed the SEC and FDIC to regulate trade and banking to protect individual investors. When the US income statement and balance sheets were in sharp decline, Roosevelt went on a hiring spree.

The finance vs. HR CEO duality we see playing out in Hoover and Roosevelt highlights the importance of holistic leadership in navigating complex and dynamic environments, and the dangers of any form of monolingual management. While his expertise in engineering and finance served Hoover well in previous roles, it proved insufficient for the multifaceted challenges of the US Presidency. Monolingual leadership isn't a new phenomenon, and it's still a significant impediment to organizational success.

---

[67] MacKenzie, D. (2010). Industrial employment and the policies of Herbert C. Hoover. *Quarterly Journal of Austrian Economics, 13*, 101; Jeansonne, G. (2011). The real Herbert Hoover. *Historically Speaking, 12*, 26–29; Rose, J. (2010). Hoover's truce: Wage rigidity in the onset of the Great Depression. *The Journal of Economic History, 70*, 843–870.

A Multilingual Approach

Departments often find themselves competing for influence, resources, and recognition. I'm not talking about co-opetition or healthy tension due to a diversity of views being shared as input-seeking behavior. I'm talking about real disputes, the kind of unhealthy internal competition that's most costly and perhaps most common. A staggering 85% of workers report experiencing some form of job-related conflict regularly, with American workers losing an average of 2.8 hours per week to these disputes. This translates to a staggering $359 billion lost annually to misunderstandings and internal conflict.[68]

Executives sometimes struggle to consider the interests of each other's departments to create productive synergy across the EXCO. This escalates the larger the company gets and the more diverse disciplines it develops. Each department comes with its own disciplinary language, priorities, and perspectives on organizational challenges.

In HR, for example, the language revolves around employee engagement, talent retention, and culture. HR people prioritize things like diversity and inclusion, employee development, and performance management, often viewing employees as the organization's most valuable asset.

The language of IT focuses on things like cybersecurity, data management, and technology infrastructure. IT people prioritize system optimization, software integration, and digital strategy, recognizing the critical role that advanced technology plays in driving operational efficiency and innovation.

Marketers speak the language of branding, customer acquisition, and market segmentation. They prioritize brand awareness, customer experience optimization, and product launches, viewing marketing as a strategic driver of business growth and competitive advantage.

---

[68] Carucci, R. (2018, November 27). How to permanently resolve cross-department rivalries. *Harvard Business Review*.

If each of these languages offers expert-level competency, then what is the responsibility of the other members of the EXCO in understanding those foreign to them? Is it really more efficient to require each of them to translate their dominant language into the CEO's preference for finance, as Paul did?

Unlearning Expertise as an Executive Function

It takes a decent amount of time and practice for an executive at the EXCO level to start viewing operations through the diverse perspectives of multiple disciplines. There is a lot of unlearning and relearning that goes on during this transition, especially in terms of the languages that the executive might choose to speak, and in some cases, the way they ideate and approach problems as well.

This challenge is a natural byproduct of a social structure where specialization is a predictor of promotion. Management rewards domain expertise, and it promotes the Subject Matter Expert as a key competitive advantage. So, the path to the EXCO is clear: immerse yourself in your chosen field, attain expert status, and climb the ladder.

But what if the prevailing wisdom that propels you up the ladder ceases to be true at the executive level? What if the domain expertise that earned you the job isn't what you really need to get the job done?

[Let's get silly for a second. Check this out!}

The quest for domain expertise has been so dominant globally that it's inadvertently resulted in the emergence of a growing group of people obsessed with the study of tree bark (rhytidome). Bark experts [rhytidologists?} are a subset of dendrologists (tree experts). They examine every detail, methodically cataloging the nooks, grooves, coloring, and texture ... of bark. No, I'm not kidding. They've mastered the bark, but staying in their lane can result in blindness to the tree in which the bark is wrapped, and too careful a study of the tree, too, risks complete ignorance of the forest in which it sits.

My point is it's often bark-level specialization that earns a specialist their first C-suite invitation, but it's competence in global forestry that will make them a success in the EXCO. That's the bait-and-switch I've been talking about. Two decades of industry and departmental expertise is often what earns you your seat on the C-suite – but *unlearning* it is what will help you succeed there.

Who in the life of the new CXO is equipped to help them value this unlearning, and step outside of the best practices that earned them their top job? Who will convince the specialist to abandon their core competency?

Specialists vs. Generalists

Ancient Greek poet Archilochus stated about 2,700 years ago that "the hedgehog knows one big thing, while the fox knows many things." Isaiah Berlin developed this idea in his 1953 essay *The Fox and the Hedgehog*, comparing hedgehogs, who "relate everything to a single, central vision," to foxes, who "pursue many ends connected ... if at all, only in some *de facto* way."[69] Which is the best evolutionary strategy: specialization or generalization?[70]

Hedgehogs have certainly taken over academia, medicine, banking, law, and a variety of other professional fields. Specialists with extensive knowledge have increasingly risen to higher levels. Specializing was the most efficient way to grow in one's job, and its effective specialization in HR, Operations, Marketing, IT, or Finance, that most often results in a C-suite offer letter.

The effectiveness of specialization quickly fades in the EXCO. I think the successful CXO role may belong to those hedgehogs that evolve into foxes. We select bark experts, but we need them to learn global forestry, fast.

---

[69] Mansharamani, V. (2020, June 22). All hail the generalist. *Harvard Business Review.*
[70] Jahanbegloo, R, (2000). *Conversations with Isaiah Berlin.* Orion Publishing.

How many bark experts are attending to potential global causes of deforestation? And how many hedgehogs inherently value the difficult metamorphosis required to become a fox? That's the CXO role in a nutshell, across all departments.

Sure, be a specialist to earn your CXO role, but then immediately and magically transform into a generalist once you get there.

[It's no wonder there's friction on the EXCO.}

The CXO Coach Toolkit

A competent CXO coach will already be aware of the departmental language challenge and be able to identify that a CXOs initial display of competence could distance them from their EXCO teammates. The competency that needs to be displayed by the new CIO isn't their mastery of esoteric technical jargon but the ability to translate their complex digital strategy into the languages, KRAs and KPIs of those speaking finance, operations, human resources, and marketing — languages that until now have been relatively foreign to the new CIO.

This challenge is also sometimes felt on the Board of Directors, where Non-Executive Directors (NEDs) often lack significant industry experience or expertise. Their range of experience from other domains makes their input innovative and valuable, but to be able to apply it, they need the highest quality of information presented to them as simply as possible. Perhaps CXOs can use the NED avatar as a rule of thumb for translation: if you're presenting to the EXCO, prepare as though you're presenting to a NED.

The OKR Framework
Imagine yourself in my shoes with Paul and Dennis. Your client, the newly appointed CIO of a large multinational corporation, seeks your guidance in ensuring that their vision for digital strategy resonates with stakeholders across finance, operations, HR, and marketing. One useful coaching toolkit here is the Objectives and Key Results (OKR)

framework.[71] It's simple to learn, so let's look at how an EC can leverage OKR to assist a new CIO (like Dennis) in effectively communicating and aligning their digital strategy with other departments.[72]

Step One

The first step in the OKR framework is to help the CIO identify the key stakeholders in each department. Then they'll need to conduct stakeholder interviews to gain a deep understanding of each department's objectives, challenges, KPIs, and existing performance metrics. The CIO needs to get out of the IT department, listen to the concerns of others in different languages, and value both the concerns *and* the languages in which they were delivered. It's a good practice for the CIO to note down specialized departmental vocabulary, including any new TLAs and FLAs (Three-Letter Acronyms and Four-Letter Acronyms) that they're certain to interact with.

Step Two

Work with the CIO to define high-level organizational objectives related to digital strategy, such as improving operational efficiency, enhancing customer experience, and driving revenue growth. These objectives should align with the overall strategic goals of the organization. Once the organizational objectives are established, encourage the CIO to collaborate with department heads to develop departmental OKRs that support the overarching digital strategy while incorporating the specific language and metrics of each department. For example,

1. Finance OKR: Increase ROI on digital investments by X%.
2. Operations OKR: Streamline processes and reduce operational costs by X%.
3. Marketing OKR: Enhance brand awareness and customer engagement through digital marketing campaigns.
4. HR OKR: Improve employee engagement and retention through digital initiatives.

---

[71] Hennigan, L. (2023, July 20). What is an OKR? definition & examples. *Forbes*.
[72] Doerr, J. (2018). *Measure what matters*. Portfolio Penguin.

Inter-departmental OKRs express success metrics for the CIO's strategy in the languages of the other departments. Using their specialized language helps those stakeholders to feel heard and valued in the CIO's strategy, and it makes the information easier for them to digest.

Step Three
Execution of the strategy is also a difficult task and should be managed in a structured format. The CIO may need to be guided to align OKRs across different levels of the organization, ensuring that individual and team objectives support departmental and organizational goals on an ongoing basis. The CIO will need to reiterate the rationale behind the OKRs in the languages of other departments regularly and solicit feedback from stakeholders. This will foster a stronger sense of ownership and accountability.

Encourage the CIO to establish a cadence for tracking progress against OKRs, conduct regular check-ins with department heads to review performance metrics, identify challenges, and make necessary adjustments to the digital strategy. This iterative, comprehensive process allows for continuous improvement and alignment across the organization.

The EC doesn't need to know all of the specialized language of their CIO client, but they should be able to ask competent questions about how to translate that language into those of other departments. By fostering alignment, engagement, and accountability, the EC can use the OKR framework to enable their CIO client to drive meaningful impact and lead the organization toward a successful digital strategy, without ever using the acronyms RPA, API, or ETL (Robotic Process Automation, Application Programming Interface, and Extract-Transform-Load).

Upskilling Hedgehogs into Foxes
Charles Babbage's 1834 creation of the analytical engine (the cornerstone of contemporary computers) was powered by punch cards. The idea came from the silk-weaving industry, which used cards with

holes to generate patterns in silk fabric.[73] Singer's sewing machines and the Swift Meatpacking Factory were similarly influenced by Henry Ford's breakthrough concept of the assembly line for making cars.[74] Major innovations like these and countless others are the result of leaders stepping outside of their dominant languages and their domains of expertise.[75]

Many studies have shown that the finest ideas come from mixing knowledge from seemingly unrelated domains.[76] For an organization to keep itself relevant to the changing times and continue the process of innovation and reinvention, there needs to be a convergence of diverse perspectives, especially on the EXCO.

An executive coach can assist a specialist CXO in transitioning into a generalist business leader by fostering self-awareness and introspection. By encouraging the specialist to reflect on their strengths, weaknesses, dominant vocabulary, departmental blind spots and areas for growth, the EC helps them gain clarity on their leadership style, communication preferences, and decision-making processes, each of which has been influenced by their department of origin.

This heightened self-awareness lays the foundation for personal and professional development, enabling the specialist to identify opportunities for improvement and leverage their strengths to drive success. Through a collaborative partnership, the EC empowers the specialist CXO to step away from the bark, to learn the tree, and to see the forest of organizational languages and disciplines as a new opportunity for personal growth.

Paul became more interested in technology, and valued Dennis' work a lot more after my engagement with them ended. Dennis is still CIO as I write this. It's worth saying again that, although I did diagnose the

[73] Bales, R. (2023). *The history of Charles Babbage's analytical engine and the birth of computers.* History of Computers.

[74] Teodoridis, F. (2018, July 31). When generalists are better than specialists, and vice versa. *Harvard Business Review.*

[75] Epstein, D. J. (2019). *Range: Why generalists triumph in a specialized world.* Riverhead Books.

[76] Burt, R. S. (2004). Structural holes and good ideas. *American Journal of Sociology, 110*(2), 349–399; Jeppesen, L. B., & Lakhani, K. R. (2010). Marginality and problem-solving effectiveness in broadcast search. *Organization Science, 21*(5), 1016–1033.

situation as a language problem, I missed an opportunity for the company by translating in only one direction. I should have convinced Paul of the need for us to work on his tech-savviness.

Ultimately, the engagement was a success because the goals defined were achieved, and I heard a few months later that the DX project was well underway. Paul and Dennis agreed that without the delay cost translation, it might have taken another year to begin execution on that piece of the project, at an additional cost of $1.2m. They are now regularly using delay cost in the organization as a tool for understanding urgency, and to mitigate against their historical tendency for analysis paralysis.

My career specializations in strategy and entrepreneurship aren't enough to equip me to coach the C-suite any more than Bob Bowman's two seasons as a swimmer in the 80s equipped him to coach Michael Phelps in the 2000s. Sure experience like that is helpful, but it would be insufficient if I were to lean on it for too long. When I shifted to executive coaching, I, too, became a generalist. I've earned academic certifications in history, finance, artificial intelligence, neurosciences, NLP, and even skydiving. Each of them has added a new set of tools to my toolbox.

Here are a few key activities and advice for an EC if they suspect a possible language barrier challenge with their client:

1. Identify communication and presentation challenges that may result from your CXO using domain-specialized language that potentially alienates them from their team.
2. Be equipped to offer a framework (such as OKR) as a potential tool for systematically translating your CXOs priorities into cross-departmental languages and success metrics.
3. Help your CXO to recognize the requirement to shift from specialization to generalization in their personal learning and development goals.
4. Inquire about how the CXOs department of origin might be operating as a filter, or a limiting frame, in their negotiations with other EXCO members.

5. Your warehouse of coaching tools should include some high-leverage finance tools like NPV and Delay Cost, especially as you work with CXOs whose backgrounds are outside of the finance function and who report to CEOs who speak finance natively.

6. You would benefit from having at least an MBA-level understanding of operations, finance, HR, marketing, and IT.

7. Read *Cultures and Organizations* by Hofstede and *Strategic Leadership Across Cultures* by House so you have some understanding of the influences national culture and cultural diversity have on decision making in leadership as well.[77]

You're the CXO coach. You don't need to be able to play the game as well as your CXO can, but you do need to be able to coach at their level to provide value – and justify your fees and their time. It's not just CXOs who need to step out of specialization into generalization: if you plan to coach in the C-suite, you need to be able to do that too.

Bottom Line

CXOs often face an unexpected language barrier when transitioning from their specialized roles to the executive level. And it's common for CXOs to feather their lingo at the EXCO table only to find that the others aren't impressed. In my experience, experts like Dennis, who are fluent in their niche, often struggle to translate that expertise into the finance-dominated conversations of the C-suite. This can result in missed opportunities and costly delays.

The most successful CXOs consciously evolve from specialists into generalists, which is often why organizations may require an MBA or some other general business studies as a prerequisite for a C-suite role. The HR function can be a catalyst for preparing high-potential leaders for C-suite roles by using tools like the MBA requirement to help them broaden their business competency beyond their own field and learn to communicate in the languages of their executive peers. By providing

---

[77] Hofstede, G., Hofstede, G. J., & Minkov, M. (2010). Cultures and organizations: Software of the mind (3rd ed.). McGraw-Hill Professional.; House, R. J., Dorfman, P. W., Javidan, M., Hanges, P. J., & Sully de Luque, M. F. (2014). Strategic leadership across cultures: The GLOBE study of CEO leadership behavior and effectiveness in 24 countries. Sage Publications.

tools and frameworks for helping to translate initiatives across departmental languages, executive coaches can also play a role in helping CXOs make this transition.

So, what's the takeaway? The days of monolingual leadership are over. If you're in the C-suite, it's time to stop peacocking your specialized knowledge and start learning to speak the languages of your peers. Your success (and your company's bottom line) depends on it. After all, being a great CXO is less about understanding the bark than it is about seeing the whole forest from above.

The language barrier certainly contributes to our next challenge, the shift from offensive to defensive career posture. Not speaking the same language isn't the only influence on the often dramatic disappointment CXOs feel when they reach the top, and it's definitely not the most sinister.

The Checklist
Formal Expertise:

- Understanding of financial, operational, HR, marketing, and IT terminologies
- Training in communication and translation of complex concepts
- Certification in cross-functional team management
- Knowledge of organizational behavior and cultural dynamics

Informal Expertise:

- Skill in translating departmental languages into common business terms
- Ability to facilitate cross-departmental communication
- Experience in diverse business functions
- Strong problem-solving and analytical skills
- Ability to build consensus and foster collaboration
- Cultural sensitivity and awareness

4.

DEFENSIVE SHIFT

"Everyone needs a coach."
– Bill Gates, Founder of Microsoft

Bill is right.

[Be like Bill. Not like Steve. I'll tell you later.}

The fourth major challenge that a CXO is likely to experience but a C-1 is less likely to have to deal with is the shift from an offensive to a defensive career posture. We know they're lonely at the top and they often speak a different language than that of their EXCO team. Well, they're also now under threat, but they don't know from whom, and it's often a blindside slap.

Perhaps it's one of their own staff eyeing up their corner office, or a competitive EXCO member looking to undermine their authority. Maybe it's the Board of Directors questioning their relevancy or performance.

Wherever the challenge comes from, the sudden need to shift from an offensive to a defensive career posture is one of the most shocking and disappointing experiences an executive can face.

[It feels like a betrayal. If you've been a CXO for any amount of time, you'll know what I'm talking about.}

Dan on the Defense

Dan was a new client of mine, a Russian in his early 50s and the CEO of a $3bn company with nearly 40,000 employees. He greeted me with a strong handshake and a big smile. I instantly liked him. His massive corner office was minimalistic in decor but it boasted floor-to-ceiling windows across two full walls.

He looked out over the city like a king. Politically, however, he was only a lord.

His company was part of a conglomerate governed by a Group Head Office based in another city. He had only been in the role for about a year, and the confidence with which he had fought mercilessly to the top of his corporate ladder was suddenly waning.

"Where would you like to begin?" I asked.

"This is my first role in the Middle East, and though I'm very good at building companies, I'm not very good at building relationships. And I think that's something I need to work on now."

"What led you to that conclusion?"

"Well, I know that about myself. I've never been known as a warm or empathetic leader. I can be a bit ruthless when I need to be. I didn't get to where I am in my career without stepping on a few heads. But I'm not reporting to the Board of Directors now, I'm reporting to a Group CEO."

"What are your priorities for building relationships? And which relationships are you looking at specifically?"

"I want to keep my job. That's my number one priority. I don't want to get blindsided by internal sabotage from my team, I want to have good relationships with my lateral colleagues in the group of companies, and I want to remain accepted by the Executive Committee and the Board of Directors."

[Wait. What? Goal #1 is "Keep my job?"}

It's in moments like this in the coaching relationship when the ability to hold space and be non-judgmental moves from a requirement of the job to a critical success factor. This was a profoundly powerful gentleman, on his heels. He was an apex predator, a 1% of the 1% giant in the corporate world and a warrior on the economic field of battle, and yet suddenly, and perhaps for the first time in his career, Dan was in a squarely defensive posture.

Was he being arrogant, or perhaps narcissistic in his individualistic and self-preservationist stance?

Or was it that, to this point in his career, he simply hadn't had to play defense like this?

I'd seen this before in other clients. Those who achieve the CEO's office have often done so by spending their whole careers looking up. In reaching the top, however (their height allegorized by the view from their top-floor windows), they often feel a sense of unease that wasn't there when they were competing for the next role.

The Shake at the Top of the Ladder

Consider a typical career in the finance department. The progression from entry-level Accountant through various Accounting Manager roles to Finance Director and eventually to Deputy CFO is always forward-facing; it's two to three decades of constantly looking to the next rung on the corporate ladder. However, once a first-time CHRO or CEO has been named, they then quickly become aware of the lack of rungs left on the ladder they've been climbing.

They also may have been one of five potential candidates for their CXO role, so once successful, they become aware that there are now four (or more) other people gunning for their top job. Those on the rungs just below remain in offensive positions, awaiting their turn. Under the right conditions, the CXO can shift subconsciously into a defensive career posture.

Instead of gunning for the top job, they're now trying to defend it.

Ok, so here's a thought … the typical ladder being climbed was already there, right? It's someone else's ladder, so maybe CXOs feel a shake at the top and grip tighter simply because it's foreign. But if the ladder was theirs, if they had built it themselves, wouldn't it be sturdier?

Well, Sam Altman, Co-founder and CEO of OpenAI, built his own corporate ladder and still got that shake at the top. In the fall of 2023 Altman was abruptly fired from his position as CEO, then reinstated within days. What more perfect example is there of a quick shift to defence?[78]

Altman's ascent in the AI industry was meteoric, pushing the boundaries of AI research and development. The ladder wasn't one he had climbed in a traditional company, but one he'd built beneath him as an entrepreneurial CEO. Yet the increasing height of his ladder brought with it the same inevitable truth: there are no more rungs left to climb, and his once offensive posture was shocked into a defensive strategy.

The Board's decision blindsided executives and employees alike. Altman was immediately on his heels, but he enjoyed massive popularity both internally (with his employees) and externally (with prominent leaders in the tech industry). The overwhelming pushback against his ouster culminated in an open letter signed by nearly all OpenAI employees who threatened to resign. The Board backed off and reinstated him as CEO.

Caught off guard, Altman was fortunate to have the social capital to defend his role and weather the political storm. Many leaders are not so

---

[78] Chafkin, M., & Metz, R. (2023, November 20). Inside Sam Altman's shock ouster from OpenAI. *Time*.

prepared. It was Altman's kind of social capital that my client Dan was looking for, and feared he didn't have.

[And Dan was right, he certainly did not have it.}

The Dark Side of Defense

Imagine Altman's disappointment at suddenly having to defend his role, and Dan's at suddenly feeling vulnerable to a similar kind of opposition.

This vulnerability can lead to feelings of isolation and protectionist strategies, which we'll go into more depth on in the next chapter. Left uncoached, the shift to defense can result in

- subconscious insecurities in communication;
- subtle slips into command-and-control leadership, out of fear of their own team; and
- posturing to the EXCO or Board of Directors, which may itself become a distraction from focusing on the challenges of the business.

In fact, it was allegations right along these lines that led to Altman's termination. His own executives cited "psychological abuse" and toxic behavior, and he was accused of being manipulative, double-crossing, and chaotic.[79] Was Altman arrogant? Narcissistic? Or were there deeper issues at play?

An autocratic or directive style, ineffective communication, and inappropriate approaches to working with employees are commonly identified in leadership research as ineffective behaviors,[80] and I've heard more than a few leaders who embody them labeled "narcissists."

---

[79] Ropek, L. (2023). *Sam Altman accused of "psychologically abusive" behavior.* Gizmodo; Barrabi, T. (2023). Senior OpenAI employees: Sam Altman was "psychologically abusive." *New York Post.*
[80] Ellinger, A. D., Hamlin, R. G., & Beattie, R. S. (2008). Behavioral indicators of ineffective managerial coaching: A cross-national study. *Journal of European Industrial Training, 32*(4), 240–257.

[In my experience, all ex-husbands are also narcissists according to their ex-wives. I'm an ex-husband, so I'm always a little cautious when I hear this label thrown around about executives.}

I'm not convinced that accusations of executive narcissism point toward a kind of exaggerated self-love, as is commonly thought. Rather, I think they are responding to insecurity in disguise.[81] Executives I've known to exhibit behavior labeled arrogant or narcissistic have often done so in a deliberate attempt to compensate for self-perceived deficits or flaws. It's more often than not a defensive posture, like puffer fish inflating themselves or dogs barking to intimidate rivals and enemies.

That's not narcissism, that's fear.

[Could be both, I suppose.}

An executive who perceives threats to their position may react to feelings of susceptibility with aggression, perhaps in the ways that Altman did. Silos can form quickly under these conditions if the CXO doesn't have a coach who is specifically competent in C-suite transitions, emotional intelligence, and senior leadership culture and politics.

It looks to me like Altman's ladder got really tall really quickly beneath him. A few people started poking at him from their offensive upward-facing positions below him, and he felt threatened ... so he barked, and the Board fired him for it.

I'm not saying that Altman should be let off the hook for bad leadership behaviors, or that the OpenAI Board made the right decision. Was it the right thing that Altman's executives turned on him, or that the Board agreed with them and fired him? Was it right that Altman's social capital applied enough pressure to reverse the decision?

I'm not proposing a right or wrong scenario here. I chose Altman's case specifically *because* there doesn't seem to be a right, or a wrong.

---

[81] Kowalchyk, M., Palmieri, H., Conte, E., & Wallisch, P. (2021). Narcissism through the lens of performative self-elevation, *Elsevier 177*.

Instead, I'm suggesting that even in organizations as globally and publicly successful as OpenAI, defensive leadership is a real consideration. While it certainly changes the political landscape of the organization, it can be viewed as either positive or negative, depending on who's looking at it. A good EC will already be aware of the conditions that can lead to these scenarios and will be prepared with tools to help mitigate potential chaos.

Defense Against Whom?

The shift to defense is most often an internal consideration. In such cases, the CXOs defensive posture isn't against the market or their competitor, but against their own colleagues. In Altman's case, it was members of his own team and his Board of Directors. In Dan's case, it was precisely the same.

Dan was a CEO lacking the EQ to manage interpersonal dynamics effectively. He was undoubtedly brilliant in his field, and he had a massive trophy case of technical expertise and financial results. He excelled at solving complex problems, optimizing processes, and driving innovation. But what got him there wouldn't keep him there, and he knew it.

His communication was curt, and his feedback was often harsh. Empathy was not a word commonly used to describe Dan's leadership style.

[But barking *was*.}

These are the conditions under which office politics can solidify cliques into silos and shift alliances. Professional conflicts simmer beneath the surface. Week after week Dan and I discussed the relationships in which he felt vulnerable, and what he could do to bring people on-side with him. But he struggled to execute on the warm leadership tools I gave him.

Unsolicited kindness and EQ without an agenda felt unnatural to him.

People management is probably the skill most needed in senior executive positions; unfortunately, it is often the most lacking. At this level, leaders aren't just responsible for driving profits or achieving targets; they're tasked with nurturing a culture of collaboration, innovation, and inclusivity, across departments and disciplines foreign to their own.

Plus, the people they're trying to collaborate with are all the kinds who fight their way up the ladder too. Many of them have the same struggles Dan did. It makes sense that the higher you climb, the more competitors and fewer collaborators you find around you.

Competition gets them to the top, but collaboration is what keeps them there. There's just no one around for them to talk to about it because they're often competing with the players they need to collaborate with.

The executive culture required for success cannot properly form if the organization's leaders are defending themselves from one another. Without skilled guidance, these top-notch competitors can escalate disagreements into turf wars, eroding trust and killing morale. Gallup's 2023 survey found that unhealthy work culture and lack of efficient leadership are why 80% of Americans are frustrated with their work environment.[82] They're frustrated with the kind of culture that forms naturally when its leaders are defending themselves against one another.

[Dan reluctantly agreed to let me tell you this next bit … but Dan is not his real name, and this is such a good illustration of the defensive shift.}

Get this: in one of our coaching sessions, Dan showed me a branded box of chocolates meant to be a holiday gift to senior staff. He pointed at the bottom of the outside of the box where logos of each of the group companies were displayed on a horizontal line. There were seven in total. He pointed at his company's logo.

Dan and I then spent forty-five minutes discussing why the logo of *his* company occurred third in line instead of second. He felt that since his business unit was second in terms of overall revenue in the group, and it had previously appeared second on other group-branded materials, it

---

[82] Smith, A.K. (2023). Here's why you have every right to be unhappy at work. *Forbes.*

should be second from the left, not third. Furthermore, he wondered who might have nefariously moved the logo from its original position, and what this logo-demon was trying to say about Dan's leadership by moving it.

Four days later he called me directly because he was still suspicious. We spent another twenty-five minutes talking about the logo positioning and whether he was being subtly dishonored.

No, I'm not kidding.

It turned out to have been just a design consideration. The graphic designer had moved the logos around because they looked more visually balanced that way.

Dan and Sam Altman both felt this social pressure in their CEO roles, and both took defensive postures, but neither of them was the first, or even the most famous to do so.

Steve Jobs on His Heels

Perhaps the most famous example of the CXO defensive shift is that of Steve Jobs preceding his ouster from Apple in 1985. While nobody doubted his status as a groundbreaking trailblazer in the tech industry, Jobs' leadership style left a lot to be desired. Many past employees have shared public accounts of what he was like to work for. There's even an official post-mortem clinical diagnosis of Narcissistic Personality Disorder for Steve published in Psychology Today.[83]

I'm not a clinical psychologist, so the diagnosis is outside my wheelhouse, but what I do know is that Jobs had a reputation for testing people, something he enjoyed doing. He was notorious for his high expectations and impatience. He was harsh, abrasive, and had frequent clashes with both the Board and his employees. His refusal to listen to differing perspectives and his propensity for berating those who disagreed with him alienated key stakeholders and eroded morale.

---

[83] Henriques, G. (2012). Was Steve Jobs' narcissism justified? *Psychology Today.*

There's an old rumor at Apple that tells of Jobs having shared an elevator with an unnamed intern. He asked the intern what they did for work, and the intern was abruptly fired for not having a clear answer by the time the two had reached their floor. It's unclear if the event actually ever happened, but former Apple employees know the story as an episode in Steve's leadership mythology.[84]

It was his harsh leadership style that led to Apple's Board removing him from management completely in 1985.

Jobs had brought in John Sculley, CEO of PepsiCo in 1983 to take over as CEO so Steve could concentrate on the Macintosh division. Two years later, Sculley pushed Jobs out of the Macintosh product group after the two got into a heated argument over lower-than-expected sales. Jobs famously lost a boardroom showdown with Sculley that played out over a week or so, after Jobs' plan of moving marketing dollars from the Apple II to Macintosh Office was rejected by the Board. Jobs attempted a coup to take over the reins of the company from Sculley, which was rebuffed and rejected by the Board. So, isolated and stripped of power, Jobs resigned.[85]

Unlike Altman, Jobs didn't have the social capital needed to defend his position and overcome the Board. Steve was a lone wolf leader.

[Because he was an asshole. A truly brilliant asshole. Light-years ahead of Dan. Why couldn't Steve have just been more like Bill?}

On the Nature of Alpha Wolves

Lone alpha wolves might be venerated in Hollywood movies, but not in the boardroom. Jobs, Altman, and Dan are all alpha wolves in the metaphorical sense. In choosing these three, I am specifically ignoring the typical association of "alpha wolf" with extroverted character traits.

---

[84] Eadicicco, L. (2015). A former Apple employee describes what it was like to work on the design team under Steve Jobs. *Business Insider.*
[85] Boogaard, K. (n.d.). What was Steve Jobs' leadership style? *Fingerprint for Success*; Silver, S. (2018, June 18). 25 years ago, Apple's board of directors pushed out CEO John Sculley. *AppleInsider.*

Jobs was notoriously introverted, Altman appears to exhibit both introversion and extroversion, and Dan (I can tell you with complete certainty) is the very definition of extroverted.

The problem is that very often the process required to achieve any CXO role favors stereotypical lone wolf behavior. Boards of Directors often hire their top profit-making and headstrong leaders as CEO ... and then are surprised to find that the results-driven, step-on-necks maverick they've hired remains perfectly in character after taking the job. The wolf isn't a sheep in disguise, or even a shepherd in a heavy fur coat. The CEO got their job by being a wolf, and a wolf they remain.

Alpha Wolf in Captivity

And wolves are territorial, predatory, aggressive and defensive, right?

Not quite.

As it turns out, the popular image of alpha wolves being ruthlessly individualistic and aggressive is true only in captivity, where wolves from different places and packs are smashed together in close quarters. When caged, they quickly and violently establish hierarchies and defend their positions on the ladder with claws and fangs. This is what gives rise to the popular image of the lone alpha wolf and its anthropomorphized narcissistic tendencies.[86]

In the wild, however, wolves are familial. They're led not by a dominant alpha male, but by a male-female breeding pair. [Hooray for gender diversity.} They only defend themselves against outsiders, not against members of their own pack. And the only time the wolf is ever "lone" is when they walk away from their pack to look for a mate to start a new pack [think: entrepreneurship}.

Alpha Wolf in the Wild

Wolves in the wild are tribal and protective.

Wolves in captivity are individualistic and defensive.

Human tribal culture, like wolf pack culture, is a top-down exercise. Leaders define the culture of their organizations, most often starting with the CEO. The CEO sets the tone for how conflict is navigated, how differing perspectives are embraced, and how open and productive conversations are fostered. Leadership requires embodying the behaviors and values that you want your team to emulate. If CXOs feel that they are free and among family, they'll typically behave tribally and protectively.

---

[86] Mech, L. D. (1999). Alpha status, dominance, and division of labor in wolf packs. *Canadian Journal of Zoology, 77*(8), 1196–1203; Turko, A. J., Firth, B. L., Craig, P. M., Eliason, E. J., Raby, G. D., & Borowiec, B. G. (2023). Physiological differences between wild and captive animals: A century-old dilemma. *Journal of Experimental Biology, 226*(23).

But if they're trapped among strangers, and threatened internally … well, claws and fangs.

So, what happens in cases like those of Dan, Sam Altman, and Steve Jobs?

Sometimes conflict resulting from a defensive posture reveals less about the wolf than their cage.

Board-CEO Conflict

Sam Altman and Steve Jobs aren't anomalies. CEO-Board conflict is more common than you might think, especially if there's outside pressure like an economic crisis or industrial disruption. Everyone thinks they know what the right thing to do is, and conflict over those decisions can erupt pretty quickly.

Since the Board holds all of the authority in the organization, they're often on the offense. This makes the CEO and their EXCO team naturally shift into defense. The CEO's leadership and communication styles aren't simply in question; they can be on trial, with the jury composed of individuals who are generally uninvolved in the day-to-day management and only selectively informed about most things related to the business. The CEO can lose confidence in the Board, and vice-versa.

So, how can a leader survive in such a defensive culture shift?

Well, as a kid I was taught that the best defense is a good offense. In this case, though, the offensive play means shifting away from the Board. If the CEO is leading an aggressive offensive play in the market, who's got time to criticize their communication style? Some of the best CEO-Board defensive plays I've seen have been offensive market shifts, like aggressive expansion and investment in disruption, both of which were brilliantly executed by Indra Nooyi.

As the first woman of color to lead a Fortune 500 company, Nooyi had to defend herself from skepticism and prejudice before she even took her first step into the corner office of PepsiCo. But she wasn't sidetracked by any of the DEI-fueled affirmative action rumors, nor was she interested in defending herself from her teammates. Her eyes were on the market.

Nooyi saw the consumer landscape shifting towards wellness, so she championed initiatives to introduce "better-for-you" snacks and low-calorie beverages.[87] While their competitors were working on new flavors, PepsiCo was lowering sugar and fat content. You can imagine how shareholders might have been a little more than irritated at her stepping away from PepsiCo's secret sauce like that. It wasn't just a shift in trajectory, but an about-face from PepsiCo's traditionally successful focus on sugary drinks and snacks.

A junk food company making healthy snacks? Yeah, investors are gonna *love* that! [sarcastic eyeroll}

Reducing water consumption and increasing environmentally friendly packaging were investment-heavy ideas, and taking sugar and fat out of snack foods was high-risk. The initial announcement sent the stock into a steady decline, from $63 to $58 over the course of 2010. Nooyi's gamble initially lost 8% of the company's value, around $7.9bn in market capital. It took more than a year for the stock to recover.[88]

The market was skeptical, investors were agitated, and that's typically when the CEO-Board relationship becomes most tense.

Internally, Nooyi faced exactly the kind of visionary incongruence that led to the ousters of Jobs and Altman, but her defensive play succeeded where Jobs and Altman had failed.

What was the difference?

First, she focused on her offensive play and doubled down on her "performance with purpose" strategy. She didn't bother defending herself, she was too busy pivoting and advancing.

---

[87] Wiener-Bronner, D. (2018). How Indra Nooyi built Pepsi for the future. *Money*.
[88] How Indra Nooyi changed the face of PepsiCo. (2020). *World Finance*; How PepsiCo is "fundamentally transforming" what it does and how it does it. (2022). *Food Navigator*.

Second was warmth and empathy. She had excellent soft skills. She was just a delight to work with, and that made it difficult for those who disagreed with her vision to scrutinize her behavior.

Nooyi's biography, *My Life in Full*, talks about the impact of the empathy, compassion, and deep relationship-building she used to weather internal politics and board conflict.[89] She connected with people, and they trusted her, even when she was leading them in a direction dramatically foreign to them.

She led like an alpha wolf does in the wild: collaboratively. And those she worked with reciprocated because leadership culture starts at the top. The extent to which the PepsiCo Board accommodated Nooyi after her resignation is a clear testament to the quality of the relationships she had built among those who represented the 7.9 billion dollars she'd initially gambled with. She writes,

> For my last meeting with Trane, Bill Roth, the CEO, chartered two planes to bring his entire executive team to our offices in Chicago. The meeting would typically have happened in his own boardroom, but I was nine months pregnant and couldn't travel. Bill wanted me to be part of BCG's final presentation to his company.[90]

By 2020, PepsiCo's better-for-you product lines accounted for 25% of total revenue, and the stock price had almost tripled from the $58 low in 2010 to $148 per share. Nooyi's long-term offensive play paid off.

Nearly all CXOs feel the dramatic shift from offense to defense in their top jobs at some point, but those who succeed in weathering the situation do so not by establishing their dominance as individuals, but by inviting collaboration, relationship, and connection. They shift from a caged-wolf worldview to a wild-wolf worldview.

This was what Dan needed to hear, but I knew he wasn't going to read Nooyi's biography. So, I encouraged him to meet with the Board

[89] Nooyi, I. (2021). *My life in full: Work, family, and our future.* Portfolio.
[90] Ibid.

members individually, and to empathize with them by trying to imagine what they were most concerned about. We mapped out a number of the key decision-makers, their personal motivations and personality types, and strategies for building warmer relationships.

I coached Dan to start all of his political and strategic conversations with the cold agenda items first, and end them with some kind of warm personal question about the other person's family, hobbies, or favorite food. This tactic would curate his interlocutor's emotional memory of Dan by taking advantage of the peak-end rule, and they would be more likely to think favorably of him when he was not in the room. I encouraged him to attend corporate social gatherings and talk about non-work-related subjects with his colleagues, executives, and Board Members.

But he didn't.

Dan missed more than one critical social gathering of the executive committee and Board of Directors, and he failed to connect intentionally with several of the key stakeholders with whom he needed to establish warmer relationships.

Upon his request, I had even given him a list of 25 warm questions with which to end his conversations with his colleagues, and in spite of the fact that the list was taped to the big oak desk in the corner of his top-floor corner office, he most often simply forgot to use them.

[facepalm}

He said it felt unnatural to seek connection when he didn't authentically want it. It felt unnatural for him to connect with people he didn't like. It felt unnatural for him to waste time at dinners he would rather avoid.

Less than six months into our coaching relationship, Dan's CEO role was dissolved, and his entire business unit was absorbed into another part of the group of companies. He was granted a generous exit package and was able to secure another CEO role within a few weeks, but it's my sneaking suspicion that he'll be paying more attention to his defensive play in his next role.

You see, amidst the turmoil and uncertainty of the shift to defense in executive politics, there lies an opportunity for growth and resilience. By fostering open communication, embracing constructive feedback, and cultivating a culture of trust and transparency, CXOs can navigate boardroom conflict with grace, as Nooyi did. In doing so, they not only strengthen their own leadership but also lay the foundation for a stronger, more resilient organization.

In this capacity, an executive coach can help shift the executive's focus to long-term strategies, informing more fruitful short-term EQ-based defensive moves. An experienced EC will be able to highlight emerging trends that the leader should be capitalizing on in order to boost the company's performance as well as solidify their position in the organization.

The CXO Coach Toolkit

The shift to defense can be traumatizing for executives. The first time they're on their heels in front of a Board of Directors (Steve Jobs), or their own executives (Sam Altman), can be very disappointing. When they feel their own team eyeing up their desk, their own executive committee challenging their authority, or their own Board of Directors questioning their relevance (Dan), it can instantly invoke a vulnerability they've not experienced to this degree before.

Sure, they've likely had a career built with other people wanting what they have, but they were looking up during those times. They might not have noticed. With nowhere "up" to look anymore, what's happening below and around them comes much more into focus. They can suddenly become like wolves in captivity, defending themselves against strangers in close quarters.

Since CXO hiring still often favors the selection of (captive) lone wolves who achieve their roles through a history of cutthroat tactics and financial results, the requirement for collaboration and empathy in the successful (wild wolf) defensive play can be shocking – worse, it may seem like an entirely foreign language to the new CXO.

I don't feel particularly successful as Dan's executive coach, though I'm confident the decision to remove him was made months prior to the announcement, and likely prior to his engagement with me. Dan probably sought the right coach, but too late to have saved his job.

The tactics and tools I worked with him on were too little too late, even if he had been more diligent in implementation. Also, I wanted to make sure this book included stories of mine that weren't great successes. Executive coaching is art and science, psychology and strategy.

[Sometimes coaches come back from the Olympics without any medals at all.}

I often feel just as human, just as vulnerable, as the CXO clients I coach. This is one of those cases where my Olympic athlete missed the medal, and I still spend time thinking through how my coaching might have been more effective.

Experiences like this one have reinforced for me that there are a few really important toolkits an EC needs to have in their warehouse when coaching a CXO through a shift to defense.

Emotional Intelligence (EI) Training
Although Dan Goleman first came up with the concept in 1995, I prefer Bradberry's treatment and presentation in *Emotional intelligence 2.0* from 2009.[91] A good EC should be able to present the four quadrants of EQ (Self-Awareness, Self-Management, Social Awareness, and Relationship Management), help their CXO identify their and others' emotional states, and suggest practical tactics for positively controlling their emotional state and influencing those of others.

Mindfulness for Stress Management
Since the shift to defense can be both emotive and stressful, a good EC will have mindfulness tools to help their CXOs maintain focus under pressure. I often use simple techniques like body scans and box breathing with my clients. I combine these with visualizations, and I

---

[91] Goleman, D. (1995). *Emotional intelligence: Why it can matter more than IQ*. Bantam Books; Bradberry, T., & Greaves, J. (2009). *Emotional intelligence 2.0*. TalentSmart.

recommend conducting them in under eight minutes, just prior to or after a challenging meeting. I know some ECs who have benefitted from having a number of advanced breathing techniques in their warehouse.[92]

Stakeholder Mapping and Analysis

Stakeholder mapping helps the CXO to think outside of themselves, and if properly employed by the EC it can result in new opportunities for empathy, sometimes even for adversarial stakeholders. This toolkit identifies key stakeholders and their interests, motivations, and potential conflicts. Mapping exercises, interest analysis, and influence diagrams allow CXOs to navigate internal and external politics more effectively and build stronger alliances intentionally.

If you are able to do it, having a third-party interview with some of your coachee's key stakeholders will give you a better understanding of how these interpersonal relationships function. In lieu of this, a DISC or MBTI profile for those key stakeholders will give you new lenses through which to see how your client is managing different personalities in their stakeholder groups.

I loved Freeman's original presentation (1984), so I recommend reading *Strategic Management: A Stakeholder Approach*,[93] but if you're new to the topic, Bridoux and Stoelhorst (2022) will give you an overview of the research so far, and you can pick the direction you'd like to go in.[94] If you prefer a program or training on the subject, Marshall Goldsmith's Stakeholder Centered Coaching is a great certification to add to your coaching warehouse.[95]

---

[92] Nash, J. (2023, September 26). 7 best breathwork techniques & exercises to use. PositivePsychology.com; Ankrom, S. (2024, February 16). Need a breather? Try these 9 breathing exercises to relieve anxiety. Verywell Mind; Johnson, C. (2024). Learn how mindful breathing helps your mind-body connection. Anahana.

[93] Freeman, R. E. (1984). *Strategic management: A stakeholder approach*. Pitman.

[94] Bridoux, F., & Stoelhorst, J. (2022). Stakeholder theory, strategy, and organization: Past, present, and future. *Strategic Organization, 20*(4), 797–809.

[95] Stakeholder Centered Coaching Ltd. (2024).

Love-Based Coaching

Though I'm still working on the actual coaching certification program, the materials are based on my book *Love@Work*,[96] and you can find most of what you need there. It's based on the idea that love is a best practice for survival from an evolutionary psychological perspective, and survival in social groups is ensured by knowing who loves us and who doesn't, who we love and who we don't. While this was historically applied in social groups based on geography, language, tribe, and religion, the Industrial Revolution gave birth to a new kind of economic tribe (companies) in which humans now invest much of their lives.

I argue that love is a natural expression of tribal allegiance among humans working co-operatively, and it is intensely profitable in the business context. To achieve this, humans connect through a consistent and measurable five-step process. Here's the nutshell version:

1. **Included**: Inclusion is level 1 in human connection. It's when you're present and feel welcome. But being included doesn't mean you've been heard.
2. **Heard**: For that, you need to feel enough psychological safety to communicate, and that communication needs to be acknowledged somehow. But being heard doesn't mean you're understood.
3. **Understood**: Most humans, most of the time, don't need to be agreed with as much as they need to be understood. For that, you'll need to hear an echo back that closely resembles what you meant in your communication. But being understood doesn't mean you're valued.
4. **Valued**: I can hear and understand your advice, but if I don't make any resulting changes, then it's not valuable advice. To feel valued in a relationship, what we contribute needs to be reflected in meaningful change.
5. **Loved**: Reciprocated meaningful change over time results in a human feeling loved. Love is the evolutionary psychological shortcut that represents the highest forms of empathy, loyalty,

---

[96] Block, C. J. (2023). *Love @ work: The final frontier of empathy in leadership.* PassionPreneur.

trust, psychological safety, discretionary effort, belonging, shared values … basically everything you read in leadership books these days.

I use this process to help my clients intentionally bring key stakeholders closer in relationship with them. The resulting connection provides a sense of free-wolf pack collaboration rather than lone-wolf captivity competition.

I think Amy Edmondson (my psychological safety guru), Simon Sinek (my empathy guru), and Stephen M. R. Covey (my trust guru) should each have written a book about the highest form of psychological safety, empathy, and trust, respectively. I wrote *Love@Work* because my gurus in the leadership space have stopped short of where I think each of them is going in their thinking. [I can't imagine why.} In any case, rather than looking at higher forms of leadership, I think we should start with every human's built-in definition of the highest form of leadership and see how that works.

People will work hard for a leader they fear, but they'll fight for a leader they respect, and they'll kill and die for a leader they love, especially one who loves them back.

Bottom Line

Executive coaches should be equipped to recognize the shift from offense to defense and help their CXOs navigate it well. Strong leaders who have achieved their top jobs by being fiercely competitive might suddenly find themselves on shaky ground, feeling vulnerable and threatened, like a wolf caged among strangers. The barking and gnashing of teeth that sometimes result are a natural and predictable byproduct of turning lone wolves into top dogs.

Wolves in the wild, however, are focused on expanding their pack's territory and defending it against outsiders, not insiders. They're not "lone" at all. They're not under attack from within, so their attention can be focused on the market around them. They lead their packs by earning trust, providing for and protecting them, and collaborating with them.

The executive shift to defense calls for a coaching playbook that includes understanding governance, mastering emotional intelligence, and learning how to build real connections with others, as Indra Nooyi did. Although aggression might have gotten them to the top, it's collaboration and empathy that will keep them there. That's a massive shift in social best-practice.

I wonder how long it takes for a captive wolf to adjust to not feeling threatened all the time when they're finally let loose into the wild?

[Oh wait, I just found it. It ranges from a few months to over a year, depending on how old they are and how long they've been in captivity. Some never successfully adapt to the wild at all.}[97]

Dan, Sam Altman, and Steve Jobs are prime examples of what can happen if this transition isn't managed well. Indra Nooyi proves that leading with empathy and relationship-building can turn this challenge into growth and success. Executive coaches will succeed by arming their clients with tools like emotional intelligence and stakeholder mapping. These keys may help CXOs survive boardroom battles and hold on to their hard-won positions at the top.

Since the defensive shift comes in response to a real or perceived challenge from within, it often amplifies and exacerbates the language barrier discussed in Chapter 3, and invariably results in a growing sense of isolation. When your colleagues are the ones picking away at your imposter syndrome and challenging your leadership, that's when it's loneliest at the top. That's where we'll go next.

---

[97] Smith, J. (2020). Reintroduction of captive wolves: Challenges and strategies. *Wildlife Conservation Journal, 15*(3), 45–58.; Johnson, L., & Brown, R. (2019). Post-release monitoring and support for reintroduced wolves. *Journal of Wildlife Management, 83*(2), 123–134.

The Checklist
Formal Expertise:

- Training in emotional intelligence and stress management
- Knowledge of stakeholder mapping and analysis
- Certification in conflict resolution and negotiation
- Understanding of organizational politics and power dynamics

Informal Expertise:

- Skill in navigating internal politics and defensive behaviors
- Ability to foster collaboration and relationship-building
- Experience in managing Board-CEO conflicts
- Strong problem-solving and analytical skills
- Ability to provide strategic advice and support
- Knowledge of leadership and team dynamics

5.

EXECUTIVE ISOLATION

"Coaching is a unique thing in the world. No other discipline demands that both people in a working relationship use everything they have—their skills, training, personal history, experience, background, personality, priorities, natural wiring—to benefit ONE PERSON in the relationship. That's the kind of thing that can change everything. And it's what the world needs."

- Jonathan Reitz, MCC, ACTC, member of the Coaches50 from Thinkers50.com

When I was younger, I was baffled by the leadership axiom "It's lonely at the top." It didn't make sense to me. It felt dismissive of a lot of people: those who worked with and for that leader, all the members of their community who helped them to reach that top position, and those in their network and on their teams who helped them stay there.

"What do you mean: lonely?" I thought. "You didn't get there alone, and you're not staying there all on your own." I was sometimes vocally critical of those who would use the axiom reflexively.

I was young. [And arrogant}

I've been the CEO a few times in my career since then, and I get it now. You can't really know this one unless you've experienced it for yourself. So the fifth major issue that a CXO is more likely to experience than a C-1 is the loneliness and isolation that accompanies being at the top of the corporate ladder.

[If you're a coach who hasn't been an executive, you really need to perk up for this.}

The Lonely CEO

"I try not to bring my office stress home, so it's not something I can talk to my wife about. Do you know what I mean?"

Albert was the CEO of a company of about 6,000 employees. He'd been hired into the role a year prior to engaging with me, just after an acquisition merged the parent company with another of about 2,000 employees. That meant a third of his employees were from a different corporate culture than the majority, and silos had formed and solidified in the interim year. Many of the executives had hired their friends and family to keep loyalty up within their departments, and cross-pollination between the OGs (the original company members) and the newbies (those in the acquired company) was discouraged on both sides, resulting in tribal information gatekeeping.

The most common disputes were procedural, and they often sounded something like this:

"That's not the way we do it here."

"Well, the way we did it at InTech is better."

"Well, you're not at InTech anymore. We bought you guys, remember? You're ProBase now. Just look at the logo on your shirt. Then do it the right way, my way."

Albert and I talked for a while about the two-culture problem, but my biggest concern was with his view of himself in all of this. So I redirected the conversation.

"Which of the two cultures trusts you the most?" I asked him.

"Neither," he sighed. "I'm still considered a foreigner by both of them. They know I was brought in to make things work, and neither side trusts me. All I seem to get is curated bickering."

"So what have you done?"

"I hired a couple of guys I've worked with before just so I could have some insight from people I trust on the inside. I thought having people I know in key roles would give me better visibility and influence."

"I'll bet that went down well."

"Not really. They're being walled off as well. The three of us are known as the 'TAs' ... Team Albert. It's annoying."

"So tell me what I can do as a coach that would help you the most right now."

"Mostly I just need someone to talk to, you know? This is the first time in my career that I'm pretty sure I'm screwing things up as the CEO, and even though I think I know what's wrong, I don't know how to fix it, and I don't have anyone to talk through it with."

"Have you tried just being honest with your EXCO?"

"Guaranteed, if I tell them I have doubts about my own leadership, they will too if they don't already. That's not going to serve them right now, or the company. They need to be able to have confidence in me, so this is one of those times where my vulnerability as a leader will likely do more harm than good. The same goes for the Board. I can't tell them I'm insecure about the next steps here. And my wife, like I said, she prefers me not to bring my work home. So, I protect her from this as well."

"Sounds lonely."

"That's exactly what it is. It's lonely at the top, I guess, but I've never felt it like this before."

"I've got you. Where would you like to begin?"

At the top of this particular ladder, Albert found himself without someone else's wisdom to lean on (**lack of mentorship**); he had a couple of old friends in the office to keep him company, but they were only telling him what he wanted to hear (**echo chamber effect**). He was surrounded by adversarial managers protecting their information from each other and from him (**information gatekeeping**), and he knew that being truthful about his insecurity would only lead to more widespread insecurity (**the authenticity paradox**).

Plus, in order to maintain healthy work-life balance boundaries, he often felt alone in his own home, with his family oblivious to the internal turmoil he hid unresolved in his heart each evening. But it was taking a toll on his relationships with his kids, and his wife suggested he see a psychologist about depression.

Cost and Causes of Isolation

Albert's case was serious, but not at all unique. And although I'm not a psychologist I could see that he wasn't depressed. He was lonely, and perhaps a little lost. Hazards of the Job.

Whether climbing the ladder or building it beneath them, executives' successful rise to the top is most often the result of thousands of hours of discretionary effort, and a sense of personal responsibility for the outcomes of the business. They earned their way up by working when no one was looking, often sacrificing social belonging in the process. Personal isolation is a common cost of professional success.

Loneliness at work was brought into sharp focus by the COVID-19 pandemic. Greater loneliness in employees is associated with poorer task, team role, and relational performance. Lonely employees feel less emotionally attached to their organization, leading to decreased performance overall. And they engage in surface acting, masking their true feelings, which distracts them from their tasks and team interactions.[98]

Now imagine that emotional detachment and surface acting at the highest executive level. Giant corporations mean magnified responsibilities, expectations, and media scrutiny; coupled with the already significant task of managing a business entity, these things can severely limit the number of people executives can trust and confide in.[99] Already back in 2009, 76% of executives reported feeling isolated in their roles.[100] There are four primary organizational dynamics that contribute to this isolationism, each of which was faced by Albert.

Lack of Mentorship

Echo Chamber Effect

Authenticity Paradox

Echo Chamber Effect

Information Gatekeeping

---

[98] Hakan, O., & Barsade, S. (2012). Work loneliness and employee performance.
[99] Henry, Z. (2016). Why Apple CEO Tim Cook doesn't think CEOs deserve any sympathy. *Inc.*
[100] De Meuse, K.P., Dai, G., & Lee, R.J. (2009). Evaluating the effectiveness of executive coaching: Beyond ROI? *Coaching: An International Journal of Theory, Research and Practice, 2*(2), 117–134.

1. **Lack of mentorship**: they don't have anyone better than they are to advise them.
2. **Echo chamber effect**: they themselves curate a monolithic team of advisors.
3. **Information gatekeeping**: those around them curate their rose-colored view.
4. **Authenticity paradox**: when being authentic undermines their own leadership.

Let's look at each of these influences on the CXO.

Lack of Mentorship

1. Lack of Mentorship

Whether they climb the ladder or build it beneath them, CXOs often earn their way into isolation by becoming the highest level of competency and authority in their organization. Coupled with a strong sense of responsibility for their company's continued growth, they become increasingly isolated when their access to mentorship from above dissolves. An important part of anyone's career is receiving input from someone more experienced. A new Deputy CFO relies on the CFO to find their way.

Upon entry into the C-suite, however, a newly hired CFO is suddenly, and for the first time in their career, expected to have the highest level of competence in their organization's finance function. This is the same for the first time CMO, CHRO, COO, CIO, and CEO. It's a brand-new challenge, one they didn't have while climbing the ladder. The language barrier is the initial challenge (Chapter 3), often rapidly followed by the shift to defense (Chapter 4). Both of these contribute to and escalate executive isolation. Plus, now they're mentorless.

At the top there are no mentors left – yet executive coaching research shows that mentorship, along with a solid ego check, are *exactly* what CXOs both need and value.[101] That's a serious vacuum.

[I know, I've been there. I was a bit of an asshole in my 20s. Impatient, arrogant, and at the top. Not a great combination, but I had coaches like Darcy and Kory. They kept me in check.}

Five years after taking over from Steve Jobs, Apple CEO Tim Cook spoke candidly about the challenges of running one of the world's most iconic companies. "It's sort of a lonely job," he admitted. Harvard Business Review reports that 61% of CEOs agree with Cook, noting that executive isolation can hinder their performance.[102] This is exaggerated for women in executive roles, as they may experience fewer opportunities for networking due to underrepresentation, and higher expectations for achieving work-life balance.[103]

Incidentally, Cook's EC was Bill Campbell. I highly recommend reading Bill's biography, *The Trillion Dollar Coach*.[104]

2. Echo Chamber Effect

I stepped into the boardroom and greeted the six gentlemen at the table. I was conducting a one-day strategy facilitation workshop so they could get aligned on their priorities for the coming year. The discussions went smoothly and consensus was found, often without much dissent or disagreement.

That's when I told them they had a serious communication problem.

[101] Grover, S., & Furnham, A. (2016). Coaching as a developmental intervention in organisations: A systematic review of its effectiveness and the mechanisms underlying it. *PLOS ONE, 11*(7); Gettman, H. J. (2008). *Executive coaching as a developmental experience: A framework and measure of coaching dimensions* [Doctoral dissertation, University of Maryland].

[102] Saporito, T. J. (2012). It's time to acknowledge CEO loneliness. *Harvard Business Review*.

[103] Catalyst. (2020). *Women in the workforce: Global*. Catalyst; Ely, R. J., Ibarra, H., & Kolb, D. M. (2011). Taking gender into account: Theory and design for women's leadership development programs. *Academy of Management Learning & Education, 10*(3), 474–493; KPMG. (2019). *Advancing the future of women in business: A KPMG women's leadership study*. KPMG; McKinsey & Company. (2020). *Women in the workplace 2020*. McKinsey & Company.

[104] Schmidt, E., Rosenberg, J., & Eagle, A. (2019). *Trillion dollar coach: The leadership playbook of Silicon Valley's Bill Campbell*. Harper Business.

"I'm sorry, Dr. Corrie," said the Chairman, "I don't know what you mean. We tend to agree on most things, and so, for the most part, we're a pretty smooth-running Board."

"That's your problem. Smooth is not profitable. And, of course, you tend to agree on things. I mean look at you. You're all a bunch of middle-aged white guys. You grew up speaking the same language, eating the same cereal, watching the same movies. You think the same because the lot of you are pretty much sharing one brain. Sure you all get along, which is a significant advantage over dinner, but it's costing you millions as a Board of Directors."

It came out that one by one each of them had received their seat at the table by invitation from someone else at the table. They had all felt a little isolated in their executive and Ministerial roles in the past, so they inadvertently turned their Board of Directors into a kind of friendship group.

If you've ever heard the terms "yes-men" or "old-boys club" used to describe a group of executives or a Board of Directors, then you know exactly what I'm talking about. The gender-bias in these terms only serves to highlight the point: same gender, same worldview.

This happens on Executive Committees, and even in departments. Leaders often subconsciously hire in line with their in-group biases in order to feel a little more affinity in the office. It's just a little less lonely at the top when you're surrounded by people who understand your jokes, watch the same sports you do, and like the same food you do.

I get it. It's lonely at the top, so keeping people next to you who look, sound, and think like you is comforting and reduces friction.

I've encountered this isolationism at the top of many of the organizations that I've worked with. And it should be said that this is not all unconscious behavior; executives are often aware they're doing it. Familiarity and similarity both improve the possibility for human connection and a sense of support. And for many isolated executives, this is a welcome compromise.

It makes sense. They feel better connected, a deeper sense of belonging, and they experience fewer challenges to their ideas that way. However, the lack of diversity that strengthens relationships weakens decision-making.

3. Information Gatekeeping
"How can we improve the sharing of information among our executives?"

Srinath was the Head of Learning and Development for a tech company with about 5000 employees. He was looking for a magic program that would somehow help his executive team to trust each other and share information more freely and proactively.

Information Gatekeeping

"There's no magic pill," I replied. "The fact is, your executives don't trust each other. They're all in this alone, and they're not sharing information because they don't believe that what they share won't be used against them in some way."

I was quickly able to diagnose the problem all the way up to the top. The Board of Directors was not empowering their CEO, who lived in fear of the consequences of reporting below expectations. The CEO curated the quality of information shared with the Board of Directors because he didn't trust them. He then put pressure on his EXCO to deliver "results, no matter how."

It was a chain of distrust and isolation that spread fear like wildfire all the way down the organization chart. Mid-level managers were trained by their department heads on how to spin and craft their messaging to present a more flattering view of their department's performance. These rosy views were then expertly honed and polished by the Executive Committee members before being sent to the CEO. The CEO then curated the best possible narrative to present to the Board of Directors, who knew better than to trust what they were being shown and responded predictably – with more disempowerment and distrust of their CEO.

Imagine for a moment that you were the Chief Marketing Officer in Srinath's company. How would you feel? You know better than to report bad sales figures to your CEO, so you pressure your team to maneuver sales numbers from one month to the next, credit pipeline sales as income at the 85% confidence level, approve deals with a negative long-term profit and a large advance payment in order to make your quarterly KPI.

All the while, you don't trust the information being provided to you by your team, and you know for a fact that your CEO can't trust what you're telling him either. That would be terribly lonely.

Information gatekeeping isn't always this obvious, though. Often CXOs will feel an increasing sense of isolation when they detect it in their teams, even if they've encouraged full transparency. It can be really hurtful, too, when an executive finds out that their CEO has been withholding vital strategic information from them.

With these three organizational tendencies in play, it's no wonder CXOs experience professional, social, and informational isolation in their top jobs. Many of my CXO clients have highlighted one or more of these three challenges as their greatest strategic concern. But even if they identify these concerns and intend to address them, they sometimes shouldn't address them out loud.

Authenticity at the top is a double-edged sword.

4. The Authenticity Paradox

Authenticity and transparency are easy buzzwords to throw around in leadership books [like this one}, but just think about the reality facing the CXO under increasing pressure to hide their growing sense of isolation. They're told by gurus like Simon Sinek to be authentic for the sake of their leadership, but what if authenticity is precisely

Authenticity Paradox

Authenticity Paradox

what they need to *conceal* for the sake of their leadership?

It's impossible for CXOs to maintain strategic confidentiality while being transparent enough in their decision-making process to ensure credibility in the eyes of the Board, investors, employees and the media. The pressure to be authentic and connect with stakeholders increases in the life of a CXO – yet if they become too honest about their isolation, stress levels, insecurities, or imposter syndrome, the very stakeholders they are meant to be authentic with may lose confidence in their leadership.[105]

Perhaps that's the most sinister type of "loneliness at the top."

Remember when the greatest gymnast of all time withdrew from the 2020 Tokyo Olympics citing mental health struggles? The world was in shock. We all knew we weren't allowed to be disappointed in Simone Biles, even if we secretly were. Her authenticity was truly brave, and she sure achieved her comeback in Paris in 2024, but tell me, what Board of Directors would respect the courage of their CEO's authenticity in stepping back from a major M&A negotiation at the eleventh hour saying, "I have to focus on my mental health and not jeopardize my health and well-being," as Biles did?[106]

---

[105] Murthy, V. (2017). *Work and the loneliness epidemic.* Harvard Business Review.
[106] Ramsey, G., Sinnott, J. & Wright, R. (2021). "I have to focus on my mental health," says Simone Biles after withdrawing from gold medal event. *CNN.*

Let's face it: CXO authenticity is often unwelcome in the business world.

Aside from personal mental health struggles, this sense of isolation and detachment can escalate into a serious business liability as well. CXOs who spend the majority of their time in executive suites or boardrooms often lose touch with the day-to-day realities of employees on the front lines. This disconnect can erode trust and morale among staff, leading to decreased engagement and productivity. Some intrepid leaders simply flee their ivory towers in search of the ground-level connection they're missing in the corner office.

Getting Re-Connected

"I'm a broken record when it comes to saying, 'We have to focus on the consumer.'"

– A.G. Lafley, former CEO of P&G

A.G. Lafley started his career in the Navy and earned a degree in history, an atypical start to a career trajectory that led to his becoming CEO of Proctor & Gamble (P&G) in 2000.[107] Lafley was a people person, and intentional about connecting all the way from the C-suite to the consumer on the street.

He'd learned his consumer orientation years prior when he was overseeing P&G's Far East operations in the 1970s. One of his most notable discoveries was learning that Japanese consumers really disliked certain foreign brands like Max Factor. He visited distributors' stores and consumers' homes himself, and refocused P&G's efforts on pushing local brands like SK-II to the front. SK-II quickly became the number one cosmetics brand in Japan, and cemented Lafley's willingness to challenge conventional wisdom and listen to the voice of the consumer.

P&G was already a massive company by the time he became CEO, and a very data-driven one. It would have been easy for him to isolate himself in the executive offices, surrounded by likeminded people, and trust the data served to him. But he saw how his executives were often buried

---

[107] Kroll, L. (2002). *A fresh face.* Forbes.

under mountains of consumer research, yet still struggled to connect with consumers on a meaningful level. And he knew better than to allow isolationism to curb his earlier learnings.

Lafley was able to bypass some of the isolating effects of the echo chamber and information gatekeeping at P&G by continuing to reach out directly to his consumers, but that didn't mean he felt totally connected. There are other aspects of isolation for the CEO of one of the world's largest companies. What about his lack of mentorship, and his authenticity paradox? Who did Lafley talk to about those things?

Ram Charan, that's who.

Charan is a world-renowned executive coach who served as an advisor to Lafley during his tenure at P&G. The two even wrote a book together about the company's success during that time.[108] Jack Welch, former Chairman of GE, once remarked of Charan that "He has the rare ability to distill meaningful from meaningless and transfer it to others in a quiet, effective way."[109]

Who was listening to the consumers? Lafley.

Who was listening to Lafley? Charan.

In most organizations, even those with healthy leadership cultures, it can be unnerving and perhaps threatening for a CXO to ask for help ... or reveal an insecurity or lack of competence ... or risk a silly question in front of the EXCO. After all, the EXCO may be complicit in the echo chamber or information gatekeeping effects (or both). So, who can a CXO talk to if they need to process something out loud with someone competent enough to understand their concern yet disconnected enough to withhold judgment?

Who can CXOs be authentic with when that very authenticity is a threat to their performance?

---

[108] Lafley, A. G., & Charan, R. (2008). *The game-changer: How you can drive revenue and profit growth with innovation.* Crown Business.
[109] Charan, R. (2024). *Ram Charan.*

Coaching the Lonely

Ben is the CEO and owner of an engineering company in Dubai. I coached him and his executive team for about a year and a half, an engagement that ended more than a year ago. But once a coach, always a coach. He reached out to me last week for an impromptu coaching session.

"I literally have no one, not one person in my life that I can talk to about this. I mean, my wife is amazing, and she knows everything. She's super supportive emotionally ..."

"But doesn't have a hot clue what you're talking about when you need to bounce around ideas for preferred stock options and graduated equity structures?" I politely added.

"Yeah," he sighed.

"I've got you."

Ben was in the middle of negotiations to arrange the buyout of one of his company's largest investors. Having put a lot of his own skin in the game, he was looking for someone he trusted to talk through the governance structure and employee equity planning. He also needed a series of sanity checks on his rationale for the deal.

Research among tech executives conducted over months of interviews by executive coach Suzan Bond highlights similar challenges. Noting both the isolating nature of their leadership roles and the loneliness stemming from situations discussed in this chapter, she concluded that these aspects of the job are driving many tech execs to seek an executive coach, as Ben did.[110]

CXOs are held to impossibly high standards; they need to present unwavering confidence and infallibility at all times. Such pressure to perform can exacerbate feelings of loneliness, especially as leaders internalize their struggles, fearing the stigma and risk of vulnerability. Friends and colleagues may offer sympathy, but they lack the context to truly understand the complexities of CXO leadership roles. Very often

---

[110] Bond, S. (2020). *Executive coaching and why leaders feel lonely.* The Vivid Minds.

the EC is quite literally the only person in their lives they can talk to about something that's both emotionally isolating and yet requires executive competency.

The CXO Coach Toolkit

An executive coach will not be able to advise a CXO better than their mentors did when they were climbing the corporate ladder to the top. But Simone Biles' coaches can't really mentor her, either. They don't have her talent or ability, but I'll tell you what they do have: coaching experience, and empathy.

Laurent Landi and Cécile Canqueteau-Landi have both competed at the top level in gymnastics.[111] They were there with full empathetic support for Biles in 2020 when she withdrew from the Tokyo games, and they were there in full empathetic support again in 2024 when she took home a silver and three gold medals from Paris. And I'll be willing to bet that neither of them could have pulled off a Yurchenko double pike on the vault, either.

But that's the nature of Olympic-level coaching. These competitors are at the top. There are no mentors left. So they'd better have a coach who's got both empathy and experience.[112]

---

[111] Sportskeeda, S.K. Desk. (2024). Simone Biles's Coach. Sportskeeda.com.
[112] Newcomb, A. (2021, August 5). Photo captures bond between Simone Biles and coach Cecile Canqueteau-Landi. TODAY.com.

Simone Biles and Her Coach at the 2020 Olympic Games

[Now go ahead and tell me that Cécile is behaving unprofessionally in this photo.}

Empathy and Experience
An EC with a solid business education and experience will know which questions to ask to help executives think through tough challenges without risking vulnerability or embarrassment in front of the other EXCO members or their Board of Directors. An EC should not only be able to hold space for discussing challenging interpersonal issues; they should also be competent enough in the business context to engage intelligently in strategy conversations   for   valuable   external processing.

Just as it is with Simone Biles, the CXO's performance will ultimately result from a combination of their intrinsic talent, learned skills, and self-efficacy.

[And coaching.}

A comprehensive literature review by Tripathy and Mangaraj emphasizes the growing role of self-efficacy in executive coaching.[113] Executives who receive multiple coaching sessions over several months

---

[113] Tripathy, S., & Mangaraj, S. (2017). A literature review on executive coaching. *Training & Development Journal, 8*(2), 117–134.

show significant improvements in self-efficacy, which is particularly relevant in addressing the lack of mentorship that many executives face. Nicolau et al. conducted a meta-analysis that demonstrates the positive impact of executive coaching on the self-efficacy, psychological capital, and resilience required by CXOs to manage their isolation, specifically.[114] By fostering self-efficacy, coaching can fill the mentorship gap and keep the loneliness at bay.

Active Listening

"Listening is not a skill; it's a discipline. Anybody can do it. All you have to do is keep your mouth shut."

– Peter Drucker

I've been critical of strict non-advisory coaches in previous chapters, but here's where these colleagues tend to excel. Non-advisory coaches tend to be very strong in active listening and critical questioning.

I'll add only two ingredients to Peter Drucker's formula that I believe are critical to the success of active listening, neither of which require you to open your mouth: curiosity and care. If you're curious about what the other person is saying and what it means to them, and you care about them as a person, then active listening is a natural byproduct of your closed mouth.

Eventually, the CXO coach will need to move beyond listening into active coaching, something that requires advisory work, even if mentoring is too tall an ask. Addressing the challenges of loneliness and isolation, however, will require adopting a particular posture: that of the critical friend.

Critical Friend

The executive coach is required to offer incisive feedback (Chapter 1) and unwavering Pygmalion optimism (Chapter 2), while maintaining trust and transparency to combat loneliness (Chapter 5). In the way it

---

[114] Nicolau, A., Candel, O. S., Constantin, T., & Kleingeld, A. (2023). The effects of executive coaching on behaviors, attitudes, and personal characteristics: A meta-analysis of randomized control trial studies. *Frontiers in Psychology, 14.*

synthesizes all of these EC competencies, I really like Costa and Kallick's (1983) concept of the critical friend. Blended from education and psychology, the critical friend is a voice of wisdom that provides both unconditional support and constructive critique.[115]

The CXO starts this process by laying out their challenges and seeking the executive coach's council. As EC, you should stick to deep questioning for as long as is needed to gain a competent understanding of the root causes and contextual nuances at play before shifting to offering external insights. Your questioning should center on having the CXO look at the same problem from a number of perspectives and then consider their response from a spectrum of possibilities.

It's important then that your client sets their desired outcomes and chooses an action plan, reclaiming their agency. Your job as a critical friend is to provide ongoing feedback in a blend of perspective-shifting insights and thought-provoking observations. They should always be aimed at highlighting potential new pathways forward.

I like this toolkit because it's advisory in nature while intentionally transcending the often transactional nature of coaching. It fosters an environment of trust, vulnerability, and mutual respect. To be a good critical friend is to tread the fine line between unwavering support and fearless critique.[116]

It can be tough, though, because this means that as an executive coach, you need to build a genuine connection. That is what your right to challenge is founded on. Simultaneously, you must resist the temptation to allow that very friendship to obscure the stark realities facing your clients. Your sympathy, while well-intentioned, can impede their progress and stifle innovation. Instead, you should be embracing the role of provocateur, by challenging assumptions and questioning their biases. That's your job. You're their most critical friend.

---

[115] Costa, A. and Kallick, B. (1983). Through the lens of a critical friend. *Educational Leadership* 51(2): 49–51.
[116] Bates, B. (2015). *The little book of big coaching models: 83 ways to help managers get the best out of people.* FT Press.

"An open rebuke is better than hidden love! Wounds from a sincere friend are better than many kisses from an enemy."
– Proverbs 27:5-6

Encourage Diversification of Input

Executive coaches should have an executive-level understanding of the effects of diversification of input on decision-making quality. Executive input-seeking behavior can be stifled both by information gatekeping and the echo chamber effect, both contributors to informational isolationism. I encourage my CXO clients to seek input diversity in five major categories:

1. **Macro-trend**: Influences like Global Climate Change, the 4th Industrial Revolution, and Generative Artificial Intelligence impact nearly all economic games. The CXO doesn't need to be an expert on these trends, but they shouldn't be ignorant of them either.

2. **Industrial**: Innovations and disruptions can cause major shifts in every industry. The CXO should know where to go for condensed, uncurated, and independent information on the latest trends affecting their industry.

3. **Role-specific**: Forums for CEOs, CFOs, CHROs and COOs (among many others) exist as communities of practice.[117] I often advise my CXO clients to belong to at least one role-specific industry-agnostic community.

4. **Demographic**: CXOs should be connecting with people of different genders, ethnicities, socio-religious backgrounds, languages, and ages. Intentionality in this not only reduces isolation but increases the diversity measure in their inputs for decision-making.

5. **Personality-based**: StrengthsFinder, MBTI, Birkmann, DISC, Big-5 Personality Traits ... the particular tool doesn't matter here. What matters is that the CXO has some understanding of who they are as a person, and they surround themselves with people

---

[117] Wenger, E. (1998). *Communities of practice: Learning, meaning, and identity.* Cambridge University Press.

whose strengths cover their weaknesses. No leader is omni-talented, but in my experience a well-curated EXCO can get pretty close.

Bottom Line

Disclaimer: it's important for the coach never to make assumptions about the quality of the coaching relationship or the level of intimacy achieved, as this too can have a negative effect. Coaches need to be sensitive to the coachee's experience and explicitly verify their level of comfort in the coaching relationship. Or as one research team found, coaches should coach with an "ongoing and deliberately maintained doubt as their only certainty."[118]

With that caveat behind us, I'll close this chapter by noting that I typically become quite good friends with my coaching clients. For many of them, I become their principal confidant.

Yes, I'm emotionally involved. No, it's not romantic. [eyeroll}

Most of them really are lonely at the top, and they have very few (if any) people they can trust with their full authentic selves. Professional distance from their EC would only add to their sense of isolation. We'll discuss in the next chapter why this sense of executive isolation requires the objectivity of an external coach. Someone not involved. Someone with uncompromised objectivity who is still willing to connect personally.

I intentionally reduce professional distance by being open about my personal life and asking about theirs. I offer transparency in order to build trust, and it works about 95% of the time. For my complete methodology on this please see my earlier book, *Love @ Work: The Final Frontier of Empathy in Leadership.*[119]

---

[118] Baron, L., Morin, L., & Morin, D. (2011). The effect of working alliance discrepancy on the development of coachees' self-efficacy. *Journal of Management Development, 30*(9), 847–864.
[119] Block, C. J. (2023). *Love @ work: The final frontier of empathy in leadership.* PassionPreneur.

Actually, I just looked at my current coaching roster and figured out that I regularly hug more than 50% of my clients. And I live in the Middle East! And half of my clients are female.

I know, I know … deeply unprofessional, right? But I wonder if my being a hugger has any mitigating effect on their sense of feeling "lonely at the top." I'll bet it does.

[jk, I know for a fact it does.}

The Checklist
Formal Expertise:

- Training in psychology or counseling
- Knowledge of executive coaching frameworks (e.g., Critical Friend, Active Listening)
- Certification in emotional intelligence and resilience training
- Understanding of organizational dynamics and leadership challenges

Informal Expertise:

- Empathy and active listening skills
- Ability to build trust and provide a safe space for executives
- Experience in dealing with high-pressure and isolating roles
- Strong interpersonal and relationship-building skills
- Ability to offer unbiased and confidential support
- Knowledge of stress management and mental health practices

6.

EXTERNAL OBJECTIVITY

"All coaching is, is taking a player where he can't take himself."
— Bill McCartney, NFL Coaching Hall of Famer and the winningest coach in Colorado history.

This is the third famous Bill I've agreed with in this book. The coach takes you to where you can't go alone. If your coach thinks all the answers you need are already inside you, then you probably have the wrong coach.

The sixth major challenge that a CXO will face that a C-1 is less likely to experience is a heightened need to process insights and actions with complete and total confidentiality, even from their own team. Internal coaching at the executive level is an organizational myth we all wish were true, but here's the hard truth: it doesn't work. When confidentiality is compromised, objectivity is blurred, and internal politics taint every interaction, how can real transformation happen? If you're serious about driving executive performance, internal coaching isn't just ineffective, it's a waste of time and resources.

What's that? I shouldn't say that out loud to your CHRO?

[Oops, too late.}

Sorry, Tata

"I'm really excited to be with you all. Thank you for inviting me, but I have some bad news."

The 20 or so CHROs in front of me represented more than a million employees in Tata Group, one of the world's largest companies. In the fall of 2023, they were in the middle of a 3-day intensive program aimed to certify each of them as ICF coaches. As a supplementary expert, they invited me to conduct a masterclass on executive coaching. I knew what they were doing was a good thing, but I also knew it was limited in application.

My dilemma: tell them what they wanted to hear or tell them what they needed to hear.

I followed Jack Welch's advice and went with the hard truth.

"You can't coach your executives, even with the ICF certification. One methodology is not enough, but more critically, you're all internal."

After discussing the limitations of non-advisory coaching for executives, and a few of the other challenges I've highlighted in previous chapters, I told them the #1 reason they would not be successful:

"They'll lie to you. Your executives. They'll look you straight in the eyes and tell you they know what they're doing, they're confident in their decisions, and they have no exit plans. They'll distract you with petty politics, team conflict, and aggrandizing their own strategic agendas, so you'll have just enough transparency to believe that they're being authentic. But here's the kicker, they didn't get to where they are by being completely authentic with anyone in the HR department, ever, especially not the kind of person that can truly influence their current role or future career."

They were stunned. Visibly disappointed. [A few looked as though I had just taken away their favorite toy and told them they weren't allowed to play with it anymore.}

It's important to acknowledge that there are very good reasons for a CXO or organization to opt for an internal coach. Many organizations start their coaching journey with external coaches and, as they see the results of coaching, seek to build internal coaching capabilities. This often stems from a desire to manage costs effectively and retain talented coaches within the company's ecosystem. Cost control and talent retention are generally good things for companies, and internal coaching effectively serves both aims.

That's what Tata Group was doing. And just as I told Tata's CHROs, that's not a bad thing, but it is limited in its application, especially at the CXO level.

Many companies, like Tata, have established internal coaching teams to offer coaching to their staff members in response to the growing popularity of coaching in general. And I agree that a coaching style of leadership at every management level is a good thing. But there are distinct advantages to a CXO in working with an external coach that simply aren't present in internal coaching relationships, or at lower levels in the management structure.

Internal to External Coaching: A Conversion Story

I've never been on staff as an internal coach myself, but Lucia Baldelli has. I challenged her in Chapter 1, and I'm taking an opportunity to honor her here to show goodwill. She spent ten years as an internal coach before leaving William Hill to become an external coach.[120] Knowing her company intimately made it easier to build trust with senior leaders and their teams, and her deep understanding of the company's culture was a notable advantage when guiding change. Plus, with young kids at home, the stability of a regular paycheck was a comforting safety net, though she couldn't help but notice that she was paid less than any external coach the company hired.

One of her last internal gigs was coaching a group of leaders who were, to put it mildly, not interested in becoming a team. Their line manager had commissioned the work, but the leaders themselves weren't exactly eager to set aside their differences and work toward a common goal. Since Lucia was already part of the organization, it wasn't unusual for some of them to try to pull her onto their side of things. This was a tough but valuable lesson for her on the importance of setting boundaries and staying neutral.

Being so closely tied to the company also made it hard for Lucia to stay impartial and avoid getting emotionally involved. She knew she needed to keep her objectivity, but when you're steeped in the culture, that's easier said than done. She often found herself dragged into conflicts or tangled in complicated dynamics, where leaders sometimes saw her as a convenient place to dump their workload, responsibilities, or stress. This forced her to draw some pretty firm lines around what her role was and wasn't.

Over time, Lucia grew frustrated. Change in the organization seemed to move at a snail's pace, and seeing the impact that lack of progress had on people made her heartache. She longed to bring fresh ideas to the table but found that her deep immersion in the company's ways limited her ability to offer new perspectives.

Balancing her roles became an ongoing challenge. She often walked the paradox between ensuring that she was offering the necessary support

---

[120] Baldelli, L. (2024, January 11). Internal vs. external coaching: Pros and cons. *Coaching Outside the Box*.

while not overstepping or creating conflicts of interest. It was exhausting.

The tensions associated with internal coaching ultimately led Lucia to pursue an external coaching career. Her transparency highlights the challenges associated with being an internal coach. While internal coaching can certainly be effective, it comes with drawbacks that aren't always limited to the C-suite.

So the question is, does the money the organization saves on coaching by using internal coaches compensate for the money it loses in lack of confidentiality, transparency, objectivity, neutrality, and fresh insights that come from external coaching? At the mid-management level perhaps it does, since there's always an executive sponsor to oversee strategy, political conflict, and budget.

But at the executive level, almost certainly it doesn't. If confidentiality, transparency, objectivity, neutrality, and fresh insights aren't available to your executives in their sessions, can it be called "executive coaching" at all?

It's for this reason I think of "internal *executive* coaching" as a kind of organizational myth. It's something we really, really, really wish was true. It would make our lives so much simpler and cheaper if it were.

[Like the Philosopher's Stone, or genies … or unicorns! Sorry, Tata.}

Why Executives Need External Coaches

Research specific to this dynamic shows that external coaching works best for top executives, and internal coaching is *only viable* when:

- There is a high level of trust in the confidentiality of the process;
- There is a large number of coaching processes to be carried out;
- The hierarchical status of the executives is *not greater* than that of their coaches, and,

- The culture of the organization views coaching as an executive responsibility.[121]

Don't get me wrong here, internal coaching at the mid-management level can be quite effective, but effective coaching at the executive level by an internal coach simply doesn't happen. It's often assumed that internal coaches have automatic affinity resulting in automatic chemistry, but what if the chemistry just isn't there? And what if the CXO tries to avoid coaching by manufacturing a lack of chemistry?

In some organizations, executives now have the option of working with the on-staff coaches or hiring an outside coach. Let's look briefly at the primary reasons CXOs tend to opt for an external coach:

1. Objectivity vs. Bias
2. Expertise vs. Range
3. Confidentiality vs. Conflict of Interest
4. Individual vs. Corporate Goals

1. Objectivity vs. Bias

Internal coaches understand the company's culture, strategies, and internal politics. They can relate quickly to the company's specialized vocabulary and cultural norms. However, the value of this high-quality information is undermined by the very position from which they have access to it.

Being internal members of the company's structure and culture also risks their coaching insights and feedback being influenced by those very same internal politics, or worse, their own internal agendas. Even if they are not individually biased, their objectivity is compromised due to internal cultural and structural biases that they themselves are a part of and may not be aware of.

External coaches can provide objective feedback unaffected by internal dynamics or biases. They offer a safe space for full transparency and

---

[121] Schalk, M., & Landeta, J. (2017). Internal versus external executive coaching. *Coaching: An International Journal of Theory, Research and Practice, 10*(2), 140–156, emphasis mine.

candid discussions on sensitive issues. Several research and case studies have found that external executive coaching for higher executive roles specifically aids in developing self-awareness and decision-making skills by making implicit organizational knowledge explicit, allowing for a new layer of critical analysis.[122]

Since the external coach is largely unaware of the implicit organizational dynamics, the coach's deep questioning forces external processing of what may otherwise remain assumptive operating models. In this frame, the external coach's relative ignorance of the company's specialized vocabulary and cultural norms becomes an asset rather than a liability in coaching effectiveness by driving innovation.

Though external coaches like me often lack a nuanced understanding of the company's internal culture and politics, I've found that the most important understanding of the internal culture and politics is the one my coachee holds when I am working with them. Their perception of reality is indistinguishable from reality as they experience it, so it's the only one I need to work with as their coach. My need for the coachee to explain their internal dynamics to me not only improves my level of understanding but invites my coachee to process those dynamics intentionally and externally, often resulting in new insights.

I'm regularly told, "This is just the way we do it here." To which I naturally respond, "How does doing it that way benefit the organization, and what might it be costing you as a leader to leave those defaults unquestioned?"

The external coach's relative ignorance, unbiased objectivity, and curiosity become catalysts for innovation.

[Even then, industry knowledge has a half-life. We'll get to that.}

---

[122] Korotov, K. (2023). Accelerated development of organizational talent and executive coaching: A knowledge management perspective. In V. Vaiman, C. Vance, & J. Ling (Eds.), *Smart Talent Management: Managing People as Knowledge Assets* (2nd ed.). Edward Elgar.; Schalk, M., & Landeta, J. (2017). Internal versus external executive coaching. *Coaching: An International Journal of Theory, Research and Practice, 10*(2), 140–156; Moen, F., & Federici, R. A. (2012). The effect from external executive coaching. *Coaching: An International Journal of Theory, Research and Practice, 5*(2), 113–131.

2. Expertise vs. Range

Internal coaches have the advantage of company-specific knowledge, processes, and strategies. But as discussed in earlier chapters, this is a double-edged sword. At the executive level, domain specific knowledge, language, and culture might be as much liabilities as assets.

If the internal coach has spent their career in the same company as their executive coachee, they may intrinsically lack the broad-range experience or coaching-specific expertise needed for high-level executive coaching. Additionally, their insights and feedback may be limited by their immersion in the company's culture. What the executive most often needs isn't more domain or industry-specific knowledge, but range exposure.

It's true that one potential weakness of an external coach is their lack of company and person-specific knowledge. For this reason, external coaches often apply more generic approaches that may not fully align with company-specific challenges. This can be ameliorated by the CXO coach who pays more attention to the warehouse-of-tools approach over the roadmap approach to coaching methodology. (This was briefly mentioned in Chapter 1 and will be addressed again in Chapter 8.) Having a broad range of experience and toolkits allows for faster adaptation and more tailored approaches to coaching.

External coaches have generally completed extensive accredited training programs specific to coaching, and they should have thousands of hours of coaching experience across a range of organizational leaders. But is it better for the external coach to have industry experience, or to bring executive experience from different industries?

Coaching organizations like CMi Merryck and 100Coaches place value on matching executives with coaches possessing extensive industrial experience. This can ease communication, but there's a specialization-for-innovation trade-off here that should also be highlighted.

An external coach with industry-specific experience will naturally carry the vocabulary and understanding needed to discuss industrial challenges, and they may bring experience in solving problems from other companies within their client's industry to offer as tactical advice. This kind of mentoring influence may be an asset for a new or inexperienced CXO. However, the more experienced the CXO is, and the higher the level at which their organization operates within their industry, the more likely it is that the coach's industry-specific experience will be outdated and ineffective in the current state of play.

What made a mentor-coach successful a decade ago is unlikely to be as valuable to their client as innovative input from cross-functional, multi-disciplinary, or multi-industrial experience in their coach today. At the highest levels of global industrial play, special expertise in the coachee's industry will be overshadowed by a coach's range of experience working with high-level leaders across multiple industries.

3. Confidentiality vs. Conflict of Interest

An internal coach is unlikely to have sufficient leadership experience to earn the respect required for a CXOs full transparency, and moreover, they are bound by the internal reporting structure of the organization. Internal coaches will likely never achieve the level of authenticity and transparency from a CXO that's required for executive level coaching.

Internal coaches are aligned with company policies and objectives, which may be seen as an advantage to the organization. However, they are often required to report certain information, potentially breaching confidentiality. This possibility makes it harder to gain full trust and transparency from executives due to potential conflicts of interest.

External coaches offer strong confidentiality. They are bound by national laws, but not by the employee handbook; by the ethical standards of the coaching profession, but not necessarily those of the organization. This ensures confidentiality. External coaches are not obligated to report internal matters, or even policy breaches, allowing for a safe space for CXOs to process what may be grey-margin decisions or potential conflicts without risking exposure.

Just this year, one of my CXO clients informed me of their decision to terminate another one of my CXO clients, about 10 weeks ahead of the announcement. A number of my CXO clients have discussed their exit plans with me (and only me), often many months before any announcement was made. Most are very open with me about their political agendas, about who they are competing with internally and who they are trying to influence, and sometimes even manipulate. Over the last twenty years, a few of my clients have even divulged information to me that might be considered cause for a gross-misconduct dismissal at some point or another.

They trust me with this information in part because I'm trustworthy, but a certain prerequisite to this level of transparency is the fact that I'm an external coach. I can maintain a level of confidentiality and objectivity that an internal coach cannot.

If a CXO is filtering the quality of information they provide to their coach, then the coach cannot hope to be able to provide the highest quality of critical feedback or tactical advice. Transparency is based on trust, and that trust is undermined by the role requirements of the internal coach.

Executives need to be able to trust that their discussions will remain private if they are going to be able to talk openly about areas of development. They need to be able to speak their minds and share what is necessary, rather than what they want others to hear. And while most internal coaching teams do promise confidentiality as a part of their programs, they often fail to live up to this commitment: they end up discussing leaders' sessions with each other, HR partners, and their managers, without consent.

The most effective executive coaching relationships are those where the organization trusts the coach, and the coach is able to work with their executives in complete confidentiality. Only in complete confidentiality can total transparency be achieved – and with it, the highest quality of coaching.

4. Individual vs. Corporate Goals

A conflict of interest, a CEO's exit plan, or a political agenda might trigger loyalty conflicts that lead the internal coach to betray the confidence of their coachee, which could be catastrophic not only for the organization's coaching program but for its bottom-line performance.

For example, a CXO resignation can impact organizational culture, strategy, and even stock price. An internal coach would have to report that intent once declared in a session, but an external coach can provide a safe space for the CXO to process the decision and transition strategy, without making the pre-emptive announcements that an internal coach would be bound to make.

And what happens when the CXO is processing their decision to restructure a department, or remove a key position or person? How can the internal coach tasked with helping them work through this decision guarantee objectivity? Or even be aware of the subconscious word choices they are using to influence such decisions?

Internal coaches work within the company's goals and frameworks and are thus naturally aligned with the organization's objectives. However, this can lead to potential conflicts of interest that may affect the coaching relationship and outcomes. And it is due to this very alignment that their quality of feedback is constrained and their advice limited by internal dynamics and reporting structures.

External coaches focus on the executive as an individual, which is why open and unbiased coaching relationships often lead to significant performance improvements in accelerated timeframes. The obvious associated risk is that, with complete confidentiality, the coachee's individual goals may be discovered to not fully align with the company's goals and culture, potentially leading to individual goal pursuit that may be less relevant from the organization's perspective. But then, the coachee's goals were misaligned anyway, just no one knew it. At least with the CXO in conversation with an external coach the organization stands a chance at potential realignment.

Organizational Non-Conformity

Humans are intensely social beings, so conformity happens naturally in groups, and over time. In an organization, though, it can quietly smother creativity and slow down progress. Social psychology studies tell us that everyone in an organization, including the internal coach, is prone to conformity shaped by the existing norms and dynamics around them.[123]

That's where an outsider's fresh set of eyes can help. External coaches don't know the company's usual way of doing things, so they can spot the nuances, roadblocks, and blind spots that might be invisible to those involved. An external view can help executives entertain and embrace new ideas and strategies, often leading to breakthroughs. This is the effect that drives organizations to aim for a healthy balance of internal and external candidates when filling key positions.

Promoting from within brings the advantages of domain-specific expertise and the stability that comes from someone who already knows the ropes. Plus, it's usually more budget-friendly. Hiring from outside, on the other hand, offers fresh ideas, innovative approaches, and broader experience, though it often comes with a higher price tag.

An internal hire is a safe bet; steady and familiar. But if you're after change and growth, it's often the outsiders who will shake things up, for better or worse. So, what's better: spending more to get fresh insights or saving by sticking with domain expertise? It really depends on the results you're after. But from my experience, your CXOs are unlikely to benefit much from access to more internal expertise in their executive coach.

An external EC is the opposite of organizational conformity. Their outsider perspective is a catalyst for challenging executives to question tradition and explore new frames. They might not fully understand the company's cultural norms, but it's that very lack of familiarity that often leads to the most valuable coaching insights.

---

[123] Schnuerch, R., & Gibbons, H. (2014). A review of neurocognitive mechanisms of social conformity. *Social Psychology, 45*(6), 466–478.

If a company is not ready to invest in external coaching at the executive level, it might be better to skip the coaching program altogether. They'll save on the program's costs and avoid wasting their CXOs' time with a coaching experience that won't deliver the impact they're really looking for.

The Gerstner Effect

I think one of the best examples of the benefits of external range over internal expertise comes from the resurrection of IBM in 1993. The once-mighty technology giant was hemorrhaging billions of dollars and had lost its footing in an industry landscape experiencing near-daily disruption.

The Board forced CEO John Akers to resign, and naturally, they looked for someone with industry expertise to replace him. John Scully from Apple, George Fisher from Motorola, and Bill Gates from Microsoft all declined the role.

[I mean, who could blame them? Who wants to captain a sinking ship?!}

So, who did the board hire to replace Akers?

From an industrial perspective, Louis Gerstner wasn't even remotely qualified when he became Chairman and CEO of IBM. He had zero experience in computers [though his brother had worked at IBM a few years back, which totally counts, right?} Instead, Gerstner had collected his range through a string of successes at McKinsey & Co., American Express, and RJR Nabisco.

Think this through. Let's take a guy with a CV in consulting, retail finance, and FMCG, and put him in charge of one of the biggest computer companies on the planet during its most critical moment of crisis.

Great idea! What could go wrong? [Also, WTF?}

Gerstner's initial days at IBM were filled with bewilderment and frustration. At his first strategy meeting he found himself surrounded by employees speaking in a foreign language, using coded jargon and obscure terminology.[124] Avoiding this language challenge is precisely the reason executives often choose coaches from within their industry; it's easier to talk.

However, facing the entrenched cultural barriers and communication breakdowns that had contributed to IBM's decline was the wake-up call Gerstner needed. His unfamiliarity with the industry and company culture produced exactly the benefits that lead executives to choose coaches from outside of their industry.

IBM needed a fundamental shift in culture, so Gerstner set out to break down the silos and build up the values of collaboration and innovation (as Indira Nooyi did with PepsiCo). He identified key team members who shared his vision for change and empowered them to drive initiatives forward. Gerstner didn't need to rely on external consultants or advisors because he *was* the external advisor!

Just like an external coach would, he developed the talent and expertise already present within IBM, and it was his new insights combined with their collective knowledge and experience that produced a meaningful transformation.

However, it took an outsider's view to identify this advantage and leverage it.

Under Gerstner's leadership, IBM emerged from the flames by transitioning from a culture of individualism and decentralization to one of teamwork and customer-centricity. By embracing open standards and focusing on delivering solutions rather than just technology, IBM regained its competitive edge and positioned itself for long-term success in the rapidly evolving technology market.

IBM's transformation under Gerstner's tenure is a brilliant example of the impact of an outsider's perspective in driving organizational change. By challenging conventional wisdom, Gerstner revitalized IBM and laid

---

[124] Gerstner, L. V. (n.d.). Gerstner: Changing culture at IBM – Lou Gerstner discusses changing the culture at IBM. HBS Working Knowledge.

the foundation for its continued growth and success. His was an external perspective, with internal authority.

He was both the coach and the executive. It's a rare circumstance, but it happens.

More often and more predictably, external executive coaches work with existing executives to produce this Gerstner effect (objectivity + authority), but with guardrails: an external view filtered through internal authority is better when the two minds are in dialogue rather than of the same mind. The external coach's fresh perspective can challenge entrenched norms within the organization, which can then be filtered and applied through the authority of the internal executive. The dialogue between coach and executive leverages both sets of advantages.

Just as Gerstner's leadership transformed IBM, external executive coaches have the potential to catalyze similar transformations through existing leaders, enabling organizations to rapidly transform, adapt, and disrupt.

But let's say you invest in the external coach, and your CXO gets the confidentiality they're looking for, but the company loses control over the coaching that they would expect from an internal coach. The best-case scenario has a worst-case scenario, too.

What happens if the level of trust and transparency is so high, and the outsider perspective so greatly valued in the executive coaching relationship, that the executive divulges potentially unethical or illegal practices to their coach?

Reporting Executive Misconduct

An external executive coach might find themselves exposed to sensitive and sometimes even unethical or illegal behavior from the executives they coach. The tricky part? The obligations around reporting executive misconduct vary depending on where you are, and with the coaching industry still largely unregulated, there isn't a clear legal framework to navigate this kind of situation.

In my research, I couldn't find any cases where an EC was prosecuted for things like insider trading, securities fraud, or failing to report serious misconduct by a client. But that doesn't mean the responsibility isn't there. I agree with Hannafey and Vitulano that there's an agency relationship between the coach and the client, where the coach acts in the interest of both the individual and their company.[125]

In many ways, the role of an EC is similar to that of doctors or lawyers. We build close, privileged relationships with our clients who trust us with confidential information. We're expected to keep the client's best interests at heart, and we often know more about the coaching process than the client does, which creates a natural imbalance of power.

But while the responsibilities may feel similar, executive coaching as a field is far less organized than the medical or legal professions. It's diverse in terms of theories, methods, credentials, and standards, without the formal structure that doctors and lawyers operate under. This makes navigating ethical and legal challenges in executive coaching a bit more complex and a lot less predictable.

In the United States, the primary legal framework for reporting executive misconduct comes from the Sarbanes-Oxley Act (SOX), which mandates internal reporting mechanisms for unethical behavior such as financial fraud, insider trading, corruption, bribery, whistleblower retaliation, and accounting misconduct. SOX emphasizes the protection of whistleblowers but doesn't explicitly mandate external parties such as executive coaches to report wrongdoing.[126]

The UK's Public Interest Disclosure Act (PIDA) protects whistleblowers who report wrongdoings in the public interest, similar to SOX.[127] The Act primarily applies to employees, but external consultants, including executive coaches, may be considered liable if they are found to be

---

[125] Hannafey, F. T., & Vitulano, L. A. (2013). Ethics and executive coaching: An agency theory approach. *Journal of Business Ethics, 115*(3), 599–603.
[126] Myers, R. (2003). Ensuring ethical effectiveness: New rules mean virtually every company will need a code of ethics. *Journal of Accountancy, 195*, 28.
[127] Hassink, H., Vries, M., & Bollen, L. (2007). A content analysis of whistleblowing policies of leading European companies. *Journal of Business Ethics, 75*, 25–44.

complicit in covering up unethical behavior. Executive coaches might be compelled to report executive misconduct if organizational policies require it, or there's significant ongoing risk to the public.

The EU Whistleblower Protection Directive mandates comprehensive whistleblower protection laws. While the Directive focuses on protecting whistleblowers, like PIDA, it doesn't impose specific reporting duties on external consultants (like executive coaches) unless there is a significant ongoing risk to the public or organizational policies dictate otherwise.[128]

The Corporations Act in Australia includes provisions for whistleblower protection as well, encouraging the reporting of misconduct. While this primarily applies to employees, external consultants, including executive coaches, may face legal and ethical pressures to report significant breaches if they are aware of them. Once again, though, executive coaches are not typically mandated to report unless otherwise dictated by organizational policies or, again, if there is a significant ongoing risk to the public.[129]

Non-disclosure agreements (NDAs) can complicate the decision to report unethical behavior as well. While NDAs are designed to protect confidentiality, they don't legally protect against reporting illegal activities. Executive coaches need to balance their legal obligations with their professional ethics and the terms of their NDAs.[130]

One of the most critical reasons executive coaches need to be qualified to a higher standard than other kinds of coaches is that they navigate complex ethical and legal landscapes, just as their executive clients do. While confidentiality is a cornerstone of our practice, certain situations may require breaking confidentiality, to prevent harm or comply with legal obligations. The key is to balance professional ethics, legal duties,

---

[128] Ibid.
[129] Ibid.
[130] Berglas, S. (2002). The very real dangers of executive coaching. *Harvard Business Review, 80*(6), 86–92, 153.

and organizational policies. Coaches must consider their ethical duty to act in the best interest of the public and the organization.[131]

Thankfully, I've never faced an instance where I've been aware of any of my clients' actions posing a significant ongoing risk to the public. However, I have on occasion been entrusted with information that might be considered cause for gross misconduct dismissal, and it's not entirely uncommon for one of my CXO clients to have a personal goal in conflict with their organization's objectives.

In almost all of those cases, I've been able to coach my clients toward a more collaborative and mutually beneficial approach to their decision-making, and I shudder to think what might have happened had they not had a coach beside them at all.

The CXO Coach Toolkit

The cost savings and benefits of internal coaching are best achieved at a mid-management level, whereas the limitations of internal coaching are most strongly felt at the CXO level. External coaching at the CXO level should be the norm because external coaches:

- are perceived as more objective;
- are better positioned to maintain confidentiality;
- have a broader range of experience due to their work across different organizations;
- provide a 'cleaner' relationship, free from internal politics or pre-existing biases;
- allow for unbiased assessments and advice;
- can foster trust and promote a more rigorous execution of coaching processes;
- can introduce fresh insights and methodologies, beneficial for organizations looking to strengthen a coaching culture; and

---

[131] King, G., & Hermodson, A. (2000). Peer reporting of coworker wrongdoing: A qualitative analysis of observer attitudes in the decision to report versus not report unethical behavior. *Journal of Applied Communication Research, 28,* 309–329.

- help in navigating the hierarchical dynamics that might challenge internal coaches.

In the Company, Not of It.
The executive coach should not be on the client company's employee payroll. While a coach is subject to national laws and to the codes of conduct issued by their coaching certification boards and professional memberships, they shouldn't be bound to the company's employee handbook. Your job is to be an outsider, and it's your external view and concurrent organizational naiveté that's perhaps most valuable to your client.

The arms-length role of the external coach provides a safe space for your client to be more transparent and authentic with you. If you're a good coach, your CXO clients will likely tell you everything that they don't want their HR departments or fellow EXCO members to know. This is important because whatever you think about the ethical or organizational implications of the information they've shared with you, you've become a competent and valued safe space for external processing during the CXO decision-making process. Honor that.

Contracts in every form are designed to govern a lack of relationship. The only time you ever read one is if there's an unmet expectation, and you're trying to figure out whose expectation it was that was unmet. Personally, I don't present my clients with a coaching contract. This way, I keep the weight of responsibility to deliver a meaningful coaching outcome on my side of the table. However, some of my client companies have asked me to sign contracts to indicate my alignment with their code of conduct. In general, I have no issues with that.

Uncompromising Confidentiality
Your client should provide you, their EC, with an NDA governing the use of confidential information. You should assume that every single word shared with you in a coaching session is subject to this agreement, and the sharing of it is a breach of confidentiality, even within the organization, unless you obtain consent from your client to use it.

As an external executive coach, it's inevitable that from time to time you'll be privy to information from your CXOs that will be ethically challenging to navigate. Again, laws governing disclosure requirements for executive coaches vary by jurisdiction. What is clear from those mentioned above is that the legal protection provided is for whistleblowers, not tattletales. The reporting protection is jurisdictional, not corporate. Your loyalty is to your coachee and to your jurisdictional laws.

Over the last two decades of coaching I've been privy to a few cringy stories from my clients. Hostile takeovers, vicious internal politics, nepotistic and oligarchical hiring and firing decisions, a few chemical-fueled benders and illicit affairs here and there, but nothing that's kept me up at night wondering if I should report it to the authorities. My rule of thumb is that if I'm not willing to call a government regulator about it, then the secret stays with me.

I've also been very careful to keep my personal financial investments completely clear of my clients and their companies. Aside from the potential for insider trading mishaps, involving my personal finances might erode my objectivity.

The only exception I've made to this is in coaching for equity with entrepreneurs. Most entrepreneurs would benefit significantly from having a top-tier EC beside them as they build their companies, but very few entrepreneurs can afford top-tier coaching fees. I have a strong history of successful entrepreneurial experience to draw from, so on rare occasions, I've offered to coach for equity. In those cases, I am aligned not just to my coachee's success, but to that of their company as well.

Expert Data Security

I often joke that I carry billion-dollar secrets on my laptop, except when it's not a joke. It is a part of the executive coach's job to maintain exceptional data privacy and protection, especially concerning communications directly with your coachee, and any notes you take during your coaching sessions.

You should be aware of any data privacy laws that exist in your jurisdiction and adhere to them. These might include the General Data

Protection Regulation (GDPR) if you're in the EU,[132] or the California Online Privacy Protection Act (CalOPPA) if you're operating in the US.[133] Your coaching credentialing body may also have particular guidelines that you need to adhere to.

In general, you should:

1. Regularly review the personal information you hold, its source, and whom you share it with.
2. Delete unnecessary data.
3. Employ encryption for emails and text messages, and secure platforms for video conferencing.
4. Clearly outline your data collection, usage, and protection practices in your privacy policy.
5. Ensure that all of your team members and third-party service providers are aware of and comply with the data protection regulations you are subject to.

Bottom Line

If you're an internal coach, you shouldn't be coaching your executives. You likely won't get what you need from them to perform well, and they certainly won't get what they need from you, no matter how good a coach you are.

If you're an external executive coach, own your role as the outsider. Your strength lies in being free from internal politics, agendas, and reporting structures. CXOs need a safe space where they can be fully transparent, and that's often something only you can provide. Remember, your value isn't just in your coaching skills but in your ability to offer objectivity, confidentiality, and a fresh perspective that internal coaches simply can't match.

---

[132] European Union. (2016). General Data Protection Regulation (GDPR) (EU) 2016/679. *Official Journal of the European Union, L119*, 1–88.
[133] California Legislative Information. (2004). California Online Privacy Protection Act (CalOPPA). California Civil Code § 22575–22579.

You're not in the company, and that's exactly why your CXOs need you. Remember, they train 10% of the time and perform on the field the other 90%, but they're not playing for a gold medal or bragging rights. The decisions they're making influence the livelihoods of perhaps many thousands of families, many thousands of investors, and maybe millions of customers. They need to get it right, each and every time. They need your objectivity because the games they play have very high stakes. That's where we'll go next.

The Checklist
Formal Expertise:

- Certification in executive coaching with a focus on confidentiality and objectivity
- Knowledge of organizational ethical guidelines and regional legal requirements for coaching
- Training in organizational behavior and cultural dynamics
- Understanding of business strategy and operations

Informal Expertise:

- Ability to maintain strict confidentiality and impartiality
- Skill in providing unbiased feedback and fresh perspectives
- Experience in working with diverse industries and organizational cultures
- Strong interpersonal and communication skills
- Ability to build trust and rapport quickly
- Empathy and active listening skills

7.

HIGH-STAKES DECISIONS

"Never argue with stupid people, they will drag you down to their level and then beat you with experience."

– Mark Twain

The seventh challenge that CXOs face that C-1s don't often face is the powerful and potentially catastrophic consequences of the decisions they make. Without a relentless pursuit of excellence in decision-making, a CXO isn't just risking their company, they're gambling with the livelihoods of thousands of families, including their shareholders.

That's right … "the buck." It stops here.

What follows is a true story, though the details have been dramatized slightly for your entertainment.

A Gap in the Bridge

The atmosphere in the grand ballroom of the Detroit Marriott Hotel was electric on March 13, 2008. The final hand of the Pairs Bridge Tournament was being dealt, and the tension flooded to the corners of the room. Among the remaining pairs vying for the win were Jimmy Cayne and Alfredo Versace, a duo known for their unspoken synergy at the table.

The dealer shuffled and dealt the cards. Alfredo was in the North seat and had picked up a hand of blended possibilities and challenges. Jimmy, in the South seat, gave a nearly imperceptible nod, a signal that he too was prepared for whatever came next.

[I'm piqued. You?}

The opening bid came from the East, who confidently placed a 1 Spade bid on the table, indicating a solid 5 Spade hand. But Alfred had a solid hand as well and countered with a 1 No Trump. The bids continued around the table, each player carefully considering their moves. The final contract was set at 4 Hearts, with Jimmy as the declarer.

The lead came from the West, a low Spade, signaling a weak suit. Jimmy's strategy was meticulous; each play was calculated to maximize their odds. He drew trumps efficiently, maneuvering through the opponents' defenses with the precision of a chess grandmaster, but the margin for error was razor thin.

The critical moment arrived with Jimmy's play of the King of Diamonds.

[King of Diamonds? What was he thinking?!}

It was a bold move, designed to force a mistake from their opponents. East hesitated for a fraction of a second, then played a low Diamond, signaling weakness in their hand. Jimmy seized the opportunity, capturing the trick and securing their position. When the final card was played, they had made their contract with an overtrick, securing vital points.

The room erupted in applause. Although Jimmy and Alfredo had only placed fourth overall, their performance in the final hand was nothing short of masterful.[134] They showcased their skill and determination, earning the respect and admiration of their peers.

But there was one critical error, Jimmy was at the wrong table, and he was playing the wrong game, and his actual peers weren't even in the room.

At that very moment, the Board of Directors of the Wall Street investment bank Bear Sterns was on a conference call, discussing the impact of the subprime mortgage defaults. The Board's Chairman, Jimmy Cayne, was busy placing fourth in a Bridge tournament in Detroit. He was late to the critical call, missed significant details of the discussion, and three days later he sold Bear Sterns to JP Morgan Chase for just two dollars per share.

[Really Jimmy? Bridge?}

I considered including Board Directors in my definition of CXO in the introduction to this book, but to be fair, most Directors don't hold a lot of individual power. The Chairman, however, is another story. Although the impact of most CXO challenges discussed in the previous chapters don't often hinge on the behaviors of the Chairman of the Board, the challenge of high-risk decision-making often does.

Though Cayne was now the Chairman, he had been CEO of Bear Sterns from 1993 to 2007 and had grown its stock price from $16 to $173 during his tenure.[135] He was well known to play a lot of golf, and he enjoyed

---

134 North America Bridge Championships. (n.d.). Spring 2008 NABC results. Cdn.acbl.org.
135 Egan, M. (2018). The stunning downfall of Bear Stearns and its bridge-playing CEO. *CNN*.

spending time in his pajamas playing bridge online. When the bank went down, Jimmy was asleep at the wheel.

Bear Sterns Collapsing (Dramatized Courtesy of AI)

So, as a nod to James (Jimmy) Cayne, please include the Chairman of the Board of Directors in my definition of CXO for the remainder of this chapter.

Developing High-Capacity Leaders

Globally, organizations are falling short on developing internal leaders like Jimmy, especially those at the top. The Corporate Executive Board (CEB) found that while 66% of businesses fund initiatives designed to identify and develop high-potential individuals, just 24% of senior executives at those businesses view the initiatives as successful. And those expressing trust in the rising leaders at their companies fell from 17% to only 13% over the three years of the study. Furthermore, 30% of newly appointed CEOs at the biggest companies in the world – all of which employ thousands of executives – come from outside the company.[136]

In high-stakes business situations, individual leaders' strategic thinking and decision-making are the foundational skills that can determine the

---

[136] Larcker, D., & Tayan, B. (n.d.). *Internal versus external CEOs.* Stanford Graduate School of Business.

success or failure of entire companies. They're the skills that CXOs need to be developing continuously. And using these toolkits involves more than just reacting to immediate challenges; it requires CXOs to adopt a forward-looking approach to long-term planning, market positioning, and competitive differentiation. These are the skills needed to develop a clear roadmap to guide the company toward future success, even amidst uncertainty and disruption as dramatic as the 2008 Global Financial Crisis.

And not having ongoing development of these critical skills in your CXOs is akin to saying that an Olympic athlete doesn't require coaching anymore once they've reached the Olympics.

[It's utterly stupid.}

Decision Coaching

Effective decision-making is a cornerstone of CXO leadership. Research by Longenecker and McCartney (2020) indicates that executive coaching significantly enhances decision-making skills among senior leaders. They found that, by offering candid feedback and objective insights, coaching provides a platform for executives to expand their thinking and improve decision-making.[137]

CXOs like Jimmy Cayne are often confronted with complex and multifaceted decisions that can have far-reaching implications for the company's bottom line. Coaching plays a crucial role in supporting executives to make better decisions, just as an Olympic coach supports their athlete in ongoing training.

Decision-making coaching, as a specialized modality of coaching, focuses on enhancing the decision-making skills and abilities of individuals. This form of coaching provides a valuable toolkit for the Olympic-caliber coach to develop in their coachee the skills, mindset, and strategies necessary to make informed choices.

---

[137] Longenecker, C., & McCartney, M. (2020). The benefits of executive coaching: Voices from the C-suite. *Strategic HR Review, 19*(1), 22–27.

In my practice, this process begins with clarifying the values and goals of the individual. This lays the groundwork for aligning decision-making with personal principles and fostering authenticity and integrity in executive leadership. By understanding a client's core values and what matters most to them, a good EC can help them navigate complex choices with confidence and clarity – because they are guided by the CXO's own sense of purpose and direction.

Clear values provide a solid foundation for decision-making; they are like True North in times of uncertainty and ambiguity. When faced with difficult choices or conflicting priorities, clients can refer to their core values to navigate complexities as they would to a compass. This anchoring effect provides a sense of stability and confidence, enabling them to make decisions with conviction and resolve. But once the values of the individual are clarified, then the context of the decision needs to be brought into focus as well.

So, in decision coaching I start with values first, then apply a decision-making framework.

Bloom's Taxonomy of Learning

I view decision-making through the lens of learning. The highest quality decisions are those made with the highest quality information. This requires a default learning posture. In the 1950s, educator Benjamin Bloom outlined six different levels of cognitive learning,[138] which were revised to this now well-known six-step process.[139]

1. **Remembering**: Recalling facts or information.
2. **Understanding**: Deriving and interpreting meaning from that information.
3. **Applying**: Practical use of knowledge in a situational context.
4. **Analyzing**: Breaking down information to understand its components.

---

[138] Bloom, B.S., & Krathwohl, D. R. (1984). *Taxonomy of educational objectives*. Addison Wesley.
[139] Ruhl, C. (2024, February 1). *Bloom's taxonomy of learning*. Simply Psychology.

5. **Evaluating**: Assessing evidence and making judgments.
6. **Creating**: Generating new ideas or original work.

These levels represent a progression from basic understanding to higher-order learning, providing a structured approach to cognitive processing. I like this progression because when applied to executive coaching, through the filter of the CXO's core values, Bloom's framework offers a systematic method for clarifying business goals and objectives, guiding leaders through deep reflection, analysis, and synthesis.

Using Bloom's framework, I'd like to take a creative shot at *posthumous* executive coaching for Jimmy Cayne, during the 3-month period from January to March 2008. I know, I know, hindsight is 20/20 … but Cayne admitted he had no idea what to do (and I take serious issue with his claim):

> The options were limited. When you become roadkill, when you happen to have lost some weight and you're not really healthy, but you know one thing – you know that you have worked your ass off and you're not smart enough to know the answer – that's tough.[140]

So, first things first. Here's what I do with the limiting beliefs of all of my clients: I call bullshit.

I get that he was a bit winded by being replaced recently as CEO, but Cayne was definitely smart enough, experienced enough, present enough, and networked enough to figure this problem out. And any decent EC with enough trust and transparency in their relationship with him should have been able to pull him out of his defeatism and into a more proactive stance.

To illustrate how important and how simple a principle this is, I'll use Bloom's very basic taxonomy, and Cayne's equally basic behavior.

---

[140] Cayne, J. (n.d.) Jimmy Cayne: In his own words. *Money.cnn.com*. Retrieved July 16, 2024, from https://money.cnn.com/galleries/2008/fortune/0808/gallery.cayne_bearstearns.fortune/index.html

Remembering

Bloom's first level is Remembering. There's a base level of information required to run a company; it includes the organization's mission, vision, and strategic priorities, as well as the CXO's own personal values and aspirations. Through targeted questioning and exploration, executive coaches help leaders remember their values and goals, ensuring alignment with the organization's objectives and strategic direction.

Jimmy failed level 1.

The reason he was Chairman of the Board in March was because he was forced out as CEO in January due to the record $1.9bn write-down he took, resulting in the reporting of an $854m loss in Q4-2007. He was blindsided and humiliated at losing about 7% of the bank's value.

[Side note: remember when Indira Nooyi lost 8% of PepsiCo's value in a single year? How did she respond? What were her leadership behaviors? Empathy, connection, collaboration, market expansion, innovation … now notice the difference in what happens with Jimmy.}

The Board told him to shift seats and let Alan Schwartz take over as CEO. Cayne himself said,

> That was a period of not seeing the light at the end of the tunnel. It was not knowing what to do. It's not being able to make a definitive decision one way or the other because I just couldn't tell you what was going to happen.[141]

[Darkness, retreat, indecisiveness, overwhelm. This is exactly when a solid coach comes in handy, BTW.}

At this point, there was no one more knowledgeable about the bank than Cayne, and in his new role as Chairman he was removed from daily operations and had the opportunity to dedicate his time and efforts to improving his sources of information. How could he better remember his 14-year tenure as CEO to help Schwartz steer through this storm?

---

[141] Ibid.

That would have been Cayne's coach's guiding question here, but I couldn't find any record of Cayne having an executive coach.

[Again, utterly stupid. Why would you show up to the Olympics without a coach?}

Understanding

Understanding is Bloom's second level. This is where business leaders are challenged to apply their knowledge in real-world scenarios. Coaches support leaders in understanding their contexts by helping them to identify potential obstacles and risks (as well as opportunities for innovation and growth) and fostering a proactive and strategic mindset.

The sub-prime mortgage crisis was already known: understanding how Bear Sterns got caught in it was now the challenge. Not only was Jimmy the best equipped to have produced an actionable strategy for saving the bank but he now had the discretionary time required to work on it after leaving the CEO's office. Any EC I know would have asked Jimmy, "What do you think contributed to your removal as CEO?"

In a transparent moment, Cayne might have indicated his hand's-off management style and growing complacency, as these were deviations from his normative values. For example, when Long Term Capital's hedge fund collapsed in 1998, Bear Sterns was the only major player untouched, as Jimmy didn't like complex or weird investments. This was the reason he had avoided the dot com bubble and its wave of bankruptcies at around that time as well.[142]

By the early 2000s, though, Cayne had given into his own Midas-touch mythology. He relaxed his oversight and cruised on the momentum of his past successes. That led to the failure of two of his hedge funds' investments in sub-prime mortgage-backed securities, undoubtedly the kind of weird investment that he'd have noticed in the 1990's. Now we understand: Cayne had abandoned his values.

---

[142] Gasparino, C. (2022, January 2). Lessons of Jimmy Cayne's Bear Stearns historic rise and fall. *New York Post.*

And with that understanding we step to the next rung on Bloom's ladder of learning.

Applying

If Jimmy remembered his past and understood his present, then what could he do to apply that knowledge to the bank's current context? It's at this point that an EC would likely be asking Jimmy, "Now that we understand the bank is in this position likely because you abandoned the leadership values that made you successful, what can you do from your new role as Chairman to help your successor avoid the same pitfalls you faced?"

Here, a quick action plan pops into view for Cayne. If being "hand's off" wasn't working so well, maybe he should have been more involved as Chairman than he'd been in his last few years as CEO. And if weird investments hadn't worked out, then maybe he should have helped Schwartz to quickly move the value of the bank into something more established, more stable.

The opportunity to do so came from repeated approaches from JP Morgan's CEO Jamie Dimon to bail Bearn Sterns out. Applied understanding, in this case, would have helped Jimmy see Dimon's offers as an opportunity to realign the bank to Jimmy's previously successful conservative values, but Jimmy refused Jamie's offers.

Jimmy's historical risk-aversion value might have saved Bear Sterns if tapped into early enough. Even as early as April 2007 when his two hedge funds were suffering, quick and decisive shifts to diversify the holdings, strengthen liquidity, and improve regulatory transparency would have significantly mitigated the impact. That is, aligning the bank's strategies with Jimmy's personal values would certainly have helped, even prior to Dimon's offers.

It didn't have to get as bad as it did. Cayne didn't remember his values, and he failed to apply what he might have understood if he'd followed this simple decision framework.

Analyzing

At Bloom's fourth level, leaders are encouraged to critically evaluate their business goals and objectives, examining the underlying assumptions, dependencies, and implications. This involves breaking down complex problems into manageable components, conducting thorough analyses, and identifying patterns and trends. Coaches facilitate this process by asking probing questions, challenging assumptions, and encouraging leaders to consider multiple perspectives.

Jimmy had a full month to do this in February 2008. Armed only with his own core values and an average EC applying Bloom's 50-year-old framework, this question might have been posed: "What were the underlying causes of your success in the past, and what is the full range of possibilities that exist for Bear Sterns given the range of resources available to you now?"

This analytical question would likely have led to the identification of the following decision-making principles that Jimmy used in the pre-crisis period: avoiding big risks, consistent performance, teamwork, loyalty, and cautious expansion.[143]

Cayne's leadership style at Bear Stearns was characterized by core values emphasizing stability, long-term relationships, and a conservative financial strategy. These principles helped Bear Stearns maintain consistent profitability and fostered a loyal and cohesive workforce.

This basic coaching analysis might have been his biggest asset in February 2008. But he didn't see it. He was busy running away from the problem. In times of crisis, Jimmy's leadership behavior wasn't empowerment, it was escapism. In fact, in July 2007, the month when his two major hedge funds finally collapsed, he spent 10 out of 21 workdays playing golf.[144]

Yes, you read that correctly. Golf.

---

[143] Wells, D. (2005, July 18). We're not betting the ranch: Bear Stearns eyes a more vigorous role in Europe – as well as the bottom line leadership. *Financial Times*. 5

[144] Kelly, K. (2007, November 1). Bear CEO's handling of crisis raises issues. *Wall Street Journal*.

Then, in February 2008, he failed to apply his extra time to evaluate the problem, the strengths he brought to the table, or how he might utilize those old strengths to address this new challenge. No applied understanding. No analysis of potential solutions.

Evaluating

The next level in Bloom's taxonomy involves integrating disparate pieces of information and ideas to create a cohesive and comprehensive understanding. Analyses are then synthesized into coherent strategies and action plans. Coaches play a crucial role in fostering innovation and creativity during this step, encouraging leaders to think outside the box, explore unconventional solutions, and evaluate them.

Cayne's coach might have asked him, "With a clear view of what you valued in the past that made you successful, what steps can you take now as Chairman to realign the bank with what you remember to be the foundational principles of your previous successes as CEO? Let's evaluate the potential impact of every reasonable possibility."

Focusing on stability, long-term relationships, and a conservative financial strategy would have been helpful. Perhaps he would have

1. Seen Jamie Dimon's early offers to bail out Bear Sterns as an opportunity instead of a threat.
2. Considered greater transparency with the US Security and Exchange Commission (SEC) to seek solutions much earlier.
3. Not let his earlier tensions with new CEO Alan Schwartz stand in the way of their working together more collaboratively on a solution for the bank.

Each of those options would have undoubtedly mitigated the impact of the Q1 crisis on Bear Sterns, but they all carried one significant price to pay: in order to align with his values, Jimmy would have to ask for help, and humility was not a quality of Jimmy's character. In fact, a 2024 study of CEO humility and narcissism lists Jimmy as a paragon of the "Destructive Narcissist" style of CEO leadership.[145]

---

[145] Spangler, W. (2024) CEO Humility, Narcissism & Competitive Advantage. *Cutter Consortium.* https://www.cutter.com/article/ceo-humility-narcissism-competitive-advantage.

Here's the evaluation then: Jimmy couldn't realign the bank to his formerly conservative values, because his character was in the way.

It's a tragedy. Still, I can't help but think that the combined talents of Alan, Jimmy, Jamie, a good executive coach, and a whiteboard during February 2008 might have made a significant difference in the outcome for Bear Sterns, its shareholders, investors, the more than 10,000 families who lost their livelihoods, and the tens of thousands of American workers whose pension and retirement funds were exposed to the bank's collapse.

Creating

Finally, business leaders are tasked in Bloom's framework with assessing the effectiveness of their strategies and decisions, measuring progress against predefined objectives and benchmarks. This involves collecting and analyzing data, soliciting feedback from stakeholders, and making adjustments as needed. Coaches support leaders in developing a culture of continuous improvement; the idea is to learn from successes and failures alike to drive iterative and creative innovation.

It was time to invite people from outside the bank into the boardroom. If Jimmy Cayne had created a new possibility for himself, and reached out to Alan Schwartz, Jamie Dimon, and the SEC, perhaps the outcome would have been dramatically different.

Rather, it was Schwartz, not Cayne, who returned Dimon's call and asked for a $30bn lifeline. But it was too late; this time Dimon refused unless the deal was federally backed. It was Schwartz, not Cayne, who reached out to then President of the Federal Reserve Bank of New York, Tim Geithner. And although the infamous midnight "fire sale" of Bear Sterns dissolved the bank and its toxic assets onto the balance sheet of JP Morgan, it was Schwartz, Dimon, and Geithner who engineered the innovation that avoided total bankruptcy.[146]

Where was Jimmy Cayne?

While the two-dollar deal was being finalized, he was having breakfast with Board Member Vincent Tese at Jackson Hole diner, at 91st and

---

[146] Financial Crisis Inquiry Commission. (2011). The financial crisis inquiry report: Final report of the National Commission on the causes of the financial and economic crisis in the United States. US Government Printing Office.

Madison Avenue, discussing bankruptcy implications. Perhaps he spent the remainder of the day playing cards with his friends. About approving the fire sale, Cayne said, "I felt nothing. You got a bad grade on your test. That's it. No appeal. I felt sad for me and sad for my Bear Stearns family."[147]

[Exactly the response you'd expect from a destructive narcissist, BTW. Textbook. Also, the PBJ Burger at Jackson Hole is life-altering, if you like craft burgers as much as I do.}

I wish for the sake of his legacy that Cayne had done things differently, though I'm glad there's a record of his eventual acknowledgment of his role in this tragedy. "I take responsibility for what happened," he said, "I'm not going to walk away from that responsibility."[148]

It's easy to play armchair quarterback with twenty years of hindsight data to draw from and a deceased subject unable to defend himself. Perhaps in that regard, this exercise seems incredibly unfair. I just can't help but think that, with a slightly above average EC in his private office and a simple coaching tool like Bloom's levels of learning, Cayne might have seen the situation for what it was: that the riskiest decision this self-styled risk-averse investment fund manager made was to show up consistently for his golfing tee-time.

[That's what happens when you go to the Olympics with a massive ego and no coach. I'm not surprised Jimmy choked under pressure. You shouldn't be either.}

Risky Avoidance

We discussed in Chapter 2 how the pressure to produce consistently positive outcomes in an ever-changing corporate environment is one of the most challenging pressures CXOs deal with. They are required to be ahead of the curve, predict market trends, and spot fresh growth prospects in their role as leaders.

---

[147] Cayne, J. (n.d.) Jimmy Cayne: In his own words (n.d.). *Money.cnn.com.*
[148] Egan, M. (2018). The stunning downfall of Bear Stearns and its bridge-playing CEO. *CNN.*

On the other hand, the speed of change is accelerating, and the threat of burnout can lead to escapism, as it had for Jimmy. Executives may experience feelings of being overwhelmed by the sheer number of decisions that need to be made each day, and their rising complexity. They often struggle to maintain a healthy work-life balance and can feel overburdened by their obligations.

Moreover, as reviewed in Chapter 5, C-suite leaders may feel stagnant due to the isolating nature of their roles. Alternatively, they may find themselves surrounded by like-minded people who have comparable experiences, backgrounds, and viewpoints to their own. This kind of unity can feel consoling, but it can also result in groupthink and a lack of diversity in input-seeking behavior. So the natural context is often either individual isolation, or collective myopia. Neither are helpful conditions for complex decision-making.

As discussed in Chapter 7, if CXOs aren't exposed to sufficiently different points of view and varied perspectives, they could get stuck in a loop of biased thinking that prevents them from questioning their norms or exploring novel directions for decision-making. The very presence of a qualified EC is a mitigating influence on all of these effects, and avoiding that critical coaching relationship is one of the highest and most easily mitigable risks an executive can take.

Cognitive Bias Risk

In behavioral economics and psychology, cognitive biases are systematic patterns of deviation from rationality in judgment and decision-making.[149] They stem from mental shortcuts, emotional influences, and ingrained beliefs, leading CXOs to make decisions that may not be based on objective analysis or logic.

For sure, a lot of executives develop biases and heuristics that lead them to make great decisions very quickly, but there's no overt expiry date on them, and the more they're used, the less conscious the executive will be that they are being used. Plus, the more the world around them

---

[149] Blanco, F. (2017). Cognitive Bias. *Encyclopedia of Animal Cognition and Behavior*, 1–7.

changes, the less relevant these mental shortcuts will become. Both effects happen naturally over time, accelerating the **bias expiry risk**.

Cognitive biases pose a risk in decision-making because they are internal functions in the CXO's mind. They likely won't even be noticed by the CXO, but they should be by their executive coach. This might have happened in the example above had Jimmy Cayne been appropriately coached.

Cognitive biases can be expressed organizationally as well, meaning the entire EXCO might be blind to them all at once, rather than just one CXO. To illustrate, let's briefly review Nokia's epic fall from the perspective of some of the most common of these cognitive biases.

In the early 1990's Nokia capitalized on innovative technologies during the digitalization and deregulation of European telecom networks, pivoting from manufacturing tires to mobile phones. However, by the mid-90s, the company faced a supply chain crisis that threatened its stability. Nokia responded by implementing stronger systems and processes that enabled rapid scaling of production and sales. Between 1996 and 2000, Nokia grew its headcount by 150% and increased its revenue by more than 500%.

But this rapid expansion came at a cost.

Two cognitive biases crept into the decision-making culture: **short-termism** and **recency bias**. As Nokia focused on rapid cycle performance metrics, it lost its innovative edge. Immediate results based on previous benchmarks were rewarded over long-term strategic planning. Managers faced mounting pressure to deliver quick wins, leaving little time or resources for R&D or long-term strategic thinking. Despite outward success, CEO Jorma Ollila grew increasingly concerned about losing Nokia's previous agility and entrepreneurial spirit. In an attempt to reignite drive and innovation, the company was significantly restructured between 2001 and 2005.

This didn't go as planned. To begin with, the restructuring plan wasn't critically evaluated, possibly attributable to a **groupthink bias**. Important leadership roles were shifted, resulting in the resignations of key executives and a decline in strategic talent. And as existing successful processes were overhauled without sufficient reason, an **action bias** likely contributed to poor execution as well.

A part of the restructuring involved shifting the entire organization into a matrix structure. But Nokia's leadership culture had been founded on decentralized decision-making, and the new organizational model proved too rigid and cumbersome. Senior managers and executives weren't adequately trained to navigate the unfamiliar complexities of a matrix organization, and different stakeholder groups wrestled over conflicting priorities, resulting in infighting and strategic stagnation.

Even by 2010 Nokia had somehow completely missed the emerging app ecosystem pioneered by Apple, continuing to rely blindly on its existing business model. This is textbook **confirmation bias**. Despite herculean attempts at realignment, Nokia continued to lose on the field of competition.

Nokia doubled down on its past successes with feature phones and failed to pivot to smartphones (**anchoring bias**). With shrinking market share and growing competitive pressures, Nokia could no longer defend its territory in mobile phones. It fell upon new CEO Stephen Elop (2010) and Chairman Risto Siilasmaa (2012) to navigate the company through this crisis.

Who was coaching these Olympic-level executives during their most high-stakes competition? I couldn't find any mention of anyone, just as it was with Jimmy Cayne.

[Olympic athletes without Olympic coaches tend to underperform in competition. Why do so many people still think it should be different in business?}

I found seven collective cognitive biases after a relatively simple analysis of the stories surrounding the decline of Nokia. I don't have the necessary space in this book to cover the full field of cognitive biases that influence executive decision-making, but Nokia's case highlights the impact of a few of the most common ones, even on collective strategic decisions. It also highlights how easy they are to recognize by a trained external executive coach. Recognizing and mitigating these biases is one of the influences that should be expected from a good EC.

[BTW, I recently met with a former Nokia executive who was present in the company throughout this whole story. He says I "nailed the analysis" here, even as an outside observer having directly interviewed exactly zero of the players involved. Haha. Thanks, Paul!}

It continues to shock me how many executives think they can play world-class economic games at their best without coaching. Just as Olympic coaches do for athletes, executive coaches provide a steady sounding board in times of uncertainty or crisis, offering reassurance and support to CXOs facing tough decisions that they may not be comfortable discussing with invested stakeholders. We also see blind spots, cognitive biases, limiting beliefs, aging heuristics, and other psychological performance improvement opportunities because that's what we are trained to do.

That's our job. That's good coaching.

The CXO Coach Toolkit

Risk is reduced and performance improves when the coach is properly qualified and equipped to recommend experiential and science-based tactics. Ultimately, the CXO will need to choose for themselves what will work in their game, but handing a CXO to an underqualified coach is an easily avoidable risk. By investing in qualified coaching, organizations can mitigate risk, enhance performance, and foster a culture of leadership excellence.

Decision-Making Frameworks

Decision-making frameworks, like Bloom's taxonomy, are essential tools for navigating complex and dynamic environments. Most executives will already be familiar with the classic SWOT Analysis, PESTEL Analysis, the BCG Matrix and Porter's Five Forces. You should be too. You don't have to be an expert in all of them, but you can't be ignorant of any of them either.[150] You should have at least two of them in your toolkit.

I also like the Ethical Decision-Making Framework because of its emphasis on aligning decisions with ethical standards and organizational values.[151] This framework works to ensure integrity to build trust and credibility with stakeholders. It promotes sustainable and responsible decision-making, focusing on long-term impacts. It also aligns with my *posthumous* coaching for Jimmy above.

Cynefin

From a Welsh word meaning a sense of familiarity or belonging, Cynefin is a great framework for helping leaders to understand the kinds of decisions they are making, and the kinds of inputs required and outputs expected.[152] Humans (including CXOs) like the world to make sense, so they naturally look for categories to put things into and cause-effect relationships to follow.

This is how we typically make sense of the world, through categorization. But what happens when the environment is so chaotic that the data doesn't seem to make sense, or fit into any of our categories? The 9-11 attack on NYC, the 2008 Global Financial Crisis, and the COVID-19 pandemic are all good examples of this.

Data was pouring in as these crises evolved, but most of the existing categories for how to deal with it were useless, so leaders in all kinds of organizations struggled to make sense of the emergent information and apply it to their particular contexts. This is where having a sense-making framework like Cynefin really helps. It provides structure for unstructured learning in complex and chaotic contexts that aren't easily

---

[150] Gurel, E. (2017). SWOT analysis: *A theoretical review. Journal of International Social Research,* *10*(51), 994–1006; Yüksel, I. (2012). Developing a multi-criteria decision making model for PESTEL analysis. *International Journal of Business and Management,* *7*(24), 52–66; Haspeslagh, P. C. (1982). Portfolio planning: Uses and limits. *Harvard Business Review,* *60*(1), 58–73; Porter, M. E. (1979). How competitive forces shape strategy. *Harvard Business Review,* *57*(2), 137–145.
[151] Pliner, E. (2022). *The ethical leader: Why doing the right thing can be the key to competitive advantage.* Wiley.
[152] The Cynefin Company. (2024). About – Cynefin Framework; Snowden, D. J. & Boone, M. E. (2007). A Leader's Framework for Decision Making. *Harvard Business Review.*

categorized. Jimmy would have benefited from having a coach who knew this tool.

I know this tool, but I thought it best to challenge Jimmy with something much more basic to highlight how easy it is for a good coach to make a significant impact with a simple tool.

Goldsmith's 6 Questions

Marshall Goldsmith's Six Question Process is another easy and effective tool for coaches to help executives process decision-making.[153] These are the questions he uses:

1. **Where are we going?** (in terms of organizational objectives and direction)
2. **Where are you going?** (this can relate to team or departmental objectives, as well as individual personal/professional goals)
3. **What do you think you are doing very well?** (current perceived strengths in context)
4. **If you were coaching yourself, what advice would you give yourself?** (clever reframing of the commonly asked question: "What do you think you can do better?")
5. **As your coach, how can I help?** (this aims to glean the resources needed from a coaching standpoint)
6. **How can I be a better enabler?** (this focuses on active leadership enablement by the coach, and invites critical feedback on the coaching process itself)

I like Goldsmith's approach because it's a toolkit that can help to decouple the executive from their biases and view their context from several different perspectives. The questions are non-confrontational, positively framed, and curiosity-driven, and they result in actionable outputs.

If you replaced my use of Bloom's Taxonomy in the case study of James Cayne above with these six questions, you'd likely come to a very similar outcome. I used Bloom to make a point about how a 50-year-old tool in

---

[153] Goldsmith, M. (2022, June 29). 6 questions for better coaching. Marshall Goldsmith.

the hands of any decent coach can be useful. But in practice I prefer Goldsmith's model for two reasons.

One advantage that Goldsmith's model has over Bloom's is that the coach is framed as an enabler, rather than just a catalyst. This invites action from the coach based on insights from the executive and honors the advisory and participatory role that coaches play at the executive level. Olympic coaches don't just train their athletes; they're right there, enabling them during competition.

[Remember the photo of Simone Biles and her coach in Chapter 5?}

The other advantage of Goldsmith's model is that it easily reveals and speaks to mindset reframing. Reaching back to the challenges of Peak Performance we discussed in Chapter 2; I can't help but wonder if Marissa Mayer would have changed her gameplay significantly had she been privately asked Marshall's Six Questions by a competent executive coach.

I suspect that the answers to Questions 1 and 2 alone would have highlighted the discrepancy between where Yahoo! was really going, and where Mayer was equipped to lead them. Perhaps the answer to Question 3 would have been shorter than she would have liked, and she might have been open to some tactical advice. And perhaps that tactical advice might have come from a Pygmalion-Olympic level EC whose positive expectations of her would have been independent of those of her team, the media, the shareholders, and her Board of Directors.

After all, it worked for Sindhu, the badminton player. Remember? No new game, and no new skills. Just a different mindset from a single coaching voice.

Maybe it would have worked for Jimmy too. This is a great tool.

Cognitive Bias Knowledge

You should also have a competent understanding of the formation and function of cognitive biases and heuristics that may present as blind spots or limiting beliefs in the CXO. You don't need to take formal training in this specifically, but you do need to do your homework. I recommend the following resources:

1. There's a great introduction to cognitive biases at https://positivepsychology.com/cognitive-biases/.[154] Read through the article, and then download, print out, and hang the codex on your wall somewhere. There are 180 cognitive biases in the codex.

2. *Cognitive Behavioral Executive Coaching* by Good, Yeganeh, and Yeganeh discusses the application of Cognitive Behavioral Therapy (CBT) in executive coaching. It's a bit more academic, but it's specifically tailored to meet the complex needs of executives. It also provides insights into cognitive biases and how structured coaching can help mitigate them.[155]

With solid understanding of cognitive biases, decision-making inputs, and strategic frameworks, executive coaches can help their clients see around corners, anticipate change, and leverage alignment between their personal and corporate values to confidently and competently navigate even the most disruptive market shifts.

Vision, Mission, Values

Simon Sinek calls it the Why statement.[156] Whether you call it Purpose, Objective, BHAG, or whatever, it's all semantics. I think it's critical for every leader to have their own vision, mission, and values clearly defined. What's important is that your CXO has a clear understanding of what they want to accomplish in their life, personally (vision); that they understand the kinds of decisions they want to make as they strive to achieve it (values); and that they know their personal best practices for success (mission).

I outline a framework for this in *Business is Personal*,[157] which focuses on integrating personal values and ethics into business practices to achieve

---

[154] Nortje, A. (2020) Cognitive biases and heuristics: How they influence our decisions. *Positive Psychology*.

[155] Good, D., Yeganeh, B., & Yeganeh, R. (2013). Cognitive behavioral executive coaching. In S. J. Armstrong & C. V. Fukami (Eds.), *Handbook of managerial learning, education and development*. Sage.

[156] Sinek, S. (2011). *Start with why: How great leaders inspire everyone to take action*. Penguin.

[157] Block, C. (2021). *Business is personal: A blueprint for unlocking meaning at work*. Passionpreneur.

sustainable success. I emphasize the importance of finding meaning at work and aligning personal and corporate vision, mission, values, and goals. The main ideas are:

1. **Personal and Professional Integration**: We all know work-life balance is a myth, so I advocate for blending personal and professional lives to create a more meaningful work experience. You'll see.

2. **Leadership and Employee Engagement**: Everyone is a little selfish, so I provide practical strategies for leaders to engage employees by aligning their personal values with the company's mission.

3. **Mental Wellness and Resilience**: I discuss techniques for maintaining mental wellness and resilience in high-stakes business environments.

4. **Holistic Success**: I encourage setting valuable personal goals that drive professional performance as well as overall individual fulfillment.

[BTW, I began my executive coaching career as a strategy consultant, so I've got a lot more toolkits here than most coaches I know … but for the record, coaching is WAY more fun!}

Bottom Line

Mitigating executive decision risk is an automatic justification for investing in executive coaching. CXOs live and breathe in the world of high-risk decision-making. The story of Jimmy Cayne, the man who played Bridge while his company imploded, serves as a big flashing warning sign. When you're coaching a CXO, there's no room for distractions or complacency – because the decisions they make can either build empires or burn them down. They faced the pressure in Chapter 2, but you'll face it here.

Yes, all CXOs will do better with an executive coach, but you have to take the need for your coaching –and its quality – as seriously as they do the game they're in. The best-case scenario is that they trust you enough to process these high-stakes decisions with you. The worst-case scenario is that you have no clue how to help them if they do.

From clarifying values to applying frameworks like Bloom's Taxonomy, your job is to help these leaders stay sharp, stay strategic, and most importantly, stay in the game. It's about guiding them to see beyond the immediate chaos and focus on what really matters: their core principles, their big-picture goals, and the decisions that align with both.

There are a lot of mind games that come with the territory. Cognitive biases, burnout, groupthink … those sneaky saboteurs that can derail even the best leaders, and sometimes entire leadership cultures. Your mission? Make sure your clients aren't just reacting but thinking strategically. And make sure that they're challenging their assumptions rather than falling into comfortable, dangerous patterns.

Your CXO clients are Olympic-level athletes in the business world, and they need you in their corner, keeping them on their toes. If they're not continuously refining their decision-making skills, they're playing with fire. And you? You're the one who makes sure they don't get burned — or burnt out.

It's your job to call out the distractions, remind them of their values, and push them to make decisions that are both bold and smart. Coasting in the C-suite is a fast track to disaster. Jimmy Cayne's Bridge game should be the cautionary tale you keep in your back pocket. The next time your client's thinking of letting up, remind them: the stakes are too high to sit this one out. You're there to keep them in the game and on top of it.

Or as my friend Marshall Goldsmith would sing, "There's *no* business like *show* business! There's *no* business I *knoooooow*!"

Get up. Get going. Game on.

The Checklist
Formal Expertise:

- Training in decision-making frameworks (e.g., Bloom's Taxonomy, Cynefin)
- Knowledge of cognitive biases and risk management
- Certification in strategic planning and crisis management
- Understanding of business strategy and operations

Informal Expertise:

- Ability to guide executives through complex decision-making processes
- Skill in aligning decisions with core values and long-term goals
- Experience in high-stakes environments and crisis management
- Strong problem-solving and analytical skills
- Ability to provide strategic advice and support
- Knowledge of leadership and team dynamics

8.

WIZARD EXPERTISE

"A good coach can change a game. A great coach can change a life."
— John Wooden, 10x NCAA Championship winning coach, a.k.a. "the Wizard of Westwood"

I n previous chapters, we've discussed challenges faced by CXOs that are unique to executive roles, or at least exponentially exaggerated in the C-suite. I trust by now I've made my case strongly enough that you'll agree with me that a CXO isn't just another manager, in the same way that an Olympic competitor isn't just another athlete. It's on this foundation that this chapter is built.

Olympians are a particular kind of athlete, requiring a certain kind of coach.

Executives are a particular kind of manager, requiring a certain kind of coach.

In the introduction to this book, I presented my definition of executive coaching:

> *Executive coaching is a co-creative process in which a coach and an executive elicit insights and actions from each other to optimize the mindset and skillset required for the executive to perform at their personal best in their executive role.*

An executive coach therefore must be:

> *A professional coach who has the mindset and skillset required to elicit insights and actions from an executive that influences the executive to perform at their personal best in their executive role.*

What then qualifies a coach in this definition? What are the mindset and skillset requirements?

The challenge of defining these in executive coaching is one that stems from the foreign language problem. We know that subject matter experts were the best sources of information and mentorship for our coachees back in the days of their specialized careers. But now, as CXOs, it's generalists they most need beside them.

It is a broad range of mindset and skillset tools that will serve the CXO best, so that's what's required of their executive coach. In this chapter I'll move the spotlight onto the range requirements of an EC, and we'll see that they constitute one of the CXOs most important resources. But make no mistake, I'm writing this particular chapter not just for the coaches out there but for the CXOs.

CXOs need to have a clear understanding of the different kinds of coaching available; they need to be able to identify the difference between a mere wayfinder and a wizard in their executive coach.

[I'm not completely thrilled with the term "wizard" as an EC qualification, but I needed something stronger than guru or guide. I took it from John Wooden's nickname, the Wizard of Westwood, meant to honor his exceptional coaching talent and the seemingly magical results he was able to elicit from his teams throughout his coaching career.}

The Whole World Is a Nail

In the last eight weeks, I've been approached by more than a dozen major coaching organizations that want to qualify me as one of their coaches. Each of them has their own psychometric tests and interpretive reports to learn. Each has a matrix, a methodology, and a number of steps that they're very certain I should be using with my coaching clients in order to achieve better results.

Many of the major coaching organizations, at least the ones I'm aware of, have their own coaching methodology. For example:

1. The Center for Creative Leadership has a set menu of programs you can choose from.[158]
2. Marshall Goldsmith has his Stakeholder Centered Coaching.[159]
3. The Leadership Circle has its own in-house developed Leadership Circle assessments and tools.[160]
4. InsideOut Development has its GROW Model.[161]
5. Hudson Institute of Coaching has its Self-as-Coach model.[162]

You get the point.

Here's my concern: if you only have a hammer in your toolkit, every problem looks like a nail.

I take no issue with coaches or their credentialing organizations producing their own coaching methodologies. I've done so too. My concern is with their inevitable presentation of their particular methodology as the only one they use, or worse, the only one required

[158] Center for Creative Leadership. (n.d.). Our Approach. Center for Creative Leadership.
[159] Goldsmith, M. (2024). Marshall Goldsmith stakeholder centered coaching. Our methodology. Stakeholder Centered Coaching.
[160] The Leadership Circle. (n.d.). The Leadership Circle.
[161] InsideOut Development. (n.d.). GROW Coaching. InsideOut Development.
[162] Hudson Institute of Coaching. (2024). Our Approach. Hudson Institute of Coaching.

for qualifying someone as an executive coach ... or much *much* worse: the only one that should ever be used by all coaches. This echoes the non-advisory coaching problem I raised earlier, but we're going to go into much more depth here.

[Buckle up.}

The competent EC should not walk into their client's office with a roadmap, but with a ring of keys to a warehouse of potential toolkits to employ. A roadmap approach is, by definition, narrow. The warehouse approach is the opposite; in fact, the warehouse that your CXO actually needs should be very, very big.

There's a broad spectrum when it comes to coaching modalities, some of which I briefly surveyed in Chapter 1. From Non-Advisory to Strategic Coaching, and Cognitive Behavioral Coaching to Positive Psychology Coaching, the list is extensive. But let's be real, if you ask a CXO managing thousands of employees vague questions like, "What haven't you tried yet?" you're probably setting yourself up to get kicked out of their corner office.

What high-powered professionals need isn't a comforting rhetorical chat but actionable strategies. And they don't just need one strategy; they need access to as many of them as possible. They're looking for Olympic level tactical input, so not just any coaching question will do – and no single methodology will suffice for all CXOs.

The #1 Executive Coach in [Wherever}

I had just shared a keynote at the SHRM conference in Dubai in the fall of 2022. It was a real honor to have the opportunity to address hundreds of the top HR professionals in the region in this private event. I shared my thoughts on the profitability of meaningful work, and how HR professionals could lead their organizations to profitability by curating more meaning at work for their employees.

I stepped off the stage on a high. The crowd honored me with a huge round of applause, which I hoped might have been an expression of gratitude for my insights, but was probably just excitement for Marshall Goldsmith, whom I had introduced to join me on stage and take over our tag-team keynote slot. After all, he's the "World's #1 Executive Coach."

[It's printed on the front cover of his books, so it *must* be true, right?}

I left the auditorium in search of a glass of water and a comfy chair to rest in and celebrate the fact that I'd remembered everything I'd wanted to say. So, I made my way to the Speaker's Lounge and sat down next to a woman in a brilliant red suit. Assuming she was also a speaker at the event, I politely introduced myself.

"Hi, I'm Corrie."

"I wouldn't put that on my stand if I were you."

"I'm sorry?"

"Your exhibition stand, it says you're the #1 Executive Coach in the UAE. I wouldn't say that if I were you. It's arrogant."

[ouch.}

I was startled. But of course, I couldn't argue with her logic. In fact, I had no set of criteria that I could use to make that claim. Even if I did have a set of criteria for determining who the #1 Executive Coach mug should go to, it wouldn't have been a widely agreed upon set of criteria, and certainly many could argue that I wouldn't have met my own criteria anyway. So, I agreed with her.

"That's probably right," I replied.

"So why do you say it?"

"Well, for the record, it wasn't me who said it. Forbes, ATD, CIPD, Marshall, and a number of other publications said it, and for obvious reasons my marketing team really loves it. But on principle, I agree with you; I can't defend the claim objectively."

"It's still arrogant. You should tell your marketing team to stop saying it."

"I'll tell you what it gets me though."

"What? Clients?"

"Not just any clients. Sometimes the most arrogant, egotistical, self-serving executives in the region feel that their leadership style would be better validated if they had an EC to tell them what they want to hear. So they search for one, but they don't want just anyone. They want the #1 executive coach. And sometimes they find me."

"Under false pretenses perhaps."

[OUCH! Ok. Breathe.}

"Maybe. I'm not sure. But then I get to meet with them. I spent about three months just listening to them and asking deep questions, and they feel like since I'm not correcting them right away, they must be a pretty good leader. Inevitably they furnish me with more than enough information for me to do my job. That's when they start to experience my unfair strategic advantage."

"What's that?"

"I know what I'm capable of in the remaining nine months, and they've got no idea. That's when I know what kinds of positive change will best impact their quality of life and the efficacy of their leadership. And that's when I've sorted out which of my toolkits will work best and produce lasting results with this particular client. It's fun, actually."

"Well, I still think it's arrogant."

"It's not arrogant if it's true, and we can agree that neither of us is qualified to make that judgment. Also, what's your name?"

"I'm Kate."

And that's how I met Kate Barker, a colleague of mine in the executive coaching space in the GCC. Kate and I became friends after that. She's strong, sharp, and very smart. She's not everyone's cup of tea, and neither am I, so I'm glad she's advancing the coaching industry with me. I really like Kate, though she sometimes doesn't make it easy to do so. She can be pretty direct.

[She gave me a lovely endorsement for this book in the Praise section at the beginning. I've included an excerpt from her on the back cover as well. Thanks, Kate!}

Later that day I asked Marshall about how he defends the "World's #1 Executive Coach" claim. I was relieved to hear much the same answer from him. He didn't say it, can't defend it, but loves the kinds of people he gets to meet because of it. And his publisher loves it.

In any case, the "#1 Executive Coach in [Wherever}" claim is only interesting if we can agree on the criteria by which that claim might be measured. But the coaching industry can't even agree on what qualifies a person to be an "executive coach" in the first place, much less the KPIs for performance.

It's also important to acknowledge and appreciate the sheer diversity of thinkers and practitioners when it comes to executive coaching. But we need a starting place for figuring out who gets the #1 EC mug, so we need some categories. I've already made my case for Advisory over Non-Advisory coaching for ECs, so we'll look at categories within advisory coaching. Broadly speaking, there are four major categories of coaching most 'hyped' in the corporate circles I'm acquainted with.

- Life coaching
- Leadership development coaching
- Organizational strategy and change coaching
- Behavioral coaching

Let's have a quick look at each of these coaching types, and you can decide for yourself which of them is the style we should use to judge who gets the #1 Executive Coach in [Wherever} trophy.

Career and Life Coaching

I can't imagine the pain that follows the sudden and tragic death of a spouse. That kind of personal tragedy in the life of an executive would understandably have a profound effect on focus, mood, optimism, and endurance, impacting decision-making quality and performance. In 2015, Facebook's COO Sheryl Sandberg found herself in exactly that position, grappling with profound grief and navigating uncharted emotional territory following the death of her husband, all of it unfolding in the public domain.

After struggling to recover her footing at home and at work, she authored a long essay about her suffering and sense of isolation and posted it on Facebook for her two million followers, igniting a global conversation about coping with tragedy.[163] Sandberg herself went through a long period of grief counseling, life coaching, and mentoring sessions to get back in shape for her professional priorities.

About two years ago, I had a similar case with one of my CXO clients. Peter was the CEO of a company of about 40,000 employees, and he was navigating the acquisition of a company with another 6,000 people. It was a billion-dollar deal. I had only been coaching him for a few months when one day, as I stepped into his office, he asked me not to open my laptop.

"No notes today, please," he sighed.

"Sure." I sat down. "What's going on?"

"My wife asked me for a divorce. She found out I've been having an affair."

"I'm really sorry to hear that. Have you talked to a therapist about it?"

"My therapist is trying to help me figure out why I had the affair, but that's not what I need right now. I'm reading through merger contracts that impact the livelihoods of 46,000 families, and I'm accountable for the outcome, but I'm doing it while my heart is actively breaking, and I'm finding it hard to stay focused. She has no tools for that. You're my coach. What have you got?"

[F*ck.}

This was another career-defining moment for me, and perhaps the moment that pushed me over the line into writing this book. I wasn't a

---

[163] Ignatius, A. (2017, July 17). Grief at work: Talking with Sheryl Sandberg and Adam Grant. *Harvard Business Review.*

therapist (at least not formally), but I had a lot of tools for managing emotions – emotional intelligence training; executing a holistic approach to biopsychosocial alignment; training and research in wellness coaching; managing biases and re-framing from NLP; managing focus from my work on Flow States – you name it. I had a warehouse.

What should I have said? "No, sorry, you'll need to talk to a counselor about that. I'm only interested in goal-setting"??? Forget that! My executive athlete faced a massive obstacle. He wasn't clear on what to do next and needed a competent tactical plan to solve his problem, so naturally he looked to his coach.

I was his coach. And I was immediately clear on what to do next.

I helped Peter prioritize his decision-making both personally and professionally. We then identified potential sources of information that would improve the quality of each of those decisions. We scheduled the time required to focus on them, and blocked his calendar accordingly to make sure he had a well-crafted plan. This gave him a sense of control. We worked on mindset, focus, flow, and mindfulness exercises. And I gave him a process for managing emotion-trigger distractions in real-time that allowed him to return to focus very quickly without bottling or suppressing them.

Sound useful? One of the differences between being a coach and a therapist is temporal focus. Therapy fixes broken people and seeks to understand the why behind emotions and experiences, often focusing on the past. That's not my job. My job is to provide mindset and skillset tools that improve performance on the field in the present context and moving forward. A lot of those tools straddle the hazy divides between personal and professional (life and career), psychological and physiological, but they're almost all goal-directed and future-focused.

Career and life coaching is holistic and inclusive, focusing on life difficulties, career development, and relationships, with a view to adding tangible value to the company. This type of coach operates more comprehensively than behavioral or strategy coaches, since they devote more of their time to personal beliefs, mission statements, and life's larger issues.

An EC will often have to address very personal life issues to find out the root cause of, or adequately address, the leadership challenge facing their client. For both Sheryl and Peter, personal challenges threatened to have a profound effect on business outcomes. Sheryl shared her experience with the world. Peter's secret struggle will die with me (Peter is not his real name). Thankfully they were both at the performance level where they had already engaged with good coaches.

Imagine the price their shareholders might have paid otherwise.

Training and experience as a career and life coach should probably be in the #1 Executive Coach in [Wherever} criteria checklist. But then balancing work and life doesn't automatically make an executive effective in leadership, so we'll need a leadership development coach as well.

Leadership Development Coaching

I suppose it's appropriate here to make a distinction between coaches who assist leaders to become more capable individuals (life and career) and coaches who assist leaders and organizations in being more effective leaders themselves, and producing better organizational leaders.

So what's your leadership style? Do you use MBTI, Birkman, DISC, Situational Leadership, 360 Degree Survey, Servant Leadership, Leadership Circle? Which leadership typology is the most accurate? Whose matrix is the best? Which leadership guru should you follow: John Maxwell, Sally Helgesen, Max DePree, Cy Wakeman, Peter Drucker, Herminia Ibarra, Henry Mintzberg?

The focus of a leadership development coach typically ranges from assisting an organization in creating a pool of outstanding coaches to assisting in the implementation of systems and programs designed to produce outstanding leaders on a continuous basis. Mostly though, leadership in all of its skillsets, theories, and matrices focuses on influence. How does one person or team in an organization influence another person, another team, or the very culture of an organization?

These coaches might work with one or more leaders individually, but often, they'll also do comparative leadership style studies across executive teams or departments to find the sources of friction and tension. They're looking for otherwise healthy tools that have devolved into unhelpful barriers to communication and collaboration. Leadership coaching focuses on individual and group behaviors that influence the behaviors of other individuals and groups, so this style should probably be included in the definition of #1 Executive Coach too, right?

But then if the coach is only looking at individual and group influence and communication, who's addressing systemic issues? Organizational strategy and change often require coaching that looks outside of individual and group behavior to see systemic and cultural patterns. While developing the leaders within them, we can't ignore the system that they're leading in.

Organizational Strategy and Change Coaching

I started out in entrepreneurship, then spent more than a decade in strategy consulting, so this naturally became my first set of coaching tools. Coaches who specialize in organizational change primarily focus on the implementation of organizational dynamics and transformation initiatives. They tackle a wide range of issues, such as the organization's ability to innovate, its collective perspective on strategic diversity, and how well it can clarify and execute new strategies. The primary characteristic of this sort of coach is their close collaboration with one or several top leaders and their teams to ensure the success of a particular transformation program.

This was the case when I lived in Yemen doing leadership training and restructuring work with the Hayel Saeed Anam family. Their patriarch, Ahmed Hayel Saeed was my next-door neighbor for five years. I remember one time when I was over at his house with some of his kids and grandkids. We were talking about leadership and business. His family left and I stayed behind with him for a while to talk.

"Can we spend a little time together?" he asked me.

"Sure. How can I help?"

"I want you to teach me how to talk to my people the way you talk to my people. They really listen to you."

I was honored, and I knew what he meant wasn't exactly what he'd said. It wasn't that his family didn't respect him, quite the contrary, it was that I had a way of influencing them that didn't require any authority. That's what he wanted. That was the moment I began my long pivot into executive coaching. Ahmed was my first unofficial client. The reason I'm an EC is not because it was a passion pursuit of mine. Coaching was something my clients requested of me because of who I was as a person – in addition to my strategy skillset.

[Ahmed passed away shortly after I left Yemen in 2012. He was a very good man, and his family is an enduring echo of his leadership.}

Right, back to it … I wasn't with Ahmed as a coach, but as a strategist, a fine line I walked for years with my clients after that. So, speaking as strategy and change management coaches, which methodology should we choose?

Personally, when I started out in strategy coaching, I really loved Lewin's Change Management Model.[164] I liked the simplicity of the three-step "unfreeze – change – refreeze" process. It worked with my clients in the 90s, but then the speed of change accelerated too much in the early 2000s. Companies stopped "refreezing" altogether and "change" evolved from a phase to a constant. So, I had to abandon Lewis in favor of Senge.

Peter Senge's Learning Organization model really appealed to me.[165] It's easy to import into the coaching world because what coaches do is very learning and development-focused, and what we do for individual leaders, Senge translates into organizational systems language. He

---

[164] Burnes, B. (2020). The origins of Lewin's three-step model of change. *Journal of Applied Behavioral Science, 56*(1), 32–59.
[165] Senge, P. M. (1990). *The fifth discipline: The art and practice of the learning organization.* Doubleday.

evolves personal mastery into a shared vision, which I've found to be really effective as a toolkit.

I also still use John Kotter's 8-Step Change Model when I'm coaching boards of directors or executive committees.[166] It's easy to follow, though too many of my clients get hung up on Step 6 – Create Small Wins – and they struggle to move on to building on the change and anchoring it properly in the company's culture.

In more recent years, I've appreciated Jason Little's Lean Change Management,[167] and Melanie Franklin's Agile Change Management,[168] as they both do a great job of marrying new tools for efficiency and knowledge stewardship to the lean and agile change models, respectively.

Working with top executives to set the tone for the organization's long-term aims, strategy coaches help guide the highest positions within the company to effectively execute meaningful systemic change. So, we probably should include some degree of strategy and change coaching on the list of criteria for the "#1 Executive Coach in [Wherever} trophy, right?

[Ahmed sure would have.}

Sometimes, though, it's not the organization that needs to change, it's just one person. And it's not their overall work-life balance or leadership style that needs to change: it's their behavior. Often, it's a specific behavior or set of behaviors in a specific context, and that's it. For that, we don't need a strategy coach, or even a life coach – we need something a little closer to a behavioral psychologist.

Behavioral Coaching

I almost never get an invitation to coach someone because they want to be transformed as a person. We often arrive at significant

---

[166] Kotter, J. P. (1996). *Leading change*. Harvard Business Review Press.

[167] Little, J. (2017). *Lean change management: Innovative practices for managing organizational change*. Happy Melly Express.

[168] Franklin, M. (2018). *Agile change management: A practical framework for successful change planning and implementation*. Kogan Page.

transformation of some aspect of their lives over the course of a few months, but that's not why they call me. They call because something in their life is broken and they want to know what to *do* to fix it. They want rapid behavioral change.

Over the last couple of decades I've been able to help hundreds of CXOs to stop yelling at their employees; start confronting abuses of power on their Boards of Directors; speak publicly with confidence; break smoking, drinking, and gambling habits; develop a new physical exercise routine or knowledge stewardship discipline; manage overwhelming complexity; collect a new competency; start reading, stop reacting, and start meditating on a regular basis. Each of these is an example of behavioral change coaching.

Behavioral coaches assist leaders in making sustained constructive shifts toward helping them build or break habits, improve their interpersonal skills, and increase their capacity for inspiring others. All leaders, even first-line supervisors, can benefit from this kind of coaching.

Behavioral Psychology

In my experience, the majority of those who identify as executive coaches are dominantly behavioral coaches, and a study by Bozer, Sarros, and Santora found that coaches with an academic background in psychology were more successful in improving coachees' self-awareness and job performance.[169] So, since the majority of coaches are behavioral and the most effective foundation for behavioral coaching is psychology, a brief introduction to behavioral psychology seems the most critical place to start.

John Watson's 1913 essay was the foundation of early behaviorism in psychology.[170] Watson suggested that our minds are empty when we are born and our behavior and learning are a product of self-selected responses to external input. We act, the world responds, and we adjust our behavior accordingly. We touch the hot stove, we experience pain,

---

[169] Bozer, G., Sarros, J. C., & Santora, J. C. (2014). Academic background and credibility in executive coaching effectiveness. *Personnel Review, 43*(6), 881–897.

[170] Watson, J. B. (1913). Psychology as the behaviorist views it. *Psychological Review, 20,* 158–178.

and we stop touching the stove. We refer to this process as classical conditioning.

A century after Watson, evolutionary biologist Robert Sapolsky suggests that not only are our heads full when we are born, but our behaviors throughout the course of our lives are predominantly influenced by the genetic and neurological material already present at birth.[171] The world does something, and our behavioral response is largely, if not completely, the inevitable result of deterministic conditions.

What I like about both classical conditioning and behavioral determinism is that both approaches agree that behavior change is primarily a response to external stimuli. This is good news for us executive coaches, because whether chosen by free will or determined by preexisting conditions, a new set of external inputs is what's required to trigger meaningful and lasting behavior change.

Watson and Sapolsky would, therefore, agree that executive coaching results in change and that it might indeed be the only possible way of eliciting change. But they would say this for very different underlying reasons. If the opposing ends of the spectrum agree with each other, then the entire spectrum must hold the same truth: there can be no meaningful change without external input.

[If you haven't yet, read *Determined* by Sapolsky. I absolutely hate that he's probably right. The science checks out. Just don't tell anyone what you know after you've read it.}

Gestalt Coaching
One of my favorite toolkits in behavioral coaching is Fritz Perls' Gestalt approach, mentioned briefly in Chapter 1.[172] Gestalt coaching places a strong focus on the value of each person's complete subjective experience at any given time. An individual's experience has cognitive, emotional, and physical components, and their behavior is determined by the meaning they assign to their particular experience, or "gestalt."

---

[171] Sapolsky, R. M. (2023). *Determined: A science of life without free will*. Penguin.
[172] Spoth, J., Toman, S., Leichtman, R., & Allan, J. (2013). Gestalt approach. In J. Passmore, D. B. Peterson, & T. Freire (Eds.), *The Wiley Blackwell handbook of the psychology of coaching and mentoring* (pp. 385–406). Wiley Blackwell.

In Gestalt Coaching, behavior change isn't a product of talking about events, rather it comes from experiencing those events differently.

I use the Gestalt approach often with my coaching clients. I ask them to describe without emotion or judgment the particulars of a past event or current context, and then to imagine a full spectrum of potential interpretations for the meaning of that event or context. After they've conceded that each potential interpretation of the event can be true without changing any of the particulars of the event, I invite my coachee to choose from among the potential interpretations a meaning that's most helpful to them at this time. The event or context doesn't change, but the experience does, and future behavior changes naturally as a byproduct of this *new* experience of a present context or an old event. It's a pretty cool set of tools.

Judy, for example, had just been promoted to Group Head of Procurement for a major multinational company, reporting to the GCFO (Group CFO). I had already been coaching her for a year when she said,

"I don't think William (the GCFO) likes me. I'm nervous that I'm not doing a good job. I try to schedule meetings with him but he often declines or reschedules. And when we do get together, the meetings are short, very deliberate."

"Okay," I replied, "that's your experience. I'd like you to separate your experience of the event from the facts of the event."

"He declines and reschedules, is quick in our meetings, and sticks to the agenda."

"All true, and you experience those facts as him avoiding you and not liking you."

"Right."

"Is there a more negative interpretation of those same facts? Let's think of the worst possible interpretation that could still be true without changing any of the facts."

"He absolutely hates me and has already planned to fire me?"

"Perfect. Now let's try the other end of the same spectrum. What's the best possible interpretation you can think of without changing any of the facts?"

"He's thrilled with my work and doesn't feel the need to either micromanage me or babysit me emotionally. And he's got so many other demands on his time that my being self-reliant is actually a gift to him."

"Great. Do you accept that along that spectrum there are an infinite number of varied meanings that can be equally true without changing any of the known facts?"

"Yes, of course."

"Ok, then which meaning would you like to choose? Which of the range of possible experiences is the most useful to you right now?"

"If he hates me there's nothing I can do about it now, haha! Let's go with William being under a lot of pressure and me being an easy maintenance teammate for him."

"How will your attitudes toward yourself and behaviors toward William change as a result of this new experience?"

"I'll assume a default of trust and empowerment from him. I'll just get on with my work, and if he cancels our meeting, I'll know it's because something mission-critical has come up, and he views his time with me as less of a fire hazard, so to speak. I'll also start informing him of what I'm doing instead of asking for approvals so often."

"Brilliant. How do you feel now?"

"Much more confident, more competent, and like I'm more of William's teammate than employee."

"Whether you're right or not about William's motivations here doesn't matter. You can't read William's mind. You can only go on what you see and hear, and the rest of the meaning you can curate for yourself. Choose the most useful meaning to you."

I think to be the #1 Executive Coach in [Wherever}, some behavioral coaching expertise should be required. What do you think?

But then which toolkit should we value the most? Gestalt? Nah. I mean, I know I just gave an anecdote about how well it worked with one client. It's certainly good, but it doesn't work for everyone, and it may not be as robust as Rational Emotive Behavioral Executive Coaching (REBEC), based on the foundational works of Albert Ellis.[173] And how about Narrative Coaching? NLP Coaching? Mindset Coaching? Peak Performance Coaching? Flow Coaching … Bio-Hacking Coaching … Advantage Coaching? Or G.R.O.W., O.S.C.A.R., C.L.E.A.R., C.A.R.E.S., and (my personal favorite) Evolutionary Neuroscientific Coaching … which is the best approach?

Each of these provides a set of tools useful enough that it has become an effective modality for behavioral coaching. They all have their own formal training curriculum, and many have their own certification processes.

Executive coaches don't have to be experts in all of the four coaching domains, but they shouldn't be ignorant of any of them either. Each of the four domains has a multitude of modalities available to address challenges common to executives, and each if properly applied will positively influence executive performance. Life coaching, leadership development coaching, organizational strategy and change coaching, and behavioral coaching all impact an executive's level of play in their business role, which in turn drives organizational performance and business outcomes.

I think that knowing any one of them is a bit like having a toolbox with one screwdriver set in it. Useful, but very limited.

But if to be an EC you need some education and/or experience in all four of the major coaching domains: behavioral, strategic, life, and leadership, isn't that a lot to ask of a coach?

Yes. Yes, it is.

---

[173] Dudău, D. P., Sălăgean, N., & Sava, F. A. (2018). Executive coaching. In M. E. Bernard & O. A. David (Eds.), *Coaching for rational living* (pp. 343–360). Springer International; Ellis, A. (1972). *Executive leadership: A rational approach*. Institute for Rational Living.; Ellis, A. (2002). *Overcoming resistance: A rational emotive behavior therapy integrated approach* (2nd ed.). Springer.

And rightly so. If you can't coach an Olympian, you have no business calling yourself an Olympic coach.

This is the Olympics of coaching in business.

Executive Coach as Competency Collector

In *The Human Behind the Coach*, authors Claire Pedrick and Lucia Baldelli, both ICF Master Certified Coaches, note that a strong profile and credentials are often what draw a client to a good coach, similarly to the way a patient might choose a surgeon. "Like the surgeon, your credentials and results won't build more trust once you are in the room."[174] I completely agree with that statement, but then, what happens to trust and credibility if the surgeon refuses to operate, waiting in silence and holding space for the patient to conduct their own surgery?

Isn't the surgeon obligated not only to know their craft, but to use what they know in service of their patient? Isn't that the surgeon's job? A coach's past credentials and results earn them the right to start coaching, but it's the application of their experience and education in service of their current client that qualifies their "coaching" as "executive."

The demand for ECs is growing, but so is the number of professionals aspiring to be one themselves. The International Coach Federation 2023 Global Coaching Study estimated that there are over 109,000 coach practitioners worldwide, with 54% growth from 2019 to 2022.[175] That's not even a third of the more than 360,000 people on Linkedin calling themselves an "Executive Coach."

---

[174] Pedrick, C., & Baldelli, L. (2023). The human behind the coach: How great coaches transform themselves first. Practical Inspiration Publishing.
[175] International Coaching Federation. (2023). ICF Global Coaching Study 1 2023 Executive Summary. (n.d.).
https://coachingfederation.org/app/uploads/2023/04/2023ICFGlobalCoachingStudy_ExecutiveSummary.pdf.

It's not surprising that I'm often asked how professionals can shift to becoming a good executive coach. They're all well-meaning people who value the field, understand that coaching is a potent means of supporting others, see the flexibility and independence that comes with running a coaching practice, and may even have benefited from coaching themselves ... but I also have to be honest with them about what's required.

The fact is that being a competent EC requires a surprising amount of hard work, a ton of reading, and a lot of experience. Just as it does for an Olympic coach, or a good surgeon.

We're not talking about hundreds of hours of foundational work here, but thousands.

And we're not talking about a single set of tools, but dozens.

A single recognized coaching credential could require up to a year of training. Passing an exam, completing at least 100 hours of client work, and engaging with a mentor coach are just some of the requirements for obtaining ICF certification, for example, and ICF is non-advisory. Almost any single coaching certification is a helpful start, but in my opinion each and every one of them is insufficient as an isolated qualification for executive coaching.

[Including mine. In fact, I don't allow coaches to take my Chief Executive Coaching program unless they already have another reputable coaching certification.}

I didn't realize how little I knew until I'd completed my second doctorate degree. I didn't accept how powerless over the world I could be until I'd gone bankrupt twice. And I didn't see how narrow my coaching methodology was until I'd learned a second one. So then I learned a third, then a fourth. Learning a new toolkit helps me to see the limitations in my previous tools. And like languages, the more you learn, the easier they are to learn.

Formal training is not the only way to learn a coaching methodology, and a strong collection of certificates doesn't make anyone a good coach *de facto*. I've learned many of my best tools from reading books. I use a lot of psychology protocols in my coaching practice, for example, and I don't have a psychology degree – but I've easily read more than a hundred books in that domain. Online courses, time with experts, experience in the field, debates with friends over dinner, all of these modes of learning have added to my coaching toolkit warehouse.

[I've learned a lot of tools from listening to Ester Perel's podcast too!}

Does Experience Expire?

I should also add here that previous in-role experience isn't enough to qualify someone as a coach either, nor is a lack of experience enough to disqualify someone. The UK Olympic cycling team has won 18 gold medals and has been coached through the last three Olympics by Dave Brailsford, whose background is in sports medicine, not competitive cycling. Gregg Troy coached the men's US Olympic swim team in 1996 and 2008 and was head coach for the 2012 Olympic games. Gregg has coached 68 Olympians, including 5-time gold medal winner Ryan Lochte. Gregg has never himself been a competitive swimmer.[176]

Marshall Goldsmith and Tony Robbins, arguably two of the world's top executive coaches, having each coached dozens of the world's top corporate CXOs, have never themselves run a large company. It wouldn't matter if they had, though; they've both been coaches for so long that their previous in-role experience would almost certainly be obsolete.

Bill Cambell, the "Trillion Dollar Coach," was the European Head of Products for Kodak, then Head of Sales for Apple in the 80s. He then became CEO of GO Corporation, which failed in 1994, so he moved into the CEO role at the tax software firm Intuit until 1998. In 2001 he started coaching the new CEO of Google, Eric Schmidt. From there, he coached the CEOs of eBay, Twitter, Flipboard, Numenta, Chegg, a number of government officials including VP Al Gore, and many others.[177]

Quick question: for how long did Bill's previous in-role experience hold its value in his executive coaching practice? After all, his last CEO role

---

[176] Meet the coaches behind the world's best Olympic teams. (2012, August 14). *BBC Sport.*

[177] Schmidt, E., Rosenberg, J., & Eagle, A. (2019). *Trillion dollar coach: The leadership playbook of Silicon Valley's Bill Campbell.* HarperCollins.

ended in 1998, before the rise of cloud computing, smartphones, ipods, FaceBook, YouTube, LinkedIn, Skype, DEI, ESG, WhatsApp, the gig economy, Google, remote work, CSR, IoT, influencers, electric cars, 3D printing, X (twitter), blockchain, AI, and every single cryptocurrency.

Do you think Bill Campbell's previous in-role CEO experience was as relevant to Google CEO Sundar Pichai in 2015 as it was to Google CEO Eric Schmidt in 2001?

He coached both CEOs (as well as the founders Larry Page and Sergey Brin).

What's the expiry date on an executive coach's previous industrial or in-role experience?

Experience Erodes as the Role Evolves

The job of a CXO is very different now than it was 20 years ago, and some industries, such as tech, finance, and telecommunications, have been completely overhauled just in the last decade. How relevant is a coach's previous CXO experience if their last post was a decade ago? In that time, we've seen massive shifts in CXO role requirements across all departments, such as:

- Digital transformation, which used to be project-based and fairly straightforward, but now requires CXOs to grapple with data analytics and AI to remain relevant;[178]
- Stakeholder management, which has broadened the requirements for CXO input-seeking behavior;[179]
- Agility, which requires CXOs to make more aggressive decisions with less time for due diligence research;[180]

---

[178] Smith, J. (2023). The impact of digital transformation on modern business. *Journal of Business Innovation, 12*(3), 45–60.

[179] Johnson, L. (2022). Balancing profit and purpose: The evolving role of CEOs. *Corporate Governance Review, 15*(2), 78–92.

[180] Brown, K. (2021). Leadership in the age of disruption: New challenges for CEOs. *Leadership Quarterly, 30*(4), 123–140.

- Diversity and inclusion, which require CXOs to pay attention to the intrinsic benefits of stronger culture and a more inclusive organization;[181] and
- Sustainability, which has grown from a fringe concern into regulatory requirements and greenwashing strategies.

I'll be the first to concede that my previous experience in entrepreneurship and corporate leadership has long since passed its best-before date. If I were leaning on that as my primary source of authority or methodology in my coaching practice today, I wouldn't be able to offer much value at all to my clients.

Don't get me wrong, I'm not throwing my earlier experience in the bin because it's old, but I am recognizing that a lot of it doesn't increase in relevance with age. If I expect my CXO clients to continuously learn and grow, I'd better be setting a good example as their coach.

Knowledge Half-Life

Knowledge half-life refers to the amount of time it takes for a particular learning to become half as relevant or applicable as it was at the time of learning. Inter-disciplinary research shows that knowledge half-life is estimated to be roughly:

- 2–3 years in the technology sector[182]
- 5–10 years in the medical sciences[183]
- 10 years in engineering[184]
- 5 years in business and management.[185]

---

[181] Johnson, L. (2022). Balancing profit and purpose: The evolving role of CEOs. *Corporate Governance Review, 15*(2), 78–92.

[182] Knudsen, E. S., & Lien, L. B. (2023). The half-life of knowledge and strategic human capital. *Human Resource Management Review, 33*(4).

[183] Chow, N. L. Y., Tateishi, N., Goldhar, A., Zaheer, R., Redelmeier, D. A., Cheung, A. H., Schaffer, A., & Sinyor, M. (2023). Does knowledge have a half-life? An observational study analyzing the use of older citations in medical and scientific publications. *BMJ Open, 13*(5).

[184] Houkes, W., & Meijers, A. (2021). Engineering knowledge. In *The Oxford handbook of philosophy of technology* (pp. 128–151). Oxford University Press.

[185] Linnenluecke, M. K. (2017). Resilience in business and management research: A review of influential publications and a research agenda. *International Journal of Management Reviews, 19*(1), 4–30.

The half-life of knowledge in the education sector varies depending on the subject. While some subjects and tools remain stable, pedagogical technology and early childhood education techniques change quite quickly.[186] The same is true in the natural sciences, where foundational chemistry and physics remain stable, but quantum mechanics and nanotechnology have developed rapidly.[187]

While fundamental principles may remain constant for decades, nearly every human domain is constantly, and rapidly, developing in terms of what can be accomplished with new discoveries and applications. At the Olympic level, access to the most recent medical research and technological developments is a stronger critical success factor than in local competition. The higher up you go in any domain, the more important ongoing development is for success.

The sharpest coaching tools I have now are in the domains of neuroscience and evolutionary psychology, neither of which I hold a degree in, and neither of which I knew anything about when I began my coaching career with Ahmed in Yemen.

I propose that the executive function in every organization is where knowledge half-life should be most highly considered as a risk factor in decision-making quality and competitive edge. What your executives knew five years ago about management will be nearly irrelevant five years from now.

Until more research is available on knowledge of half-life in the coaching industry specifically, I propose we use the same business and management benchmark of about five years. A coach's previous in-role experience should be considered about 25% useful a decade out of the role, and this principle should be applied to degrees, certifications, books read, conversations had, and ideas conceived.

---

[186] Biwer, F., Egbrink, M. G. A. o., Aalten, P., & de Bruin, A. B. H. (2020). Fostering effective learning strategies in higher education – A mixed-methods study. *Journal of Applied Research in Memory and Cognition, 9*(2), 186–203.

[187] Chow, N. L. Y., Tateishi, N., Goldhar, A., Zaheer, R., Redelmeier, D. A., Cheung, A. H., Schaffer, A., & Sinyor, M. (2023). Does knowledge have a half-life? An observational study analyzing the use of older citations in medical and scientific publications. *BMJ Open, 13*(5).

Everything you know about coaching today will be roughly half as valuable in five years' time. So, what are you doing between now and then to remain relevant as an executive coach?

Personally, I'm collecting competencies.

[Come with me.}

The CXO Coach Toolkit

In previous chapters, I've used this section to make recommendations for the kinds of tools that coaches should consider having to address specific challenges of their executive clients. But because this chapter was written for the *coach*, I've reserved this section for the CXO. The question here is, what should a CXO be looking for in their coach's warehouse of tools before signing on for executive coaching?

Before we get to that, though, we need to know if there's any point at all for you to even start executive coaching. Because if you're not coachable, then it's all a waste of time.

Are You Coachable?

In *Becoming Coachable*, the authors discuss the four biggest determinants of success in coaching, and none of them has to do with the qualifications of your coach. They are qualities in the executive, specifically:[188]

1. Openness to Change
2. Openness to Feedback
3. Openness to Take Action
4. Openness to Accountability.

These four qualities in the CXO's posture toward coaching will be the biggest success factors in executive coaching.

Ultimately, no matter how educated and experienced the coach is, the coachability of the CXO and their relationship with their coach will be

---

[188] Osman, S., Lane, J., & Goldsmith, M. (2023). *Becoming coachable: Unleashing the power of executive coaching to transform your leadership and life.* 100 Coaches Publishing.

the highest determinants of success. CXOs indicate that coaching "helpfulness is much less predicted by technique or approach than by factors common to all coaching, such as the relationship, empathic understanding, positive expectations etc."[189] None of the tools will be useful if the relationship isn't good to begin with or the coachee isn't open to change.

Additionally, regardless of the experience level or credentials of the coach, the CXOs perception of dominance in the relationship is positively correlated with coaching success.[190] Although the EC needs to have wizard-like competency, the CXO's needs to hold the throne in the relationship. This is an echo of the Gerstner Effect from Chapter 6. Your coach needs to hold their objectivity, and you need to hold your authority.

So once you can answer yes to the four openness categories above, then you, the CXO, can start to look for someone you trust to speak truth to you when no one else will. Remember, you're choosing a critical friend here, someone you like as a person but also has the courage and competency to call you out on your bullshit.

Minimum Formal Qualifications for an EC

As for their CV, in my personal opinion and as a starting place for qualifications, coaches at the CXO level in companies of 1,000+ employees should have a minimum of:

1. A decade of executive business experience;
2. Five years or 500 hours of coaching experience;
3. A master's degree in business, leadership, psychology, or a related field;
4. Independent coaching accreditations in at least two of the four coaching domains mentioned above; and

---

[189] De Haan, E., Culpin, V., & Curd, J. (2011). Executive coaching in practice: What determines helpfulness for clients of coaching? *Personnel Review, 40*(1), 24–44.
[190] Ianiro, P. M., Lehmann-Willenbrock, N., & Kauffeld, S. (2015). Coaches and clients in action: A sequential analysis of interpersonal coach and client behavior. *Journal of Business and Psychology, 30*(3), 435–456.

5. A new toolkit being added to their warehouse at least every two years.

Are my expectations too high? What do you think? Honestly. If you had to decide if someone was "qualified" to coach the CEO of a company that governed the livelihoods of more than a thousand families, what would be on your list? After all, this may be the highest level of play in business, but it isn't the Olympics. If the executive misses a play, we don't just lose the gold medal, we might lose ten million dollars, and a thousand families might lose their primary source of income. The stakes are much higher, so shouldn't the qualifications be higher as well?

Again, this criteria set is my recommendation, not a regulatory requirement. I know great executive coaches without any executive experience at all. And I know others without a master's degree. However, I don't know any great executive coaches who have neither.

Continuous development is also an important consideration for vetting a good executive coach. Look for competency collectors. In the public domain you might find they've completed a certification, published an academic article, authored a book, delivered a major keynote, or collected a formal degree from time to time. You'll probably find these on LinkedIn.

If these kinds of public domain artifacts aren't visible in the coach's recent life, then there are two ways to know if the coach is still self-developing. First, ask them what books they're reading, which conferences they're attending, who they're being coached by, and how they're staying sharp enough to keep up with their high-performing clients.

Second, look at their clients. While the best Olympic coaches are competency collectors too, their success as a coach is not judged by their list of learnings but by the successes of their clients. Look for referrals, endorsements, and impact or ROI statements from current or former clients.

If an EC has been coasting on past learning and past successes for 24 months, they're almost certainly sliding down the relevance ladder. If it's been a decade since they've done anything truly novel, they're almost certainly completely outdated.

The world is changing rapidly, and so are the tools needed to help executives to continue to perform at Olympic levels in their ever-evolving economic games. How could one size (or credential, or book, or idea) ever fit all? And how could any decent executive coach ever say they've finished honing their craft?

In domain terms, I recommend that every EC be able to demonstrate an above-average level of understanding of the following:

- Fitness, recovery and nutrition
- Psychology and mindset
- Business structure and processes
- Leadership and management
- Organizational behavior
- Organizational governance and office politics
- Executive personal branding and presentation skills
- Interpersonal communication and negotiation
- Personality type models
- Team building tactics

And yes, it's a lot of work to get there. But several organizations have already started on this path. Personally, I like the coaching qualifications required by CoachSource.[191] Their top-tier coaches must demonstrate the following pre-requisites (as taken directly from their website):

1. **Leadership Effectiveness Coaching**: Specializing in helping leaders achieve positive, long-term change in leadership behavior over time.
2. **Advanced Degree**: MBA, MA, MS or PhD in org. development, org. psychology, business or related fields.

---

[191] CoachSource. (2024). *Become A CSQ™ Coach*. CoachSource.

3. **Extensive Experience Coaching Senior Leaders**: C-level, EVP/SVP, VP, Director coaching experience.
4. **Business Experience**: Prior senior leadership positions in organizations, line management and Fortune/FTSE 500 preferred.
5. **Fortune/FTSE 500 Client List**: Client experience with similar caliber to our clients.
6. **Years of Experience Coaching**: Minimum five years as practitioner, 10+ years preferred, minimum two years independent, specific coach training and certification.
7. **Executive Presence**: Demonstrates the overall presence of a seasoned, senior executive coach.

I'm grateful for organizations like CoachSource, CMi Merryck, 100 Coaches, and others who are setting higher objective standards for the qualifications of executive coaches.

If you want to become a CXO coach, stop looking for a roadmap to wayfind with. Instead, start filling your competency warehouse with a broad range of wizard-like toolkits.

Burch's Hierarchy of Competency
By this stage in the book, I'm hoping to have helped both CXOs and coaches uncover some new information that will help coaches learn to be better executive coaches, and CXOs learn how to choose and engage with good executive coaches. Burch's hierarchy of competence gives us a framework for looking at this enlightenment process.[192]

---

[192] Innovation Training. (2023, April 26). *The Four Stages of Competence Model – Innovation Training | Design*. Innovation Training | Design Thinking Workshops.

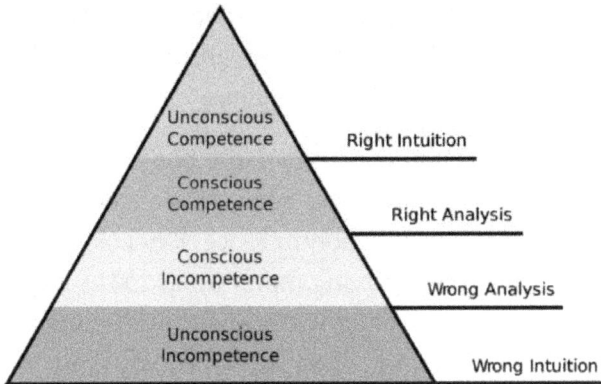

Burch's Hierarchy of Competency

It's my sincere hope that I've been able to shine some light on the unconscious incompetence of both those CXOs who don't think they need executive coaching, and those coaches who may innocently and yet quite unhelpfully think they are qualified to coach executives.

CXOs who think they don't need coaching are like Olympic athletes who think they don't need coaching. They're a joke, and worse, they're gambling with their peoples' livelihoods and their shareholders' value. I accept that it's sometimes tough for an executive to find a coach capable of coaching at their level of play, but I do not accept that an executive can ever perform better without a coach than they could with one.

Coaches, too, might think of themselves as "good enough" to coach executives with a single coaching credential or a decade-old stint as a CEO, and this, too, is equally misguided.

If you find yourself in one of these categories, I hope you'll accept that this is not an insult, it's an education. I wrote this book because it was necessary. The fact is, we all have things we are unconsciously incompetent in. We don't know what they are because we are unconscious of them. Once we become conscious of them, that doesn't make us competent, just conscious that we're not competent. We were always incompetent, but now we know it.

[I feel that way about fatherhood, pretty much all the time. I don't know how incompetent I am. Sometimes though, one of my kids loves me enough to let me know. Then I know. Haha.}

The next step is to make a plan to become consciously competent. As either a CXO or a coach, reading this book should have helped with that. To help with the climb out of incompetence, I've provided seven major challenges that CXOs face, and one major uplift to the expectations we all should have of anyone calling themselves an executive coach. With enough time, effort, education, and experience, my hope is that you will turn these lessons, and many of the tools I've recommended in them, into second languages for yourself.

I typically don't have to think through which of my warehouse of tools to use, because most of them are second nature to me. They are unconscious competencies. The same will happen for you, if you're willing to put the effort in to earn that level of expertise.

One of my coaching colleagues just reminded me that if a person calling themselves an EC isn't actively engaged in continuous learning, "it may be that they don't know that they don't know, because they think they already know, you know?" If you run into these coaches, my advice is to run *away* from them. If you think that's too sharp a response, perhaps consider giving them your copy of this book, as a gift.

[Incidentally, if someone gave you this book as a gift, it might be because they care about you enough to not let you look stupid in front of your colleagues, or your industry. Thank them! Or it might just be because you're awesome. Who knows?}

Bottom Line

In the high-stakes world of executive leadership, one-size-fits-all coaching is like showing up to a sword fight with a butter knife. CXOs need wizards, not way finders; they need coaches who bring an arsenal of skills, strategies, and perspectives. To be the #1 Executive Coach even in your own eyes, you've got to be relentless in your pursuit of a broad range of knowledge and constantly upgrading your toolkit. The best coaches aren't defined by their experience in a single industry, or expertise in a single methodology, but by their ability to pivot, adapt, and pull the right strategy out of the hat when the stakes are highest.

If you want to know if you're The #1 Executive Coach in [Wherever}, don't look at your client list, your revenue, or the number of followers you have on social media. Look at your warehouse, and judge for yourself. Can you truly wield both advisory and non-advisory toolkits in all four of the coaching domains: life, leadership, strategy, and behavior? Can you work across industries ranging from oil and gas to luxury shoes, in cultures as varied as the UK and Yemen, or across disciplines such as HR and finance? Are you the multi-dimensional wizard your clients need, or just a way finder with a slick roadmap?

The Checklist (this time it's for the CXO)
Resources for understanding the majority of the competencies discussed in this chapter are in the online compendium, just follow the QR code in Chapter 1 or at the end of the Conclusion.

Here we concentrate on the six absolutely mandatory criteria for CXOs to know if their coaching engagement is likely to work:

1. Are you open to making change?
2. Are you open to receiving feedback?
3. Are you open to taking action based on that feedback?
4. Are you open to accountability for your commitment to take action?
5. Do you trust your coach to speak the truth to you even when you don't like it?
6. Do you trust your coach not to try to control you in the relationship?

If all six answers are "yes," then you're good to go.

So go!

CONCLUSION

"**A**re you a god, a coward, or a liar?"

Seventeen GCXOs and CXOs of a multinational bank sat in stunned silence as I began an offsite workshop on executive leadership. I had invited them to talk about their mistakes openly with each other. I'd asked for any volunteer to "tell me the story of a major mistake you've made in the last twelve months."

None volunteered.

"I know you're under a lot of pressure to consistently perform," I continued. "Your industry is changing rapidly, and you are all at the top of your game. There are only two kinds of leaders at your level who make no mistakes: gods and cowards. If you're a god, then you need to tell me now because I'll need to start worshipping you and that will make our relationship super awkward."

They laughed.

"But if you're not a god and you're not making any mistakes, it's probably because you're not doing anything truly challenging, remarkable, innovative, or disruptive. In your industry, and at your level of play, that qualifies you as a coward."

They stopped laughing.

"But let's say you *are* moving fast enough to break things, and you're just not telling the rest of us about it when that happens. If that's the case, you're robbing your team and the organization as a whole of the learning opportunity that comes from your undesired outcome. You're pretending to be perfect, when you know you're not, and we all know you're not, and that qualifies you as a liar."

They were properly offended now.

"So which is it? Coward or liar? Because I'm pretty sure you're not gods."

"We know we're not gods, Dr. Corrie," barked Ralph (the GCFO), visibly frustrated by what I'd said. And that's when the breakthrough happened. Ralph continued, "We just don't feel safe with each other. We're afraid to talk about those things in this room because the pressure to perform is so high, and we're forced to pretend like everything is going as planned and that things that don't go as planned are always outside of our control or someone else's fault."

"Thank you, Ralph." I sighed.

Perfect.

He was spot on. That's exactly what everyone knew and no one said. Executives like Ralph are culturally curated to present themselves as tiny gods, somehow always doing the right thing, taking calculated risks, innovating and pushing the edge of their industry, and yet never making any mistakes.

It's not just unfair, it's irrational. And to ask someone to live that myth as a lifestyle, well, it's inhumane.

This is the pressure that most executives face in their daily lives, and it's a difficult reality to empathize with unless you've lived in it yourself.

What followed was an amazing conversation about humanity in executive leadership, celebrating undesired outcomes, and knowledge stewardship in a learning organization. And, of course, executive coaching as a critical investment in both individual and team performance. They needed a safe space.

A coaching space.

The relationship between a CXO and their coach is characterized by trust, confidentiality, and mutual respect. It provides that safe space for CXOs to process mistakes, explore sensitive decisions, grapple with strategic challenges, and confront personal and professional dilemmas. In this context, the coach serves as a sounding board, a strategic advisor, and a confidant, offering insights and perspective to inform the CXOs leadership character and behavior, bypassing the unrealistic expectations of the tiny-god executive culture.

Throughout this book, I've presented the role of an executive as entailing several challenges that are not as commonly or dramatically shared by their direct reports outside of the C-suite. In response to the specialized nature of CXO roles, executive coaching emerges as a specialized field of coaching. Let's briefly review the main thread.

The Overview

The narrative of the preceding chapters ran like this: Executives need

1. **Advisory Coaching** tailored for
2. **Peak Performance**, where the
3. **Language Barrier** contributes to a
4. **Defensive Shift**, resulting in
5. **Executive Isolation**, which requires
6. **External Objectivity**, because
7. **High-Stakes Decisions** reinforce the case for ...

Advisory Coaching. What kind of advisory coaching exactly?
8. **Wizard Expertise**.

We began by highlighting the critical shift from non-advisory to **advisory coaching** when working with CXOs. Executives at the highest level don't need vague questions but actionable insights. Non-advisory coaching has its place in the mid and senior management layers of an organization, and as a management style at all levels; but it's not for CXOs, who require strategic value and tactical advice to navigate their complex roles. The impact here is clear: to be an effective executive coach, you must provide more than just thought-provoking questions, you must deliver meaningful guidance.

The intense pressure for **peak performance** faced by CXOs was viewed through the internal and external forces that can either drive or derail them. Drawing parallels with elite athletes, we looked at the importance of mindset coaching and the Pygmalion Effect in fostering executive self-efficacy. For coaches this means helping executives reframe their internal narratives to overcome pressure and succeed at the highest levels.

Newly appointed CXOs often face **language barriers**, especially when their expertise in one area doesn't translate to other departments. ECs can help executives bridge these departmental and domain-specific language gaps, enhancing cross-departmental collaboration and helping to ensure that executives communicate effectively across their organization.

Over time, CXOs often shift from a proactive, offense-oriented mindset to a **defensive shift**, driven by the weight of responsibility and external pressures once they reach the C-suite. ECs should be ready to help executives regain their offensive edge by focusing on emotional intelligence, mindfulness, and stakeholder management. An EC's impact lies in helping executives maintain their strategic agility rather than become overly cautious and protectionist.

Executive isolation is a reality that coaches, too, must address. We looked at how echo chambers, corporate protectionism, and a lack of mentorship, can contribute to the loneliness that CXOs experience. ECs play a vital role in breaking through this isolation, providing not just guidance but a critical, trusted relationship that executives often lack. For those aiming to qualify as executive coaches, here's the call: you are more than a coach – you are a confidant and a mentor in the lonely terrain of executive leadership. Connect deeply or get out of the way.

Though internal coaching can be effective at mid-level and some senior-level management positions, internal coaching lacks the **external objectivity**, confidentiality, and range expertise needed by CXOs at the top level. So this is a reminder of the unique value an EC brings as an external advisor who can offer unbiased, confidential, and expert guidance that internal coaches simply cannot provide.

Attending to all of these executive challenges is important because of the high-risk nature of executive decisions. Good ECs help executives navigate these **high-stakes decisions** by applying decision-making frameworks and providing objective feedback that helps mitigate cognitive biases. An executive coach is crucial in helping executives make better, more informed decisions that drive long-term success for their organizations.

Executives need coaches who can offer deep expertise and transformative insights across a range of disciplines, not "way finders" who just help them navigate a single generic methodology. In my view, the #1 Executive Coach in [Wherever} award goes to the competency collector with **wizard expertise**, the coach who amassed a diverse toolkit that can be adapted to meet the specific needs of each CXO individually. If that's your goal, then you need to continually expand your knowledge, skills, and experience ... not just your coaching hours. That will ensure you continue to offer high-value, specialized advice that transcends typical coaching methods.

If you're a coach aiming to provide value as an executive coach, I hope I've provided you with an overview of some of the tools, strategies, and mindsets necessary for you to succeed in coaching at the highest levels of business. Each key challenge faced by CXOs, from overcoming loneliness and pressure to making high-stakes decisions, requires a different set of advisory coaching tools. Your journey as an EC isn't just about asking questions; it's about delivering value, offering strategic insights, and transforming the lives and careers of top-level executives. Now, armed with this knowledge, I hope you feel better prepared to step into the EC role with confidence, clarity, and a powerful warehouse of tools at your disposal.

You'll need to decide what kind of tools you'll need to collect from this point forward. I've given you a number of suggestions, but I've not indicated any of them specifically as mandatory. And my suggestions are exemplary but not exhaustive, there's a lot more out there that I'm unaware of myself. It doesn't matter how long you've been coaching, what corporate or life experience you have, or how good your profile used to be. If you're not actively engaged in your own professional development outside of your coaching sessions, you should probably retire.

If you're not getting sharper, you're getting duller.

Who's the #1 Executive Coach?

I've stopped short of writing criteria for achieving or defending any kind of #1 EC claim, including that on my own LinkedIn profile. However, gun to my head, it would have to be that the #1 EC mug should probably be awarded to a

> *Multidisciplinary industry agnostic external advisory coach with at least two formal coaching certifications and significant enough experience and education that they'll have their CXO client's trust and respect from day one, and move seamlessly been mindset and skillset optimization toolkits that result in positive sustainable and measurable progress toward the CXO performing at their personal best in their executive role.*

The problem with this definition is that each CXO is different. What each CXO needs in terms of skillset and mindset is different. So, the definition of the #1 EC isn't based on the coach's qualifications, their clients' job titles, or their fee structure but rather the "good fit" between coach and coachee.

Regardless of what my marketing team tells you online, I'm the #1 EC not *in* any geographical region, but *for* a kind of executive client. I was clear in Chapter 8 about what I think the minimum qualifications for an EC should be. However, the highest form of qualification as an EC isn't measurable by region; or a certain kind, combination, or volume of either education or experience. It's measured against the ideal match between coach and executive. This is because

> *Executive coaching is a co-creative process in which a coach and an executive elicit insights and actions from each other to optimize the mindset and skillset required for the executive to perform at their personal best in their executive role.*

Each executive has a #1 EC specifically tailored for them, someone with a wizard-like range of toolkits in their skillset and mindset warehouse, the combination and application of which provides the ideal critical friend required by that particular executive to reach their maximum potential in their role.

Principles of Coaching

I've given a lot of thought to how we might leverage coaching principles from Olympic-level athletics. I've come up with these 10 principles that I think might help us:

1. Nearly all high-performance athletes have high-performance coaches: that's how they got there, and that's how they stay there.
2. Coaches for individual athletes are most often chosen by the athletes themselves.
3. Coaches for teams are most often chosen by the team's owners, not the athletes.
4. The coach doesn't have to play the game as well as the athlete but should understand the game just as well, and be more knowledgeable than the athlete about mindset, behavior, and strategic exercises for development.
5. High-performance coaches don't ask their athletes, "What do you think you should do?" or "What else haven't you tried?" At the highest level of athletic performance, coaches come

    prepared with experience, education, and a warehouse of science-based tactics to employ.

6. If the coach doesn't push an athlete outside of their comfort zone regularly, they're the wrong coach.

7. If an athlete doesn't get frustrated with their coach from time to time, they have the wrong coach.

8. If an athlete is engaged in coaching but their performance doesn't improve, they have the wrong coach.

9. If an athlete refuses to engage in coaching, they're the wrong athlete.

10. Now, replace the word "athlete" with "executive," in all of the above statements.

Though this book has been primarily focused on individual executive coaching, I've included here a couple of the foundational principles of coaching for teams. I'd love to hear your thoughts, including those that challenge these principles or any of my other suggestions. Whether you agree with me or not on all these ideas, I'm sure we can now agree that handing over a top executive (or EXCO, or Board of Directors) to an underqualified coach is a significant gamble that no organization should be willing to take.

Like an Olympic athlete with a junior league coach, the risk of injury and failure increases. In business, that could mean a thousand families lost in layoffs or a million dollars off the bottom line. Olympic athletes need Olympic coaches, and even though gold medal coaches can't play the game as well as their athletes can, they can all coach at their athlete's level of play.

Remember, Brian Pinkerton (Webcrawler) had the first mover advantage, but Larry Page and Sergey Brin (Google) had Bill Campbell. Executives will never know their potential unless they have a coach equipped to help them reach it. And as the executive goes, so goes the company. It's stunning to me that shareholders don't insist on executive coaching more often.

[Don't they want to make more money?}

The Kicker

For executives, the process of finding a coach who can do more than just ask questions is akin to finding a kind of professional platonic life partner who brings depth, challenge, and growth into the relationship. For coaches, this book has been about preparing you to be that partner, the one who isn't just a good match on paper but who can step into the arena and help your clients achieve the extraordinary. Great partnerships don't happen by accident; they happen when both parties show up ready to challenge each other, grow together, and push boundaries. Now, it's your turn to become that partner in the corner office.

Aside from my brief list of core prerequisites at the end of Chapter 8, I'm not here to tell you whether you're qualified to be an EC or not.

There's no regulatory body qualifying Olympic coaches either, because at the top level of human performance, only the top performers, their competitors, and their coaches know what they really need.

[Read that last sentence again.}

You'll have to look in the mirror and decide for yourself if you're qualified, but here's a shortcut: If you're reading this and still unsure whether you're ready to coach at the top, then you probably aren't.

[Perhaps I'm the one you should trust to tell you the truth when no one else will. After all, I'm an executive coach. That's my job.}

The CXOs of the world aren't looking for someone to ask rhetorical questions. They need someone who knows the game, who has the guts to say, "Here's what you need to do," or "Let's try this." If you want to coach CXOs, you'd better be ready to add serious value. No excuses, no half-measures. Because at this level, there's no room for average. Be the coach who brings actionable knowledge that drives results.

Be as Olympic in your craft as Bob Bowman is in his.

Then, and only then, please feel free to call yourself an Executive Coach.

SCAN ME

www.learn.corrieblock.com/courses/CECresources

REFERENCES AND FURTHER READING

Anderson, M., & Metrixglobal. (n.d.). Executive briefing: Case study on the return on investment of executive coaching. *GVA Success*. https://gvasuccess.com/articles/ExetutiveBriefing.pdf.

Ankrom, S. (2024, February 16). Need a breather? Try these 9 breathing exercises to relieve anxiety. *Verywell Mind*. https://www.verywellmind.com/abdominal-breathing-2584115.

Athanasopoulou, A., & Dopson, S. (2016). *Executive coaching outcomes and how organizations can capitalize on them.* In *2016 AOM Symposium on Coaching & Competencies*. Said Business School – University of Oxford.

Babad, E. Y., Inbar, J., & Rosenthal, R. (1982). Pygmalion, Galatea, and the Golem: Investigations of biased and unbiased teachers. *Journal of Educational Psychology, 74*(4), 459.

Bachkirova, T. (2009). Cognitive-developmental approach to coaching: An interview with Robert Kegan. *Coaching: An International Journal of Theory, Research and Practice, 2*(1), 10–22.

Baldelli, L. (2024, January 11). Internal vs. external coaching: Pros and cons. *Coaching Outside the Box.*

Bales, R. (2023). *The history of Charles Babbage's analytical engine and the birth of computers.* History of Computers.

Bandura, A. (1997). *Self-efficacy: The exercise of control.* Freeman.

Baron, L., Morin, L., & Morin, D. (2011). The effect of working alliance discrepancy on the development of coachees' self-efficacy. *Journal of Management Development, 30*(9), 847–864.

Barrabi, T. (2023). Senior OpenAI employees: Sam Altman was "psychologically abusive." *New York Post*. https://nypost.com/2023/12/08/business/senior-openai-employees-sam-altman-was-psychologically-abusive/.

Bates, B. (2015). *The little book of big coaching models: 83 ways to help managers get the best out of people.* FT Press.

Berglas, S. (2002). The very real dangers of executive coaching. *Harvard Business Review, 80*(6), 86–92, 153.

Biwer, F., Egbrink, M. G. A. o., Aalten, P., & de Bruin, A. B. H. (2020). Fostering effective learning strategies in higher education – A mixed-methods study. *Journal of Applied Research in Memory and Cognition, 9*(2), 186–203. https://doi.org/10.1016/j.jarmac.2020.03.004.

Blanco, F. (2017). Cognitive Bias. *Encyclopedia of Animal Cognition and Behavior*, 1–7. https://doi.org/10.1007/978-3-319-47829-6_1244-1.

Block, C. (2021). *Business is personal: A blueprint for unlocking meaning at work.* Passionpreneur.

Block, C. (2022, March 16). 12 reasons your digital transformation will fail. *Forbes*. https://www.forbes.com/councils/forbescoachescouncil/2022/03/16/12-reasons-your-digital-transformation-will-fail/.

Block, C. J. (2023). *Love @ work: The final frontier of empathy in leadership.* PassionPreneur.

Bloom, B.S., & Krathwohl, D. R. (1984). *Taxonomy of educational objectives.* Addison Wesley.

Bond, S. (2020). Executive coaching and why leaders feel lonely. *The Vivid Minds*. https://thevividminds.com/suzan-bond-on-executive-coaching-and-why-leaders-feel-lonely/

Boogaard, K. (n.d.). What was Steve Jobs' leadership style? *Fingerprint for Success*. https://www.fingerprintforsuccess.com/blog/steve-jobs-leadership-style

Borgschulte, M., Guenzel, M., Liu, C., & Malmendier, U. (2021). *CEO stress, aging, and death*. https://doi.org/10.3386/w28550

Bowman, B., & Butler, C. (2016). *The golden rules: 10 steps to world-class excellence in your life and work.* Little, Brown Book Group.

Boyce, L. A., Jackson, R. J., & Neal, L. J. (2010). Building successful leadership coaching relationships: Examining impact of matching criteria in a leadership coaching program. *Journal of Management Development, 29*(10), 914–931.

Boysen, S., Cherry, M., Amerie, W. & Takagawa, M. (2018). Organisational coaching outcomes: A comparison of a practitioner survey and key findings from the literature. *International Journal of Evidence Based Coaching and Mentoring, 16.* 159–166. https://doi.org/10.24384/000475.

Bozer, G., Sarros, J. C., & Santora, J. C. (2014). Academic background and credibility in executive coaching effectiveness. *Personnel Review, 43*(6), 881–897.

Bradberry, T., & Greaves, J. (2009). *Emotional intelligence 2.0.* TalentSmart.

Bridoux, F., & Stoelhorst, J. (2022). Stakeholder theory strategy and organization: Past, present, and future. *Strategic Organization, 20*(4), 797–809. https://doi.org/10.1177/14761270221127628.

Brown, K. (2021). Leadership in the age of disruption: New challenges for CEOs. *Leadership Quarterly, 30*(4), 123–140.

Bungay Stanier, M. (2016). *The coaching habit: Say less, ask more & change the way you lead forever.* Box of Crayons Press.

Burnes, B. (2020). The origins of Lewin's three-step model of change. *Journal of Applied Behavioral Science, 56*(1), 32–59. https://doi.org/10.1177/0021886319892685.

Burner, David. (1996) [1979]. *Herbert Hoover: The public life.* Easton Press. Originally published as Burner, David. (1979). *Herbert Hoover: The public life.* Knopf Doubleday.

Burt, R. S. (2004). Structural holes and good ideas. *American Journal of Sociology, 110*(2), 349–399. https://doi.org/10.1086/421787.

California Legislative Information. (2004). California Online Privacy Protection Act (CalOPPA). California Civil Code § 22575–22579. Retrieved from https://leginfo.legislature.ca.gov/faces/codes_displayText.xhtml?lawCode=CIV&division=3.&title=1.81.5.&part=4.&chapter=&article=.

Carucci, R. (2018, November 27). How to permanently resolve cross-department rivalries. *Harvard Business Review.* https://hbr.org/2018/09/how-to-permanently-resolve-cross-department-rivalries.

Cascio, C. N., O'Donnell, M., Tinney, F. J., Lieberman, M. D., Taylor, S. E., Strecher, V., & Falk, E. B. (2016). Self-affirmation activates brain systems associated with self-related processing and reward and is reinforced by future orientation. *Social Cognitive and Affective Neuroscience, 11*(4), 621–629.

Catalyst. (2020). *Women in the workforce: Global.* Catalyst. Retrieved from https://www.catalyst.org/research/women-in-the-workforce-global/.

Cayne, J. (n.d.). Jimmy Cayne: In his own words. *Money.cnn.com*. Retrieved July 16, 2024, from https://money.cnn.com/galleries/2008/fortune/0808/gallery.cayne_bearstearns.fortune/index.html.

Center for Creative Leadership. (n.d.). Our approach. Center for Creative Leadership. Retrieved July 12, 2024, from https://www.ccl.org/our-approach/.

Center for Substance Abuse Treatment. (1999). Motivational interviewing as a counseling style. In *Enhancing motivation for change in substance abuse treatment* (Treatment Improvement Protocol (TIP) Series, No. 35, Chapter 3). Substance Abuse and Mental Health Services Administration. Retrieved from http://store.samhsa.gov.

Chafkin, M., & Metz, R. (2023, November 20). Inside Sam Altman's shock ouster from OpenAI. *Time*. https://time.com/6337437/sam-altman-openai-fired-why-microsoft-musk/.

Charan, R. (2024). *Ram Charan.* https://ram-charan.com/.

Chow, N. L. Y., Tateishi, N., Goldhar, A., Zaheer, R., Redelmeier, D. A., Cheung, A. H., Schaffer, A., & Sinyor, M. (2023). Does knowledge have a half-life? An observational study analyzing the use of older citations in medical and scientific publications. *BMJ Open, 13*(5), e072374. https://doi.org/10.1136/bmjopen-2023-072374.

CoachSource. (2024). Become a CSQ™ coach. CoachSource. Retrieved July 12, 2024, from https://cs.coachsource.com/become-a-coach/.

Co-Active Coaching and Leadership Training. (n.d.). Retrieved June 6, 2024, from https://coactive.com/.

Controversial magazine cover features Yahoo CEO. (n.d.). *ABC7 San Francisco*. Retrieved May 29, 2024, from https://abc7news.com/marissa-mayer-variety-magazine-shown-as-jesus-yahoo-ceo-christ-cover-featuring/1353732/.

Costa, A. and Kallick, B. (1983). Through the lens of a critical friend. *Educational Leadership, 51*(2), 49–51.

Cox, E., & Bachkirova, T. (2016). A cognitive-developmental approach for coach development. In *The complete handbook of coaching* (3rd ed.). Sage.

Cox, E., Bachkirova, T., & Clutterbuck, D. (Eds.). (2023). *The complete handbook of coaching* (3rd ed.). Sage.

The Cynefin Company. (2024). About – Cynefin Framework. Retrieved from https://thecynefin.co/about-us/about-cynefin-framework/.

De Haan, E., & Burger, Y. (2014). *Person-centred coaching: Facilitating the coachee.* In *Coaching with colleagues.* Palgrave Macmillan. https://doi.org/10.1057/9781137359209_7.

De Haan, E., Culpin, V., & Curd, J. (2011). Executive coaching in practice: What determines helpfulness for clients of coaching? *Personnel Review, 40*(1), 24–44.

De Meuse, K. P., Dai, G., & Lee, R. J. (2009). Evaluating the effectiveness of executive coaching: Beyond ROI? *Coaching: An International Journal of Theory, Research, and Practice, 2*(2), 117–134.

Doerr, J. (2018). *Measure what matters.* Portfolio Penguin.

Drake, D. B. (2017). *Narrative coaching: The definitive guide to bringing new stories to life* (2nd ed.). CNC Press.

Ducharme, M. J. (2004). The cognitive-behavioral approach to executive coaching. *Consulting Psychology Journal: Practice and Research 56*(4), 214–224. https://doi.org/10.1037/1065-9293.56.4.214.

Dudău, D. P., Sălăgean, N., & Sava, F. A. (2018). Executive coaching. In M. E. Bernard & O. A. David (Eds.), *Coaching for rational living* (pp. 343–360). Springer International.

Eadicicco, L. (2015). A former Apple employee describes what it was like to work on the design team under Steve Jobs. *Business Insider.* https://www.businessinsider.in/a-former-apple-employee-describes-what-it-was-like-to-work-on-the-design-team-under-steve-jobs/articleshow/47656644.cms.

Effron, M., & Ort, M. (2010). *One page talent management: Eliminating complexity, adding value.* Harvard Business Review Press.

Effron, M. (2018). *8 steps to high performance: Focus on what you can change (ignore the rest).* Harvard Business Review Press.

Egan, M. (2018). The stunning downfall of Bear Stearns and its bridge-playing CEO. *CNN.* https://edition.cnn.com/2018/09/30/investing/bear-stearns-2008-crisis-jimmy-cayne/index.html.

Ellinger, A. D., Hamlin, R. G., & Beattie, R. S. (2008). Behavioral indicators of ineffective managerial coaching: A cross-national study. *Journal of European Industrial Training, 32*(4), 240–257.

Ellis, A. (1972). *Executive leadership: A rational approach.* Institute for Rational Living.

Ellis, A. (2002). *Overcoming resistance: A rational emotive behavior therapy integrated approach* (2nd ed.). Springer.

Ely, R. J., Ibarra, H., & Kolb, D. M. (2011). Taking gender into account: Theory and design for women's leadership development programs. *Academy of Management Learning & Education, 10*(3), 474–493. https://doi.org/10.5465/amle.2010.0046.

Epstein, D. J. (2019). *Range: Why generalists triumph in a specialized world.* Riverhead Books.

European Union. (2016). General Data Protection Regulation (GDPR) (EU) 2016/679. *Official Journal of the European Union, L119,* 1–88. Retrieved from https://eur-lex.europa.eu/eli/reg/2016/679/oj.

Fernández-Llano, C., Bernardo Vilamitjana, M., & Kasperskaya Riabenko, Y. (2023). Assessing the impact of executive coaching on business results applying a Balanced Scorecard Framework. *International Journal of Evidence Based Coaching and Mentoring 21*(1), 4–16.

Financial Crisis Inquiry Commission. (2011). *The financial crisis inquiry report: Final report of the National Commission on the Causes of the Financial and Economic Crisis in the United States.* US Government Printing Office. https://www.govinfo.gov/content/pkg/GPO-FCIC/pdf/GPO-FCIC.pdf.

Fisher, J., & Silverglate, P. H. (2022). The C-suite's role in well-being. Deloitte Insights. https://www2.deloitte.com/us/en/insights/topics/leadership/employee-wellness-in-the-corporate-workplace.html.

Flow Research Collective. (2023). Performance neuroscience coaching certification – Apply now. https://www.flowresearchcollective.com/high-flow-coaching/overview.

FourFourTwo. (n.d.). World Cup icons: Roberto Baggio – The miss that haunted a career (1994). https://www.fourfourtwo.com/features/world-cup-icons-roberto-baggio-miss-haunted-a-career-1994.

Franklin, M. (2018). *Agile change management: A practical framework for successful change planning and implementation.* Kogan Page.

Freeman, R. E. (1984). *Strategic management: A stakeholder approach.* Pitman.

Galinsky, A. D., Stone, J., & Cooper, J. (2000). The reinstatement of dissonance and psychological discomfort following failed affirmations. *European Journal of Social Psychology, 30*(1), 123–147.

Gallup. (2024).CliftonStrengths. Retrieved August 20, 2024, from https://www.gallup.com/cliftonstrengths.

Gallwey, W. T. (1974). *The inner game of tennis.* Random House.

Gasparino, C. (2022, January 2). Lessons of Jimmy Cayne's Bear Stearns historic rise and fall. *New York Post*. https://nypost.com/2022/01/01/lessons-of-jimmy-caynes-bear-stearns-historic-rise-and-fall/.

Gettman, H.J. (2008). *Executive coaching as a developmental experience: A framework and measure of coaching dimensions* [Doctoral dissertation, University of Maryland]. Available from ProQuest Dissertations and Theses database. (UMI No. 3324934).

Gerstner, L. V. (n.d.). Gerstner: Changing culture at IBM – Lou Gerstner discusses changing the culture at IBM. *HBS Working Knowledge*. https://hbswk.hbs.edu/archive/gerstner-changing-culture-at-ibm-lou-gerstner-discusses-changing-the-culture-at-ibm.

Goldsmith, M. (2022, June 29). 6 questions for better coaching. Marshall Goldsmith. https://marshallgoldsmith.com/articles/6-questions-for-better-coaching/.

Goldsmith, M. (2024). Marshall Goldsmith stakeholder centered coaching. Our methodology. Stakeholder Centered Coaching. Retrieved July 12, 2024, from https://www.marshallgoldsmith.com/methodology/.

Goldsmith, M., & Reiter, M. (2007). *What got you here won't get you there: How successful people become even more successful*. Hyperion.

Goleman, D. (1995). *Emotional intelligence: Why it can matter more than IQ*. Bantam Books.

Good, D., Yeganeh, B., & Yeganeh, R. (2013). Cognitive behavioral executive coaching. In S. J. Armstrong & C. V. Fukami (Eds.), *Handbook of managerial learning, education, and development*. Sage.

Greenberg, C. C., Ghousseini, H. N., Pavuluri Quamme, S. R., Beasley, H. L., & Wiegmann, D. A. (2015). Surgical coaching for individual performance improvement. *Annals of Surgery, 261*(1), 32–34. https://doi.org/10.1097/SLA.0000000000000776.

Greene, J., & Grant, A. M. (2006). *Solution-focused coaching: Managing people in a complex world*. Momentum.

Grimley, B. N. (2016). What is NLP? The development of a grounded theory of Neuro-Linguistic Programming, (NLP), within an action research journey. Implications for the use of NLP in coaching psychology. *International Coaching Psychology Review, 11*(2), 166–178.

Grover, S., & Furnham, A. (2016). Coaching as a developmental intervention in organisations: A systematic review of its effectiveness and the mechanisms

underlying it. *PLOS ONE, 11*(7), e0159137.
https://doi.org/10.1371/journal.pone.0159137.

Gurel, E. (2017). SWOT analysis: A theoretical review. *Journal of International Social Research, 10*(51), 994–1006.

Hamill, P. (2013). *Embodied leadership: The somatic approach to developing your leadership* (1st ed.). Kogan Page.

Hannafey, F. T., & Vitulano, L. A. (2013). Ethics and executive coaching: An agency theory approach. *Journal of Business Ethics, 115*(3), 599-603.

Hakan, O., & Barsade, S. (2012). Work loneliness and employee performance. https://faculty.wharton.upenn.edu/wp-content/uploads/2012/05/Work_Loneliness_Performance_Study.pdf

Haspeslagh, P. C. (1982). Portfolio planning: Uses and limits. *Harvard Business Review, 60*(1), 58–73.

Hassink, H., Vries, M., & Bollen, L. (2007). A content analysis of whistleblowing policies of leading European companies. *Journal of Business Ethics, 75*, 25–44. https://doi.org/10.1007/S10551-006-9236-9.

Hennigan, L. (2023, July 20). What is an OKR? Definition & examples. *Forbes.* https://www.forbes.com/advisor/business/what-is-an-okr-definition-examples/.

Henriques, G. (2012). Was Steve Jobs' narcissism justified? *Psychology Today.* https://www.psychologytoday.com/us/blog/theory-knowledge/201201/was-steve-jobs-narcissism-justified.

Henry, Z. (2016). Why Apple CEO Tim Cook doesn't think CEOs deserve any sympathy. *Inc.* https://www.inc.com/zoe-henry/tim-cook-says-running-apple-is-a-lonely-job.html.

Herbert Hoover: The engineer-president. (2023, October 31). *Washington Examiner.* https://www.washingtonexaminer.com/magazine/187736/herbert-hoover-the-engineer-president/.

Hofstede, G., Hofstede, G. J., & Minkov, M. (2010). *Cultures and organizations: Software of the mind* (3rd ed.). McGraw-Hill Professional.

Hoover's Gold. (2005). Australian Broadcasting Corporation. https://www.screenaustralia.gov.au/the-screen-guide/t/hoovers-gold-2005/20810/.

Houkes, W., & Meijers, A. (2021). Engineering knowledge. In *The Oxford Handbook of Philosophy of Technology* (pp. 128–151). Oxford University Press. https://doi.org/10.1093/oxfordhb/9780190851187.013.10

House, R. J., Dorfman, P. W., Javidan, M., Hanges, P. J., & Sully de Luque, M. F. (2014). *Strategic leadership across cultures: The GLOBE study of CEO leadership behavior and effectiveness in 24 countries*. Sage Publications.

How Indra Nooyi changed the face of PepsiCo. (2020). *World Finance*. Retrieved September 16, 2024, from https://www.worldfinance.com/markets/how-indra-nooyi-changed-the-face-of-pepsico

How PepsiCo is "fundamentally transforming" what it does and how it does it. (2022). *Food Navigator*. Retrieved September 16, 2024, from https://www.foodnavigator.com/Article/2022/09/15/How-PepsiCo-is-fundamentally-transforming-what-it-does-and-how-it-does-it.

How PV Sindhu definitively shed off the tag of second best. (2019). *Times Now News*.

Hudson Institute of Coaching. (2024). Our approach. Hudson Institute of Coaching. Retrieved July 12, 2024, from https://hudsoninstitute.com/about-us/our-approach/.

Ianiro, P. M., Lehmann-Willenbrock, N., & Kauffeld, S. (2015). Coaches and clients in action: A sequential analysis of interpersonal coach and client behavior. *Journal of Business and Psychology, 30*(3), 435–456.

Ignatius, A. (2017, July 17). Grief at work: Talking with Sheryl Sandberg and Adam Grant. *Harvard Business Review*. https://hbr.org/2017/05/above-all-acknowledge-the-pain.

India Today. (n.d.). PV Sindhu's new Korean coach Kim Ji-hyun focused on producing champions. *Sportstar*. https://www.indiatoday.in/sports/badminton/story/bwf-world-championships-pv-sindhu-wins-gold-first-indian-korean-coach-kim-ji-hyun-1592421-2019-08-28.

Innovation Training. (2023, April 26). *The Four Stages of Competence Model – Innovation Training | Design*. Innovation Training | Design Thinking Workshops. https://www.innovationtraining.org/the-four-stages-of-competence-model.

InsideOut Development. (n.d.). GROW coaching. InsideOut Development. Retrieved July 12, 2024, from https://insideoutdev.com/solutions/grow-coaching.

International Coaching Federation. (2020). PCC Markers. Retrieved from https://coachingfederation.org/credentials-and-standards/performance-evaluations/pcc-markers.

International Coaching Federation. (2023). *ICF Global Coaching Study 2023 Executive Summary*.

https://coachingfederation.org/app/uploads/2023/04/2023ICFGlobalCoachingStudy_ExecutiveSummary.pdf

International Coaching Federation (ICF). (2024). *International Coaching Federation: Empowering the world through coaching.* https://coachingfederation.org/.

Jahanbegloo, R. (2000). *Conversations with Isaiah Berlin.* Orion Publishing.

Jeansonne, G. (2011). The real Herbert Hoover. *Historically Speaking, 12,* 26–29.

Jeppesen, L. B., & Lakhani, K. R. (2010). Marginality and problem-solving effectiveness in broadcast search. *Organization Science, 21*(5), 1016–1033. https://doi.org/10.1287/orsc.1090.0491.

Johnson, C. (2024). Learn how mindful breathing helps your mind-body connection. Anahana. https://www.anahana.com/en/breathing-exercise/mindful-breathing

Johnson, L. (2022). Balancing profit and purpose: The evolving role of CEOs. *Corporate Governance Review, 15*(2), 78–92.

Johnson, L., & Brown, R. (2019). Post-release monitoring and support for reintroduced wolves. *Journal of Wildlife Management, 83*(2), 123–134.

Jung, C. G. (1964). *Man and his symbols.* Doubleday.

Kantaro, S. (2024). Carlos Yulo's former Japanese coach proudly watches from Paris Games sidelines. *Rappler.* https://www.rappler.com/sports/exclusive-carlos-yulo-former-coach-munehiro-kugimiya-watches-sidelines-paris-olympics-2024/.

Kaufman, S. B. (2021). Center for human potential. Retrieved from https://centerforhumanpotential.com/

Kelly, K. (2007, November 1). Bear CEO's handling of crisis raises issues. *Wall Street Journal.*

Kierein, N. M., & Gold, M. A. (2000). Pygmalion in work organizations: A meta-analysis. *Journal of Organizational Behavior, 21*(8), 913–928.

Kimblin, A. (2009). The inner game of coaching. *International Journal of Evidence-Based Coaching and Mentoring Special Issue 3,* 38–50.

King, G., & Hermodson, A. (2000). Peer reporting of coworker wrongdoing: A qualitative analysis of observer attitudes in the decision to report versus not report unethical behavior. *Journal of Applied Communication Research, 28,* 309–329. https://doi.org/10.1080/00909880009365579.

Kirubashini, R. (2024, July 31). Jin Wei wins cheers after going down fighting in Olympics debut. *The Star.* https://www.thestar.com.my/sport/badminton/2024/07/31/jin-wei-wins-cheers-after-going-down-fighting-in-olympics-debut.

Klein, G. A. (1999). *Sources of power: How people make decisions.* MIT Press.

Knudsen, E. S., & Lien, L. B. (2023). The half-life of knowledge and strategic human capital. *Human Resource Management Review, 33*(4), 1–10. https://doi.org/10.1016/j.hrmr.2023.100989.

Kotter, J. P. (1996). *Leading change.* Harvard Business Review Press.

Korotov, K. (2023). Accelerated development of organizational talent and executive coaching: A knowledge management perspective. In V. Vaiman, C. Vance, & J. Ling (Eds.), *Smart talent management: Managing people as knowledge assets* (2nd ed.). Edward Elgar.

Kowalchyk, M., Palmieri, H., Conte, E., & Wallisch, P. (2021). Narcissism through the lens of performative self-elevation, *Elsevier 177.* https://www.sciencedirect.com/science/article/pii/S0191886921001550?via%3Di hub

KPMG. (2019). *Advancing the future of women in business: A KPMG women's leadership study.* KPMG. Retrieved from https://home.kpmg/xx/en/home/insights/2019/03/advancing-the-future-of-women-in-business.html.

Kroll, L. (2002). A fresh face. *Forbes.* https://www.forbes.com/.

Lafley, A. G., & Charan, R. (2008). *The game-changer: How you can drive revenue and profit growth with innovation.* Crown Business.

Larcker, D., & Tayan, B. (n.d.). *Internal versus external CEOs.* Stanford Graduate School of Business. https://www.gsb.stanford.edu/sites/gsb/files/publication-pdf/cgri-research-spotlight-08-internal-versus-external-ceos.pdf

Laske, O. E. (1999). An integrated model of developmental coaching. *Consulting Psychology Journal: Practice and Research 51*(3), 139–159. https://doi.org/10.1037/1061-4087.51.3.139.

Lawrence P., & Whyte A. (2014). Return on investment in executive coaching: a practical model for measuring ROI in organisations. *Coach Int J Theory Res Pract 2014,* 7(1), 4–17.

The Leadership Circle. (n.d.). The Leadership Circle. Retrieved July 12, 2024, from https://leadershipcircle.com/.

Leuchtenburg, W. E. (2009). *Herbert Hoover.* Times Books (Henry Holt and Company).

Leung, A., & Sy, T. (2018). I am as incompetent as the prototypical group member: An investigation of naturally occurring Golem Effects in work groups. *Front. Psychol., 9*, 1581.

Linnenluecke, M. K. (2017). Resilience in business and management research: A review of influential publications and a research agenda. *International Journal of Management Reviews, 19*(1), 4–30. https://doi.org/10.1111/ijmr.12076.

Little, J. (2017). *Lean change management: Innovative practices for managing organizational change.* Happy Melly Express.

Longenecker, C., & McCartney, M. (2020). The benefits of executive coaching: Voices from the C-suite. *Strategic HR Review, 19*(1), 22–27.

MacKenzie, D. (2010). Industrial employment and the policies of Herbert C. Hoover. *Quarterly Journal of Austrian Economics, 13*, 101.

Mansharamani, V. (2020, June 22). All hail the generalist. *Harvard Business Review.* https://hbr.org/2012/06/all-hail-the-generalist.

McGovern, J., Lindemann, M., Vergara, M., Murphy, S., Barker, L., & Warrenfeltz, R. (2001). Maximizing the impact of executive coaching: Behavioral change, organizational outcomes, and return on investment. *Manchester Review, 6*(1).

McKinsey & Company. (2020). *Women in the workplace 2020.* McKinsey & Company. Retrieved from https://www.mckinsey.com/featured-insights/diversity-and-inclusion/women-in-the-workplace.

Mech, L. D. (1999). Alpha status, dominance, and division of labor in wolf packs. *Canadian Journal of Zoology, 77*(8), 1196–1203. https://doi.org/10.1139/z99-099.

Meet the coaches behind the world's best Olympic teams. (2012, August 14). *BBC Sport.* https://www.bbc.com/sport/olympics/19253531.

Merton, R. K. (1968). *Social theory and social structure.* Free Press.

Moen, F., & Federici, R. A. (2012). The effect from external executive coaching. *Coaching: An International Journal of Theory, Research and Practice, 5*(2), 113–131. https://doi.org/10.1080/17521882.2012.708355

Murthy, V. (2017). Work and the loneliness epidemic. *Harvard Business Review.* https://hbr.org/2017/09/work-and-the-loneliness-epidemic.

Myers, R. (2003). Ensuring ethical effectiveness: New rules mean virtually every company will need a code of ethics. *Journal of Accountancy, 195*, 28.

Nagel, C. (2019). *Psychodynamic coaching: Distinctive features* (1st ed.). Routledge.

Nash, J. (2023, September 26). 7 best breathwork techniques & exercises to use. PositivePsychology.com. https://positivepsychology.com/breathwork-techniques/

Neenan, M., & Palmer, S. (2001). Cognitive-behavioral coaching. *Stress News, 13*(15), 15–18.

Newcomb, A. (2021, August 5). Photo captures bond between Simone Biles and coach Cecile Canqueteau-Landi. *Today.com*. https://www.today.com/news/photo-captures-bond-between-simone-biles-coach-cecile-canqueteau-landi-t227483.

Nicolau, A., Candel, O. S., Constantin, T., & Kleingeld, A. (2023). The effects of executive coaching on behaviors, attitudes, and personal characteristics: A meta-analysis of randomized control trial studies. *Frontiers in Psychology, 14*.

https://doi.org/10.3389/fpsyg.2023.1089797.

Nooyi, I. (2021). *My life in full: Work, family, and our future*. Portfolio.

North America Bridge Championships. (n.d.). Spring 2008 NABC results. Cdn.acbl.org. Retrieved July 16, 2024, from https://cdn.acbl.org/nabc/2008/01/results/March13.html

Nortje, A. (2020). Cognitive biases and heuristics: How they influence our decisions. *Positive Psychology*. Retrieved August 23, 2024, from https://positivepsychology.com/cognitive-biases/.

Osman, S., Lane, J., & Goldsmith, M. (2023). *Becoming coachable: Unleashing the power of executive coaching to transform your leadership and life*. 100 Coaches Publishing.

Oxford Bibliographies. (n.d.) Self-fulfilling prophecy and the Pygmalion effect in management (Abstract). *Obo*. Retrieved May 29, 2024, from https://www.oxfordbibliographies.com/abstract/document/obo-9780199846740/obo-9780199846740-0014.xml.

Page, N., & de Haan, E. (2014). Does executive coaching work? *The Psychologist, 27*(8), 582–587.

Palmer, S., & Cavanagh, M. (2006). Editorial – Coaching psychology: Its time has finally come. *International Coaching Psychology Review, 1*(1).

Palmer, S., & Green, S. (Eds.). (2018). *Positive psychology coaching in practice* (1st ed.). Routledge.

Passmore, J., & Rowson, T. S. (2019). Neuro-linguistic-programming: A critical review of NLP research and the application of NLP in coaching. *International Coaching Psychology Review, 14*(1), 57–69.

Pedrick, C., & Baldelli, L. (2023). *The human behind the coach: How great coaches transform themselves first.* Practical Inspiration Publishing.

Performance Neuroscience Coaching Certification – Apply Now. (2023). Flowresearchcollective.com. https://www.flowresearchcollective.com/high-flow-coaching/overview.

Pliner, E. (2022). *The ethical leader: Why doing the right thing can be the key to competitive advantage.* Wiley.

Porter, M. E. (1979). How competitive forces shape strategy. *Harvard Business Review, 57*(2), 137–145.

PV Sindhu's new Korean coach Kim Ji-hyun focused on producing champions. (n.d.). *India Today.* https://www.indiatoday.in/sports/badminton/story/bwf-world-championships-pv-sindhu-wins-gold-first-indian-korean-coach-kim-ji-hyun-1592421-2019-08-28.

PV Sindhu response on her final phobia. (2018). *YouTube.* https://www.youtube.com/watch?v=VvCX9KICfZ4.

Rath, T. (2007). *StrengthsFinder 2.0.* Gallup Press.

Ratiu, L., David, O. A., & Baban, A. (2017). Developing managerial skills through coaching: Efficacy of a cognitive-behavioral coaching program. *Journal of Rational-Emotive & Cognitive-Behavior Therapy 35*, 88–110. https://doi.org/10.1007/s10942-015-0225-8.

Rhythm Systems. (n.d.). *The ROI of business coaching: Executive coaching ROI statistics (2023 updated).* https://www.rhythmsystems.com/blog/the-roi-of-executive-coaching.

The ROI of business coaching: Executive coaching ROI statistics (2023, updated). www.rhythmsystems.com. https://www.rhythmsystems.com/blog/the-roi-of-executive-coaching.

Ropek, L. (2023). Sam Altman accused of "psychologically abusive" behavior. *Gizmodo.* https://gizmodo.com/sam-altman-ceo-psychologically-abusive-openai-1851082091.

Rose, J. (2010). Hoover's truce: Wage rigidity in the onset of the Great Depression. *The Journal of Economic History, 70*, 843–870.

Rosenthal, R. (2003). Pygmalion in the classroom. *American Psychologist, 58*(3), 839.

Rosenthal, R., & Rubin, D. B. (1978). Interpersonal expectancy effects: The first 345 studies. *Behavioral and Brain Sciences, 1*(3), 377–415. https://doi.org/10.1017/S0140525X00075506.

Ruhl, C. (2024, February 1). *Bloom's taxonomy of learning.* Simply Psychology. https://www.simplypsychology.org/blooms-taxonomy.html.

Sandler, C. (2011). *Executive coaching: A psychodynamic approach.* Open University Press.

Sapolsky, R. M. (2023). *Determined: A science of life without free will.* Penguin Press.

Saporito, T. J. (2012). It's time to acknowledge CEO loneliness. *Harvard Business Review.* https://hbr.org/2012/02/its-time-to-acknowledge-ceo-lo.

Schalk, M., & Landeta, J. (2017). Internal versus external executive coaching. *Coaching: An International Journal of Theory, Research, and Practice, 10*(2), 140–156.

Schmidt, E., Rosenberg, J., & Eagle, A. (2019). *Trillion dollar coach: The leadership playbook of Silicon Valley's Bill Campbell.* Harper Business.

Schnuerch, R., & Gibbons, H. (2014). A review of neurocognitive mechanisms of social conformity. *Social Psychology, 45*(6), 466–478. https://doi.org/10.1027/1864-9335/a000213.

Schwarz, R. (2002). *The skilled facilitator: A comprehensive resource for consultants, facilitators, managers, and coaches.* Jossey-Bass.

Seligman, M. E. P. (2011). *Flourish: A visionary new understanding of happiness and well-being.* Free Press.

Senge, P. M. (1990). *The fifth discipline: The art and practice of the learning organization.* Doubleday.

Silver, S. (2018, June 18). 25 years ago, Apple's board of directors pushed out CEO John Sculley. *AppleInsider.* https://appleinsider.com/articles/18/06/18/25-years-ago-apples-board-of-directors-pushed-out-ceo-john-sculley.

Siminovitch, D. (2017). *A gestalt coaching primer: The path toward awareness IQ.* Dorothy Siminovitch.

Sinek, S. (2011). *Start with why: How great leaders inspire everyone to take action.* Penguin.

Smith, A.K. (2023). Here's why you have every right to be unhappy at work. *Forbes.* https://www.forbes.com/sites/annkowalsmith/2023/12/15/heres-why-you-have-every-right-to-be-unhappy-at-work/?sh=3d70098c1309.

Smith, J. (2020). Reintroduction of captive wolves: Challenges and strategies. *Wildlife Conservation Journal, 15*(3), 45–58.

Smith, J. (2023). The impact of digital transformation on modern business. *Journal of Business Innovation, 12*(3), 45–60.

Snider, J. S., & Mike. (n.d.). Marissa Mayer's diminishing legacy at Yahoo. *USA Today.* Retrieved May 29, 2024, from https://www.usatoday.com/story/tech/columnist/2016/10/18/marissa-mayers-diminishing-legacy-yahoo/91547536/.

Snowden, D. J. & Boone, M. E. (2007). A Leader's Framework for Decision Making. *Harvard Business Review.*

Souders, B. (2019). *17 Motivational Interviewing Questions and Skills.* Retrieved from 17 Motivational Interviewing Questions and Skills (positivepsychology.com).

Spangler, W. D. (2024). CEO Humility, Narcissism & Competitive Advantage. *Cutter Consortium.* https://www.cutter.com/article/ceo-humility-narcissism-competitive-advantage.

Sportskeeda, S.K. Desk (2024). Simone Biles's coach. https://www.sportskeeda.com/gymnastics/simone-biles-coach

Spoth, J., Toman, S., Leichtman, R., & Allan, J. (2013). Gestalt approach. In J. Passmore, D. B. Peterson, & T. Freire (Eds.), *The Wiley Blackwell handbook of the psychology of coaching and mentoring* (pp. 385–406). Wiley Blackwell.

Stakeholder Centered Coaching Ltd. (2024). https://mgscc.net/.

Stanier, M. B. (2016). *The coaching habit: Say less, ask more & change the way you lead forever.* Box of Crayons Press.

Stewart, L. J., Palmer, S., Wilkin, H., & Kerrin, M. (2008). The influence of coaching on self-efficacy. *International Journal of Coaching in Organizations, 6*(1), 13–22.

Strickland. B. (2024, January). From CFO to CEO: An increasingly popular path. *Journal of Accountancy.* URL: https://www.journalofaccountancy.com/news/2024/jan/from-cfo-to-ceo-an-increasingly-popular-path.html.

Strozzi-Heckler, R. (2014). *The art of somatic coaching: Embodying skillful action, wisdom, and compassion*. North Atlantic Books.

Szabó, P. (2012). Making a positive change: A randomized study comparing solution-focused vs. problem-focused coaching questions. *Journal of Systemic Therapies, 31*(2), 21–35.

Teodoridis, F. (2018, July 31). When generalists are better than specialists and vice versa. *Harvard Business Review*. https://hbr.org/2018/07/when-generalists-are-better-than-specialists-and-vice-versa.

Thomas, J. S. (2012). The dangers of executive coaching: Pitfalls for coaches and coachees. *International Coaching Psychology Review, 12*(4), 210–225.

ThoughtCo (2017). Everything you need to know about new Yahoo! CEO Marissa Mayer. *ThoughtCo*. https://www.thoughtco.com/biography-profile-of-marissa-mayer-3533914.

Tobak, S. (2016, July 26). RIP Yahoo: Why Marissa Mayer failed. *FOXBusiness*. https://www.foxbusiness.com/features/rip-yahoo-why-marissa-mayer-failed.

Tripathy, S., & Mangaraj, S. (2017). A literature review on executive coaching. *Training & Development Journal, 8*(2), 117–134.

Turko, A. J., Firth, B. L., Craig, P. M., Eliason, E. J., Raby, G. D., & Borowiec, B. G. (2023). Physiological differences between wild and captive animals: A century-old dilemma. *Journal of Experimental Biology, 226*(23). https://doi.org/10.1242/jeb.246037.

van Zyl, L. E., Roll, L. C., Stander, M. W., & Richter, S. (2020). Positive psychological coaching definitions and models: A systematic literature review. *Frontiers in Psychology, 11,* 793. https://doi.org/10.3389/fpsyg.2020.00793.

Vaiman, V., & Vance, C. (2013). *Smart talent management: Building knowledge assets for competitive advantage*. Edward Elgar.

Watson, J. B. (1913). Psychology as the behaviorist views it. *Psychological Review, 20,* 158–178.

Weill, P., Woerner, S. L., & Shah, A. M. (2021, March 3). Does your C-suite have enough digital smarts? *MIT Sloan Management Review*. https://sloanreview.mit.edu/article/does-your-C-suite-have-enough-digital-smarts/.

Wells, D. (2005, July 18). We're not betting the ranch: Bear Stearns eyes a more vigorous role in Europe – as well as the bottom line leadership. *Financial Times*. Retrieved from https://www.proquest.com/newspapers/were-not-betting-ranch-bear-stearns-eyes-more/docview/249652825/se-2?accountid=150425.

Wenger, E. (1998). *Communities of practice: Learning, meaning, and identity.* Cambridge University Press.

Whitler, K. A. (2019, October 14). New study on CEOs: Is marketing, finance, operations, or engineering the best path to CEO? *Forbes.* https://www.forbes.com/sites/kimberlywhitler/2019/10/12/new-study-on-ceos-is-marketing-finance-operations-or-engineering-the-best-path-to-the-C-suite/?sh=54379245e07f.

Whitmore, J. (2002). *Coaching for performance: GROWing people, performance, and purpose.* Nicholas Brealey.

Who is Marissa Mayer? Everything you need to know. (n.d.). www.thefamouspeople.com. https://www.thefamouspeople.com/profiles/marissa-mayer-50204.php.

Wiener-Bronner, D. (2018). How Indra Nooyi built Pepsi for the future. *Money.* https://money.cnn.com/2018/08/07/news/companies/indra-nooyi-legacy/index.html.

Wilson, C. (2021). *Mastering coaching: Practical insights for developing high performance.* Routledge.

World Cup icons: Roberto Baggio – The miss that haunted a career (1994). (n.d.). *FourFourTwo.* https://www.fourfourtwo.com/features/world-cup-icons-roberto-baggio-miss-haunted-a-career-1994.

Yahoo's false prophet: How Marissa Mayer failed to turn the company around. (2016, May 24). *Yahoo Entertainment.* https://www.yahoo.com/entertainment/yahoo-false-prophet-marissa-mayer-failed-turn-company-160630052.html.

Yüksel, I. (2012). Developing a multi-criteria decision making model for PESTEL analysis. *International Journal of Business and Management, 7*(24), 52–66.

www.ingramcontent.com/pod-product-compliance
Lightning Source LLC
Chambersburg PA
CBHW031954190326
41520CB00007B/243